"T. F. Torrance's theology is currently attractin[...] and rightly so. This book makes a major con[...] tually rigorous and highly readable, the study Sherrard has given us shows well how the implications of Torrance's work extend much further than we might initially think. Highly recommended."

Jeremy Begbie, Duke University

"Reflecting upon the recent turn to missional theology, Sherrard brings to the discussion the resources of Christian dogmatics, mediated through the work of T. F. Torrance. The practical and evangelical aspects of Torrance's work have often been overlooked. Sherrard corrects this imbalance and shows how a well-considered systematic theology has a lot to offer the missional conversation. Theologians have always thought they had something worthwhile to offer the church, and Sherrard shows this to be the case by drawing out of Torrance's corpus the red thread of missional theology. This is a theological manifesto, of sorts, for missional theology, and one which retrieves Torrance as a missional theologian par excellence. This work will have wide appeal across denominational and theological divides."

Myk Habets, senior lecturer in theology at Laidlaw College, Auckland, New Zealand

"Missional theology can benefit from engaging the work of the Reformed theologian Thomas F. Torrance, and the theology of Torrance demands perceptive analysis. Joseph Sherrard serves us well by providing both for the introduction of Torrance to missional thought and then also a critical examination of ways in which Torrance's theology should be refined. In so doing, a host of key ideas are put to work in the missional conversation, including the ascension, the threefold office of Christ and the church's participation therein, and apostolicity. Sherrard moves the missional conversation quite a way forward by beginning the examination several theological steps back, not simply with church and mission but ultimately with the triune God of the gospel. Conversant with cultural and churchly trends, patient in its exposition, critical without being censorious, biblical and historical in its orientation, Reformed and yet appreciatively catholic, this is a wise book and a great guide for thinking about mission in theological terms."

Michael Allen, John Dyer Trimble Professor of Systematic Theology and academic dean, Reformed Theological Seminary, Orlando

"Throughout T. F. Torrance's corpus, he draws on the resources of systematic theology to inform the church's mission. Employing Torrance as a neglected conversation partner in missional theology, Joseph Sherrard encourages us to faithfully reconnect theology and mission, holding together the God who acts with the church's witness in this world. From the Trinity to the *munus triplex* of Christ, from the Lord's Supper to the church's relations to the state, Sherrard helps us see how Torrance's objective realism provides an abundance of fresh insight for the life and mission of the church. Since we are far too often tempted to reduce missional theology to mere sociological observation, this is a timely and needed work."

Kelly M. Kapic, professor of theological studies at Covenant College, author of *The God Who Gives*

"Anyone who wants to think intentionally and theologically about the present and future work of the church will find this work to be an asset. Sherrard brings Torrance, the missional church movement, and Jesus' threefold office as prophet, priest, and king into dynamic conversation, all with an eye toward effective ministry in a post-Christian world."

Esau McCaulley, assistant professor of New Testament at Wheaton College, author of *Reading While Black*

"Joseph H. Sherrard's *T. F. Torrance as Missional Theologian* delivers on its title's promise. By engaging one of the late-twentieth-century's leading theologians, Dr. Sherrard not only fills a lacuna in missional theology but also presents a compelling reading of Torrance's entire theological project. Sherrard demonstrates that Torrance's corpus can be read in light of his deep-seated and long-standing missional concern to evangelize the entire culture. This fine study will naturally be of interest to theologians and students of Torrance. But it will also be of value to pastor theologians and other thoughtful practitioners who want better to understand the theological dimensions of the church's mission in the world—and God's work in that mission. Highly recommended!"

Todd Wilson, cofounder and president of the Center for Pastor Theologians

NEW EXPLORATIONS IN THEOLOGY

T. F. TORRANCE AS MISSIONAL THEOLOGIAN

THE ASCENDED CHRIST AND THE MINISTRY OF THE CHURCH

JOSEPH H. SHERRARD

FOREWORD BY ALAN TORRANCE

ivp
Academic

An imprint of InterVarsity Press
Downers Grove, Illinois

InterVarsity Press
P.O. Box 1400, Downers Grove, IL 60515-1426
ivpress.com
email@ivpress.com

©2021 by Joseph H. Sherrard VI

All rights reserved. No part of this book may be reproduced in any form without written permission from InterVarsity Press.

InterVarsity Press® is the book-publishing division of InterVarsity Christian Fellowship/USA®, a movement of students and faculty active on campus at hundreds of universities, colleges, and schools of nursing in the United States of America, and a member movement of the International Fellowship of Evangelical Students. For information about local and regional activities, visit intervarsity.org.

Scripture quotations, unless otherwise noted, are from The Holy Bible, English Standard Version, copyright © 2001 by Crossway Bibles, a division of Good News Publishers. Used by permission. All rights reserved.

The publisher cannot verify the accuracy or functionality of website URLs used in this book beyond the date of publication.

Cover design: Cindy Kiple
Interior design: Beth McGill

ISBN 978-0-8308-4920-8 (print)
ISBN 978-0-8308-4921-5 (digital)

Printed in the United States of America ∞

InterVarsity Press is committed to ecological stewardship and to the conservation of natural resources in all our operations. This book was printed using sustainably sourced paper.

Library of Congress Cataloging-in-Publication Data
A catalog record for this book is available from the Library of Congress.

| P | 26 | 25 | 24 | 23 | 22 | 21 | 20 | 19 | 18 | 17 | 16 | 15 | 14 | 13 | 12 | 11 | 10 | 9 | 8 | 7 | 6 | 5 | 4 | 3 | 2 |
| Y | 43 | 42 | 41 | 40 | 39 | 38 | 37 | 36 | 35 | 34 | 33 | 32 | 31 | 30 | 29 | 28 | 27 | 26 | 25 | 24 | 23 | 22 | 21 |

For Kate

Contents

Foreword by Alan Torrance   ix

Acknowledgments   xi

Introduction: T. F. Torrance as a "Missional Theologian"   1

  1 Dualism and the Doctrine of God   11
     *T. F. Torrance's Trinitarian Theology
     and the Gospel Within Western Culture*

  2 The Lord of Mission   60
     The Threefold Office and Ascension of Jesus Christ

  3 The Mission of the Body of Christ   101
     Ecclesiology, Mission, and the Deposit of Faith

  4 The Ministry of the Ascended Lord   143
     The Church's Participation in Christ's Kingly Office

  5 The Ministry of the Ascended Lord   180
     *The Church's Participation in Christ's Prophetic
     and Priestly Offices*

Conclusion   217

Bibliography   229

General Index   237

Scripture Index   239

Foreword

Alan Torrance

⊕

T. F. Torrance was born in West China to parents who had travelled individually to China as missionaries driven by a passion for the outreach of the church. His parents met there and married. Tom was one of their six children. All three boys were ordained into the ministry and all three girls married ministers, two of whom became missionaries themselves. In short, Tom was raised within a family that shared a common passion for the mission of the church and made remarkable personal sacrifices to that end. Indeed, Tom didn't see his father for most of his teenage years because his father remained in China to continue his work while his family had to return home to Scotland given the violence and unrest in the region.

During the Second World War, Tom served as a chaplain in Italy. While there, he insisted on a change of army policy to allow him to be present with his men as they fought on the edge of the enemy lines. His view was that he couldn't preach the gospel and minister to the men if he wasn't able to be present with those who were making the ultimate sacrifice. I remember him telling me a story, which Sherrard also recalls in this book, of a nineteen-year-old soldier who had been mortally wounded. As he lay dying, he asked Tom what God was really like. "God is exactly what we see in Jesus. When we look at him, we see who God is." The young lad died with the sense of assurance that those words provided.

While an undergraduate, I had the privilege of spending a year living with T. F. and his wife, Margaret. What became clear to me during that year was that the way he read the Bible and led prayers before breakfast, approached his work as an army chaplain, and dedicated himself to his academic vocation were driven by the same all-embracing passion for the mission of the church. As a dogmatic theologian, his commitment to mission was evident in his extensive work with the Church of Scotland in drafting their statements on baptism, his theological engagement with contemporary science for which he was awarded the Templeton Prize, his groundbreaking achievements in ecumenical dialogue with the Orthodox Church, and of course his decades of teaching candidates for the ministry.

In this impressive study, Joey Sherrard goes to the theological heart of Tom's passion for the gospel and his missionary commitment. As illustrated not only by his published work but his preaching and wider ministry, the key focus of Tom's missional theology was Jesus Christ and his ongoing mission to this world interpreted in light of Christ's threefold office. He is the King through whom and for whom all things were created and who reigns as the Lord who out of love for a broken humanity came to us as a suffering servant. He is the Prophet who not only declares the arrival of the kingdom of God but mediates knowledge of God to us in his very person as the eternal Word made flesh. And he is the sole Priest of our confession who reconciles us to God, sanctifies our humanity and ever lives to intercede for us—taking our worship and intercessions in all their frailty, and presenting them to the Father as his. To understand the person and work of Christ in these terms is to recognize that every facet of the mission, worship, and outreach of the church requires being seen as sharing in his mission to this world. It is also to grasp that there is no higher or more relevant calling that we can be given than to share in this by the Spirit.

This study is a profoundly perceptive analysis of T. F.'s trinitarian theology of mission that is not only thoroughly and extensively researched but also clearheaded and lucid—more so, perhaps, than some of T. F.'s own writing! For this is a constructive analysis, not hagiography, and Sherrard does not shy away from asking the critical questions that need to be raised. At every point, however, he addresses them fairly and perceptively. This is anything but a dry, academic study. It has been undertaken by a pastor-theologian whose own passionate vision for the mission of the church does not simply replicate that of T. F. Torrance but faithfully seeks to press further and deeper.

Acknowledgments

THE END OF ALL THEOLOGICAL WORK is the praise of the triune God and the upbuilding of his church, and it is to that end that this work is directed. In the fittingness of God's providence and wisdom, this work is itself the result of God's faithfulness through many different branches of his church, many men and women who have played indispensable roles in bringing this work to completion.

The counsel of pastors and the love of churches have been significant in this journey. At an impressionable moment Allan Poole provided for me an example of a pastor whose vocation married a beautiful vision of the everyday life of pastoral ministry with intellectual curiosity and energy. Andrew Purves spoke into my life at a crucial moment in my discernment about further studies and encouraged me to take a next step. And Mark Stirling provided for me and my family both encouragement and counsel during our time in St. Andrews. The good people of First Presbyterian Church of Starkville, Mississippi, overwhelmed me and my family with their generosity in celebrating and then supporting our family in these studies. Their love and care for our family has and continues to be a sign of God's goodness in our lives. Cornerstone Church was an ideal community for the marriage of heart and mind while we lived in St. Andrews, and the open homes of our pastors and friends there helped sustain us during our time away from friends and family in the States. And the family of Signal Mountain Presbyterian Church has supported and encouraged us as this work has drawn to a close. It is a joy and privilege to partner with that congregation in ministry.

So many men and women have stepped in at crucial moments to support and to encourage this work to completion. Forrest Buckner was a faithful partner in prayer during our time together in St. Andrews, and the many prayers we prayed together on the West Sands sustained our common hope that our work would bless God's people. Kenny Robertson likewise encouraged, pastored, and prayed me through our time in St. Andrews. Esau McCaulley was a steadfast friend through our time in St. Andrews and a constant reminder of the pastoral implications of the work we undertake. Kavin Rowe, Douglas Campbell, and Jeff McSwain provided early encouragement to seek further studies and guidance along the way. The community of the Roundel was the ideal environment for mutual edification, and lunchtime conversations with Tim Baylor, Jordan Hillebert, Andrew Kaethler, Jonathan Lett, Jared Michelson, and Tyler Wittman have sharpened this work considerably. It is difficult to imagine a more supportive and encouraging faculty than what I experienced at St. Andrews, and John Webster, Stephen Holmes, Mark Elliott, Scott Hafemann, and David Moffitt each went above and beyond in giving time to meet with me and strengthen this work. And my supervisor, Alan Torrance, was a great encouragement to me throughout this process. There is no better endorsement of the theology of the Torrance family than his joyful concern for the church and concern regarding its articulation of the gospel. Finally, David McNutt's service as an editor has strengthened this work considerably, and I am grateful for his support of this project.

Neither could this project have been completed without the support of our family. My grandparents, Joe and Anne Sherrard, played no small role in making our time in St. Andrews possible, and it is surely a fitting thing that their generosity sent me to "the home of golf." Kate's parents, Dean and Beth Norman, blessed us in our move overseas even when it meant that they would see their daughter (and perhaps more worryingly, their grandsons) with significantly less frequency. My father's intellectual curiosity and questioning had no small part in guiding me along my vocational path, and it brings a smile to my face to think of the pride I know he would feel in this work being published. My sister, Stephanie, will always have my gratitude in blessing our move to St. Andrews as she cared for our mother, care that only increased in its demands as her health increasingly worsened. And my mother's excitement over our move to St. Andrews made a world of difference to us. That the timing of our move back to the States allowed me to be with her in her final days and hours was a generous gift from God.

My sons, Joseph and James, brought joy that lightened the load of this project. It is an immense privilege to be a father to two men who are so full of life, and their constant tugs to see their latest Lego creation or to play soccer in the backyard were a constant reminder of the blessings of life outside of the office (and outside of my own head). And the chief acknowledgment belongs to my wife, Kate. Her courage in taking the momentous step of leaving behind all the familiarities of our life in order to move, sight unseen, across the ocean to Scotland, was then and still is an incredible thing to contemplate. Her steadfast encouragement and prayers sustained me over those four years, and it is a joy to share in life's ventures with a companion with such courage and wisdom.

Introduction

T. F. TORRANCE AS A "MISSIONAL THEOLOGIAN"

IN 1986 LESSLIE NEWBIGIN posed the prescient question, "What would be involved in a missionary encounter between the gospel and this whole way of perceiving, thinking, and living that we call 'modern Western culture'?"[1] The prescience lay in Newbigin's perception of the declining state of Christianity in Europe and North America. Christendom's day in Western culture was moving swiftly toward dusk, and the Western church was largely unaware and unequipped to address the advance of secularism and that culture's drift away from its moorings. Although by no means a lone voice in the wilderness, Newbigin clarified for many an issue that would determine a significant amount of self-criticism and constructive attempts to mount an answer to this pressing question.

By the turn of the twenty-first century, Newbigin's question had catalyzed an entire discipline: "missional theology." Identifying itself self-consciously with Newbigin's legacy, missional theology sought to recast theology's work within the new Western context and in so doing reclaim fundamental truths about the nature of theology and the church's existence. Thus in the introduction to a central publication of the movement, *Missional Church: A Vision for the Sending of the Church in North America*, Darrell Guder writes, "We have come to see that mission is not merely an activity of the church. Rather, mission is the result of God's initiative, rooted in God's

---

[1] Lesslie Newbigin, *Foolishness to the Greeks: The Gospel and Western Culture* (Grand Rapids, MI: Eerdmans, 1986), 1.

purposes to restore and heal creation. 'Mission' means 'sending,' and it is the central biblical theme describing God's action in human history."[2] Under the banner of the Gospel and Our Culture Network[3] and other entities, a number of other publications followed that emphasized the need for theology to understand "mission" neither as a topic peripheral to the church's theology nor as synonymous with the activity of foreign missionaries, but rather an essential element of the church's articulation of the message with which it has been entrusted. Thus in another central text of the movement, David Bosch writes, "The entire Christian existence is to be characterized as missionary existence."[4]

Arguments for the significance of missional theology have typically traded along three similar but distinct lines. There is first a sociological argument: the church no longer enjoys the place of privilege it once did within Western Christendom. With the advance of secularism and the disappearance of a culture which is amiable to the claims of the Christian faith, the church must renew its articulation of the gospel so as to witness winsomely, faithfully, and effectively to the risen Lord Jesus and his claims. When missional theology is pursued along this line, it focuses its energies upon helping the church employ the proper kinds of practices of mission, repositioning itself within current intellectual and cultural environments and of contextualizing the gospel message so as to communicate effectively within this new moment in Western culture. While there is reflection upon Christian doctrine within this stream, these kinds of projects are done chiefly with the reformulation of Christian practice in mind.[5] This strain of

---

[2]Darrell L. Guder, ed., *Missional Church: A Vision for the Sending of the Church in North America* (Grand Rapids, MI: Eerdmans, 1998), 4.

[3]Alongside *Missional Church,* other important publications in this series include Darrell L. Guder, *The Continuing Conversion of the Church* (Grand Rapids, MI: Eerdmans, 2000); Darrell L. Guder, *Called to Witness: Doing Missional Theology* (Grand Rapids, MI: Eerdmans, 2015); Craig Van Gelder, *Confident Witness—Changing World: Rediscovering the Gospel in North America* (Grand Rapids, MI: Eerdmans, 1999); and Lois Y. Barret, ed., *Treasure in Jars of Clay: Patterns in Missional Faithfulness* (Grand Rapids, MI: Eerdmans, 2004).

[4]David J. Bosch, *Transforming Mission: Paradigm Shifts in Theology of Mission,* 20th anniv. ed. (Maryknoll, NY: Orbis Books, 2011), 10.

[5]Examples of this range widely. See Newbigin, *Foolishness to the Greeks*; Michael Frost and Alan Hirsch, *The Shaping of Things to Come: Innovation and Mission for the 21st-Century Church* (Peabody, MA: Hendrickson, 2003); James Davidson Hunter, *To Change the World: The Irony, Tragedy, and Possibility of Christianity in the Late Modern World* (Oxford: Oxford University Press, 2010); Barrett et al., *Treasure in Clay Jars.*

argument is demonstrated in Guder's introduction to *Missional Church* where he writes, "The obvious fact that what we once regarded as Christendom is now a post-Constantinian, post-Christendom, and even post-Christian mission field stands in bold contrast today with the apparent lethargy of established church traditions in addressing their new situation both creatively and faithfully."[6]

The second approach follows along the lines of biblical theology. Rather than addressing the church's mission primarily by way of the pressing need for a more missional theology or by way of the sociological conditions which affect its witness and practice, here we find a reading of the biblical text which places mission as one of Scripture's core themes. As we follow the narrative of the people of God we see that God's people were always on mission, and that the church will do well to recognize that in some sense every book of the Bible is a book about mission.[7] When Christopher Wright states that "*the whole Bible is itself a 'missional phenomenon,'*"[8] he is representative of this strain of missional theology.

And there is finally, and most significantly for our own purposes, an approach that draws from the resources of systematic theology. In this view, missional theology is pursued through a return to the church's doctrine so as to emphasize the particular resources that the various loci of systematic theology possess. Perhaps the example par excellence of this argument is the concept of the *missio Dei*. Mission, it is argued, is a concept that finds its origin not in ecclesiology, but rather in the doctrine of God. God's mission to the world is demonstrated first and foremost from his triune nature through the sending of the Son and the Spirit in their external missions. Thus Ross Hastings writes, "The core of theology and the gospel is that God is a sending God, and . . . we can only know this because of God's two missions: the sending of the Son and the sending of the Spirit. That is, it was mission that led us to understand God as Trinity, and if Trinity is the distinctively Christian understanding of God, then mission, the mission of

---

[6]Guder, *Missional Church*, 7.
[7]The most impressive example of this approach is undoubtedly Christopher J. H. Wright, *The Mission of God: Unlocking the Bible's Grand Narrative* (Downers Grove, IL: IVP Academic, 2006).
[8]Wright, *Mission of God*, 22.

God that determine all mission, is the mother of theology."⁹ While such reflection necessarily unfolds into discussions of the nature of the church's practice, they do so only after lingering upon the nature of God's triune life,[10] the incarnation,[11] or ecclesiology.[12] A great dependence upon and a more robust reflection upon Christian theology is exhibited in this approach.

What is striking about the current state of this third approach to missional theology is its underdevelopment. In view of the wealth of the church's doctrinal tradition, the recent revival of and controversy surrounding trinitarian theology, and the christological vocabulary and resources available to theologians, missional theology remains strikingly and unnecessarily impoverished. Concepts such as the *missio Dei* are often utilized carelessly and without reference to the extensive tradition of theological reflection on the doctrine of God within the church. The incarnation is rightly given a central place in the church's self-understanding of its mission, but is done so without reference to the lessons learned through the various christological controversies. This lack of engagement with systematic theology has been noted by Jason Sexton in an essay titled, "Missional Theology's Missing Ingredient: The Necessity of Systematic Theology for Today's Mission." There, he argues not only that missional theology remains relatively uninformed by the resources of systematic theology, but also that this lacuna negatively impacts missional theology:

> Without [systematic theology], missional thinking robs itself of the very impulse essential to mission. In doing so, it ultimately fails to drum up the categorical reach that faithfully testifies to Jesus' exclusive lordship within the church and the public arena, tending instead towards a ghettoized iso-disciplinarity that nurtures an unhealthy form of pluralism and arrogance whilst forsaking the mission the church has already been summoned by and sent on. . . . If missional theology wishes to display the strengths it seeks, generating a coherent structure and kerygma lending to distinctly evangelical gospel-proclamation,

---

[9]Ross Hastings, *Missional God, Missional Church: Hope for Re-Evangelizing the West* (Downers Grove, IL: IVP Academic, 2012), 249.
[10]John Flett, *The Witness of God: The Trinity, Missio Dei, Karl Barth, and the Nature of Christian Community* (Grand Rapids, MI: Eerdmans, 2010).
[11]Darrell L. Guder, *Be My Witnesses: The Church's Mission, Message, and Messengers* (Grand Rapids, MI: Eerdmans, 1985).
[12]Hastings, *Missional God, Missional Church*.

it will need to take much better account of systematic theology, and the way mission has always been and is really done.[13]

Missional theology, it would seem, is a discipline that could be significantly strengthened through the resources of the catholic church's theological tradition.

T. F. Torrance as a "Missional Theologian"

The argument of this book is that the theology of T. F. Torrance is a significant attempt to address this perceived deficit within the discipline of missional theology. Torrance's stature and significance as a theologian has long been recognized, with scholars such as Bruce McCormack stating that he was "the most significant theologian of the late-twentieth century."[14] Less attention, however, has been given to the motivations that drove Torrance and the perspective this gives to his corpus. From very early on Torrance understood his vocation as a theologian to be a missionary vocation. Reflecting upon the effect of his early life as the child of missionary parents in China, Torrance stated, "I look upon my life as dedicated to the spreading of the gospel, evangelizing in different areas of human life and thought."[15] Torrance initially understood that this vocation would lead him to follow in the footsteps of his mother and father,[16] but he later came to understand his calling as that of a theologian and professor. In turning aside from a life as a foreign missionary, Torrance did not believe he was removing himself from this evangelical calling. Rather, Torrance understood the calling of the theologian to be that of an evangelist of every aspect of culture: "The theologian has to do what the ancient bishops often had to do in the early church. They had to be, among other things, evangelists. The theologian needs to help the church evangelize *the entire culture*."[17]

That statement bears further scrutiny. Torrance's concern is the evangelization of culture, but there is an ecclesial emphasis to this concern: "to help

---

[13]Jason S. Sexton, "Missional Theology's Missing Ingredient: The Necessity of Systematic Theology for Today's Mission," *Mission Studies* 32 (2015): 395.
[14]Bruce L. McCormack, cover endorsement of Alister E. McGrath, *T. F. Torrance: An Intellectual Biography* (New York: T&T Clark Ltd, 2006).
[15]I. John Hesselink, "A Pilgrimage in the School of Christ: An Interview with T. F. Torrance," *Reformed Review* 38.1 (1984): 49.
[16]Hesselink, "Pilgrimage in the School of Christ," 52.
[17]Michael Bauman, "Interview with Thomas Torrance," in *Roundtable: Conversations with European Theologians* (Grand Rapids, MI: Baker, 1990), 114 (emphasis original).

the church evangelize." Throughout Torrance's life, he was consistently concerned with the church, its articulation of the gospel, and the effectiveness of its mission within his own Western culture. Early in his career, Torrance was involved in the beginning of the Faith and Order Movement, a branch of the World Council of Churches and the institution that incubated the conversations that would later become the missional movement. While teaching at New College, Torrance trained Church of Scotland pastors and would later serve as the Moderator of the Church of Scotland's General Assembly. During his time in that office, Torrance named as a primary concern the church's task of proclaiming the gospel to a skeptical and unbelieving world.[18] For Torrance, the practice of theology and the theologian's role are not to be found merely in the advancement of the frontiers of knowledge, but instead in equipping the church for the pressing task of proclaiming the gospel.

Previous engagements with Torrance have focused upon his work on the relationship between science and theology as the prime example of the "intellectual evangelism" that is so central to this proclamation. Torrance's demonstration of the common epistemological commitments of science and theology deserves the attention it has received, but thus far few studies have drawn attention to the extent to which Torrance presents a comprehensive vision of the church, its missional nature, and its service and ministry to the world. In their surveys of Torrance's thought, both Elmer Colyer[19] and Paul Molnar[20] give attention to Torrance's ecclesiology, but this attention is limited in proportion to his doctrine of the Trinity, his christology, and his understanding of atonement, with little attention given to the place of mission within Torrance's theology and ecclesiology. Kye Won Lee devotes a chapter to Torrance's ecclesiology in his study of the theme of union with Christ in Torrance's theology, but the missional implications of Torrance's thought are examined only in passing and within a more fundamental

---

[18]See "An Urgent Call to the Kirk," a letter Torrance wrote while serving as Moderator and which was circulated throughout the Church of Scotland: www.tftorrance.org/call-to-kirk.php.
[19]Elmer M. Colyer, *How to Read T. F. Torrance: Understanding His Trinitarian and Scientific Theology* (Eugene, OR: Wipf & Stock, 2001), 259-282.
[20]Paul D. Molnar, *Thomas F. Torrance: Theologian of the Trinity* (Burlington, VT: Ashgate, 2009), 265-323.

exploration of the doctrine of union with Christ.[21] Stanley S. MacLean's *Resurrection Apocalypse, and the Kingdom of Christ* notes the ecclesial and missional implications of Torrance's developed eschatology, but these ideas are neither developed nor explored.[22]

The most complete study of Torrance's ecclesiology is Albert L. Shepherd's dissertation, "The Body of Christ: T. F. Torrance's Ecclesial Ontology."[23] This careful analysis examines the place of Torrance's central metaphor for the church, "The body of Christ," within his wider theological architectonic. Aspects of the nature of the church and the place of sacramental ministry are considered as well. But Torrance's particular account of the church's mission is not within the purview of Shepherd's excellent work. Kate Tyler has also recently contributed a survey of Torrance's ecclesiology, and her work includes some consideration of the significance of the missional elements in his thought.[24] But beyond these relatively brief engagements the specifically missional implications of Torrance's ecclesiology have not received significant attention.

In response to this lacuna, this work presents two interrelated arguments. First, it is argued that Torrance's extensive and wide-ranging theological corpus presents a coherent and comprehensive missional theology. Beginning with the doctrine of God, continuing through christology, and finally in ecclesiology, Torrance's thought is consistently informed by missional concerns and is directed toward answering the challenges the church faces in its proclamation of the good news of Jesus Christ for the world. This missional theology, while not without weaknesses, is a compelling and overlooked contribution to the current conversation about the nature and source of the church's mission. In contrast to proposals which trade heavily on sociology and cultural analysis, Torrance offers a *theological* account of the church's identity and its place in the ascended Christ's continuing mission to the world.

---

[21] Kye Won Lee, *Living in Union with Christ: The Practical Theology of T. F. Torrance* (New York: Lang, 2003), 251-293.

[22] Stanley S. MacLean, *Resurrection, Apocalypse, and the Kingdom of Christ: The Eschatology of Thomas F. Torrance* (Eugene, OR: Wipf & Stock, 2012).

[23] Albert L. Shepherd, "The Body of Christ: T. F. Torrance's Ecclesial Ontology" (PhD diss., University of Aberdeen, 2015).

[24] Kate Tyler, *The Ecclesiology of Thomas F. Torrance: Koinonia and the Church* (Lanham, MD: Lexington Books/Fortress, 2019).

Second, this book argues that Torrance's stature as a theologian of mission has been overlooked thus far. At the beginning of his theological career, Torrance worked alongside the early forerunners of the missional movement—Lesslie Newbigin, Willem Visser 't Hooft, and Hendrik Kraemer, among others—as a part of the Faith and Order Movement. The collection of writings that Torrance published from this time have not been given significant attention by Torrance scholars thus far. The concerns Torrance addressed during this period of his life never left him, and even as Torrance moved on to address the relationship between science and theology and, as this study demonstrates, he articulated his doctrine of the Trinity, these initial impulses were never left behind.

To make these arguments, the first chapter examines Torrance's doctrine of the Trinity. One of missional theology's central tenets has been the location of mission first within the doctrine of God as opposed to primarily in christology, pneumatology, or ecclesiology. The concept of the *missio Dei* argues that the centrality of mission within the life of the church is to be "derived from the very nature of God"[25] because of its centrality within the doctrine of God. Within this context, Torrance's own doctrine of God is considered. The historical theology that undergirds his trinitarian theology is explored, and it is noted how Torrance's handling of the Nicene, Reformation, and contemporary sources with which he engaged was undertaken with an eye to the particular problem of dualism. The resulting theological realism has significant epistemological and soteriological implications on Torrance's theology and reveal the missional concerns that drive his thought. Torrance's thought is compared with a recent similar proposal, that of John Flett in his *The Witness of God*, and the two projects are contrasted with one another.

The second chapter discusses Torrance's christology. Because of his christocentric methodology, the shape of Torrance's christology lays important groundwork for his subsequent ecclesiological and missional work. Torrance's description of the work of Christ by way of the threefold office is examined, and we explore Torrance's use of the scriptural witness to describe Christ's redeeming work and how his proposal is both similar to and

---

[25]Bosch, *Transforming Mission*, 390.

divergent from other Reformed proposals. Torrance's doctrine of the ascension is also considered, and we explore how the ascension creates space for the church's participation in Christ's ongoing activity.

The third chapter focuses upon the central ecclesiological concept in Torrance's theology, the body of Christ. Torrance utilizes classical christological grammar in order to deploy this concept within his christology, and we examine how Torrance does this in such a way that he can argue in a number of different but complementary ways that mission is essential to the nature of the church. Torrance's ecclesiology is then compared with that of Lesslie Newbigin. Newbigin is a figure who is in many ways similar to Torrance, in his biography as well as in theological instincts. Interestingly, though, Newbigin draws different conclusions about the church's mission. Out of this contrast the relative strengths of Torrance and Newbigin's missional ecclesiologies are assessed. In this chapter, Torrance's understanding of apostolicity is also evaluated. His use of the deposit of faith as a central concept in understanding the nature of the church's mission is a unique contribution to the concept of apostolicity, the significance of which has not yet been recognized.

The fourth and fifth chapters explore the shape of Torrance's missional ecclesiology as the church participates in the ascended Christ's ongoing ministry. Because the church's work can only be understood through Christ's threefold office, the nature of the church's royal, prophetic, and priestly work is considered. Torrance's unique contribution to each of these areas is considered and assessed. Aspects of the church's royal work are compared with that found in Oliver O'Donovan's work, and Torrance's argument for embedding the doctrine of Scripture within the prophetic office is also considered, while the thinness of his description of the act of preaching is also explored. The centrality of the priestly office within Torrance's ecclesiology is described at some length, and the resulting argument for the centrality of the Lord's Table to the church's mission is discussed.

The concluding chapter summarizes the work of the book and appraises the unique contribution of Torrance's thought, considering its strengths and weaknesses. The result is a detailed argument for how missional concerns drove Torrance's thought from his doctrine of God, to his christology, his ecclesiology, and on to his understanding of the church's mission. Torrance's missional theology is a significant constructive proposal that, while not without weaknesses, offers an important model for the practice of responsible and robust theological engagement with the church's mission while also enriching the current debate about the nature of the church's mission and the God who calls and enables the church to do that work.

1

Dualism and the Doctrine of God

T. F. Torrance's Trinitarian Theology and the Gospel Within Western Culture

---

The *Missio Dei* and the Doctrine of God

In our introduction we noted the recent appearance of a number of arguments for the fundamental importance of the category of mission within the discipline of systematic theology. These attempts are often gathered under a single descriptive heading: *missio Dei*. This term and the conceptual framework attached to it, often (apparently erroneously) traced back to Karl Barth,[1] describes the fundamental conviction that unites all these recent projects. In *Transforming Mission*, a foundational text for both strands of biblical and theological reflection upon mission, David Bosch describes the conviction in this way: "Mission was understood as being derived from the very nature of God. It was thus put in the context of the doctrine of the Trinity, not of ecclesiology or soteriology.... As far as missionary thinking was concerned, this linking with the doctrine of the Trinity constituted an important innovation."[2]

---

[1] See John G. Flett's helpful historical study of the term *missio Dei* in chapters three and four of his *The Witness of God: The Trinity, Missio Dei, Karl Barth, and the Nature of Christian Community* (Grand Rapids, MI: Eerdmans, 2010). Flett argues that while Barth is an important contributor to the church's reflection on its mission, the specific term *missio Dei* was neither used nor defined by Barth.

[2] David J. Bosch, *Transforming Mission: Paradigm Shifts in Theology of Mission*, 20th anniv. ed. (Maryknoll, NY: Orbis Books, 2011), 390.

Yet recent work has questioned to what extent these proposals were ever properly grounded in the doctrine of God. In his analysis of the genesis of the term *missio Dei* and its historical development, Flett offers a critical assessment of the *missio Dei*'s development and history: "Both the decisive force and fatal flaw of the *missio Dei* rests in its relationship to the doctrine of the Trinity. As propounded to date, the concept is deficiently Trinitarian, and the wide range of its contemporary problems is a direct result of this single lack."[3] In Flett's analysis, the relation between various *missio Dei* proposals and the doctrine of God was primarily defensive and apologetic in nature, rather than robustly constructive: "The doctrine of the Trinity plays only a negative role, distancing mission from improper alignments with accidental human authorities. This afforded a needed corrective to the phenomenological approach to mission so compromised by the colonialist endeavor, and established a theological means for distancing a local church from her host culture, that is, identifying her as a missionary community."[4]

This claim is certainly vindicated by a survey of the literature that surrounds the *missio Dei*. While many of the recent proposals that connect God's triune life with the church's practice of mission are quite helpful and elegant, there is a certain thinness to their accounts of the doctrine of God. Let us take as an example of a significant milestone in missional reflection upon the Trinity: the work of Lesslie Newbigin. The value of Newbigin's work on this topic, found first in the pamphlet *Trinitarian Doctrine for Today's Mission* and then later expanded in *The Open Secret: Sketches for a Missionary Theology*, is difficult to overstate. Newbigin, in many ways ahead of the "trinitarian revival" of the second half of the 20th century, cleverly applies elements of basic trinitarian theology to key problems facing the church in the face of secularism's advance. There is little that one can find to criticize here. Yet it should be noted that Newbigin's work is devoid of any deeper reflection on God's immanent life and how the conclusions he draws about the economic activity of the Father, Son, and Holy Spirit is to be understood and coordinated within that light. Bosch's *Transforming Mission* demonstrates a similar reticence to speak about the relation between the claims about God's economic activity and God's immanent triune relations.

---

[3]Flett, *Witness of God*, 9.
[4]Flett, *Witness of God*, 76.

We should not lay blame at the feet of a missionary and a missiologist for a failure to apply the tools of systematic theology. But we should nonetheless ask, with Flett, that the claims of *missio Dei* theology be given greater scrutiny as they relate to the church's theological tradition, and that the missional resources already available might be supplemented even more so that possible error is identified and corrected. There have been recent gestures in this direction,[5] but I would argue that more can be done to draw from the church's tradition. T. F. Torrance is an underutilized resource that can make a significant contribution to this conversation. As we have already discussed, Torrance's life was informed and shaped by missional concerns, and these concerns in turn shaped his work. In this chapter, we will make explicit the deep resonances between Torrance's thought and the concerns of *missio Dei* theology, bringing the two into fruitful conversation.

Our objective in this chapter is therefore two pronged. First, we will demonstrate how Torrance's doctrine of the Trinity is informed by missional concerns. The content of Torrance's trinitarian theology is supplied by theologians from the catholic tradition of the church such as Athanasius, Gregory of Nazianzus, and Basil of Caesarea. But Torrance's appropriation of these sources is shaped by his distinctly modern concerns about the intelligibility of the gospel in the West and his concern for the church's mission. Second, we will also demonstrate how Torrance's doctrine of the Trinity is an important, constructive voice in the articulation of the church's participation in Christ's reconciling work.

The Shaping of Torrance's Trinitarian Theology

In 1980, Torrance published what would be the first of three books on the Trinity which were in many ways the culmination of his theological career. This book, *The Ground and Grammar of Theology*, is at first glance a somewhat curious approach to the doctrine of the Trinity. The first four of the six chapters of Torrance's book have comparatively little to do with the doctrine of the Trinity, but are instead a survey of the intellectual conditions of science

---

[5]See for example Ross Hastings, *Missional God, Missional Church: Hope for Re-Evangelizing the West* (Downers Grove, IL: IVP Academic, 2012), 80-118, 243-267; Jason Sexton, "A Confessing Trinitarian Theology for Today's Mission," in *Advancing Trinitarian Theology: Explorations in Constructive Dogmatics*, ed. Oliver D. Crisp and Fred Sanders (Grand Rapids, MI: Zondervan, 2014), 171-189. See also the examination and critique of Flett, *Witness of God*, below.

and theology in the West. Throughout these chapters, Torrance is particularly attentive to what he calls in the preface to the second edition "the two great dualist cosmologies of the past, the Ptolemaic and Copernican-Newtonian, and to the non-dualist cosmological outlook arising out of the radical change in the basic rationality of science which we owe to Einstein."[6] In the final two chapters, however, the discussion pivots to the nature of Christian theology and to the doctrine of the Trinity. Far from a digression, these final chapters are in fact integral to Torrance's understanding of his attempt in the book "to clarify the trinitarian structure of Christian theology."[7] Torrance moves naturally from an analysis of the dualistic intellectual conditions of Western culture to a discussion of the Trinity.

The progression of Torrance's argument in *The Ground and Grammar of Theology* gives us a view into the concerns that shape his doctrine of the Trinity. Torrance's trinitarian theology was not developed in an intellectual vacuum, but rather emerges in coordination with other concerns—in particular, the problem of dualism. Recent studies of Torrance's theology have helpfully demonstrated the importance of the doctrine of the Trinity in his thought[8] as well as the nature of his handling of the patristic sources that provide the substance of Torrance's doctrine of God.[9] But in their inattention to the concerns that accompany this doctrine, a more complete understanding of Torrance's trinitarian theology has been occluded. In what follows, we will first demonstrate the significance of the problem of dualism for Torrance's theology and then follow how this influence shapes his doctrine of the Trinity.

Dualism. The theological career of T. F. Torrance was worked out in the context of the collapse of Christendom in Europe, and Torrance committed his considerable theological ability to a winsome and formidable presentation of the Christian faith within these social and intellectual conditions. In contrast to contemporaries with similar fundamental concerns—for example, Lesslie Newbigin—Torrance focused his response not on the

---

[6] Thomas F. Torrance, *The Ground and Grammar of Theology: Consonance Between Theology and Science* (Edinburgh: T&T Clark, 2001), vii.
[7] Torrance, *Ground and Grammar of Theology*, vii.
[8] Paul D. Molnar, *Thomas F. Torrance: Theologian of the Trinity* (Burlington, VT: Ashgate, 2009).
[9] Jason Radcliff, *Thomas F. Torrance and the Church Fathers: A Reformed, Evangelical, and Ecumenical Reconstruction of the Patristic Tradition* (Eugene, OR: Wipf & Stock, 2014).

advance of secularism but instead on the intellectual conditions of Western life and the dualistic philosophy he perceived to be a cause of its problems.

One would be hard pressed to find a work of Torrance's that did not contain an explicit or implicit reference to the concept of dualism, and this is particularly evident whenever Torrance deals with the doctrine of God. In the aforementioned *The Ground and Grammar of Theology*, Torrance states his overwhelming concern with "dualist modes of thought that drive a wedge between Christ and God, and correspondingly between the message of Christ and Christ himself."[10] In *The Christian Doctrine of God*, Torrance draws attention to the problem of "the menace of the dualist structure of thought."[11] And in *The Trinitarian Faith*, Torrance describes how "the biblical teaching about God's providential and saving activity in history, and the Christian message of incarnation and redemption in space and time, had to struggle with the underlying assumptions of a dualist outlook upon God and the world in order to be heard aright and take root."[12] Thus in each of the volumes on the Trinity that come at the climax of Torrance's theological career we see evidence of his concern with the problem of dualism.

Torrance's focus on dualism clearly springs from his concern about the mission of the church. In a speech which Torrance gave to the Scottish Church Theology Society (later titled "Preaching Christ Today"), Torrance gives what he calls "a plea to return to Christ-centered teaching and preaching."[13] Speaking out of his concern with the plight of the church in the West, Torrance identifies dualism as one of the most significant contemporary obstacles to the proclamation of the gospel: "We are still in the midst of this struggle to maintain the supreme truth of the unbroken relation in being and act between Jesus Christ and God the Father against insidious dualist or dichotomous ways of thinking."[14] An oft-recounted story from Torrance's experience as a WWII army chaplain further demonstrates the extent to which this concern shapes his thinking on the

---

[10]Torrance, *Ground and Grammar of Theology*, 41.
[11]Torrance, *The Christian Doctrine of God: One Being, Three Persons* (Edinburgh: T&T Clark, 2016), 130.
[12]Torrance, *The Trinitarian Faith: The Evangelical Theology of the Ancient Catholic Church*, 2nd ed. (London: T&T Clark, 2016), 47-48.
[13]Torrance, *Preaching Christ Today: The Gospel and Scientific Thinking* (Grand Rapids, MI: Eerdmans, 1994), viii.
[14]Torrance, *Preaching Christ Today*, 21.

church's proclamation of the gospel. In the aftermath of a battle in Italy, Torrance came across a mortally wounded nineteen-year-old soldier. As he lay dying, the young man asked Torrance, "Is God like Jesus?" Reflecting upon the encounter, Torrance wrote, "I assured him that he was—the only God that there is, the God who had come to us in Jesus, shown his face to us, and poured out his love to us as our Savior."[15] This event, and another like it from his time as a pastor in Aberdeen, was formative for Torrance: "When I thought about that afterwards, I asked myself, what has been happening, what has come in between Jesus Christ and God to obscure God from people?"[16] Torrance's answer? "The insidious effect of dualism."[17]

The overall shape of Torrance's theology is polemically, or perhaps better put evangelically, directed at the problem of dualism in the theological and scientific culture of the West. But despite the importance of the term for Torrance's theology and its ubiquity within his corpus, it can at times be difficult to identify precisely how Torrance utilizes the term *dualism*. We can begin with a definition that Torrance approved, which is found in the endnotes to *Belief in Science and in Christian Life*. There, Torrance provides this description:

> *Dualism*: the division of reality into two incompatible spheres of being. This may be cosmological, in the dualism between the sensible and an intelligible realm, neither of which can be reduced to the other. It may also be epistemological, in which the empirical and theoretical aspects of reality are separated from one another, thereby giving rise to the extremes of empiricism and rationalism. It may also be anthropological, in a dualism between the mind and body, in which a physical and mental substance are conceived as either interacting with one another or as running a parallel course without affecting one another.[18]

These realms may either be clearly separated or perhaps touching upon one another in a limited sense. But whether they are "adjacent to one another but with a clear gap between them" or "touching one another

---

[15] Quoted in Alister E. McGrath, *Thomas F. Torrance: An Intellectual Biography* (Edinburgh: T&T Clark, 1999), 74.
[16] Torrance, *Preaching Christ Today*, 56.
[17] Torrance, *Preaching Christ Today*, 56.
[18] Torrance, ed., *Belief in Science and in Christian Life: The Relevance of Michael Polanyi's Thought for Christian Faith and Life* (Eugene, OR: Wipf & Stock, 1998), 136.

tangentially,"[19] they are, according to Torrance, fundamentally separate and therefore dualist.

Other interpreters offer differing definitions of Torrance's understanding of dualism, all focusing upon the cosmological and epistemological aspects of the above description. In his survey of Torrance's theology, Elmer Colyer describes dualism as "the division of reality into two incompatible or independent domains" and identifies two main species of dualism —epistemological and cosmological.[20] Titus Chung proposes that when Torrance uses dualism in a theological context, he indicates "an internalized mode of perceiving reality into two opposing poles of the Creator and the creation, negating any real relation between them and rendering God's revelation and mediation in Christ null."[21] In our discussion of Torrance's understanding of dualism, we will follow Colyer in his identification of epistemological and cosmological dualism as of particular significance to Torrance.[22] As we shall see, these two kinds of dualism inform and form important aspects of Torrance's dogmatic project.

In order to understand the formative influence of dualism in Torrance's thought, we require more than a definition of dualism but rather an understanding of how dualism functions and how the catholic church has responded to its challenge throughout the ages. And that sense can be best gained by looking to Torrance's historical theology. In so doing, we will not focus on the accuracy of Torrance's reconstruction of the theologies of Athanasius, Calvin, and others. Recent work by scholars such as Lewis Ayres and Richard Muller[23] raise questions about the adequacy of Torrance's work

---

[19]Torrance, *Preaching Christ Today*, 51.
[20]Elmer M. Colyer, *How to Read T. F. Torrance: Understanding His Trinitarian and Scientific Theology* (Eugene, OR: Wipf & Stock, 2001), 58.
[21]Titus Chung, *Thomas Torrance's Mediations and Revelation* (Farnham, England: Ashgate, 2011), 41.
[22]Torrance's concern about anthropological dualism, as demonstrated in his own definition of dualism, is worth noting. This concern, however, isn't fully developed in his writings and are tangential to our argument here.
[23]Lewis Ayres's *Nicaea and its Legacy: An Approach to Fourth-Century Trinitarian Theology* (Oxford: Oxford University Press, 2004) demonstrates just how much more complicated the history that surrounded Athanasius and other pro-Nicene theologians is than what Torrance describes. See in particular pp. 430-435 for a summary of the twists and turns of this period of church history. Muller's criticisms of the interpretation of the school of Calvin, that includes Torrance, appears throughout his work. But for an example of his most direct engagement, see "The Barth Legacy: New Athanasius or Origen Redivivus? A Response to T. F. Torrance," *The Thomist* 54.4 (1990): 673-704.

qua historical scholarship. But as his historical theology reveals the mind of Torrance himself, it provides a window into precisely what dangers Torrance saw in dualism and how elements of the doctrine of the Trinity serve to redress these dangers and thereby provide safe passage for the church. In his historical theology, Torrance identifies three key moments where the church overcame the problems of a dualist epistemological, and cosmological, framework: the Arian controversy, the Protestant Reformation, and the theology of Karl Barth. This historical theology is not original to Torrance. In his 1934 essay "Revelation,"[24] Karl Barth proposes the same narration of church history. Almost certainly Torrance read this essay and it provided the foundation for his own work. But in Torrance's writing we find the idea developed beyond what is seen in Barth's initial suggestion, and with an eye trained specifically on the concept of dualism.

Key moment one: the insight of Athanasius. To have even the most casual acquaintance with the theology of T. F. Torrance is to know the significance of the heroes and villains of the Arian controversy. Torrance's most in-depth account of this chapter of church history is seen in *The Trinitarian Faith*, where we find his analysis of the fourth century debates of the early church. In this account, Torrance identifies the conflict primarily as what took place when "the preaching and teaching of the Gospel came up against a radical dualism of body and mind that pervaded every aspect of Graeco-Roman civilisation."[25] This dualism finds its genesis first in Plato, who endorsed a fundamental separation between the sensible world and the intelligible world. That dichotomy is compounded by Aristotle, whom Torrance (following his philosopher friend and fellow Scotsman Donald MacKinnon) believed offered a basically similar cosmology, with abstract forms "prescinded" from the concrete expression of matter.[26] When the apostolic and post-apostolic church proclaimed its good news within this dualist cosmology, friction was both inevitable and immediate. The Greco-Roman philosophical understanding of the universe presumed "to shut God out of

---

[24]Karl Barth, *God in Action: Theological Addresses*, trans. Elmer George Homrighausen and Karl J. Ernst (New York: Round Table Press, 1936), 3-19.
[25]Torrance, *Trinitarian Faith*, 47.
[26]Torrance, "Theological Realism," in *The Philosophical Frontiers of Christian Theology: Essays presented to D. M. MacKinnon*, ed. Brian Hebblethwaite and Stewart Sutherland (Cambridge: Cambridge University Press, 1982), 193n1.

the world of empirical actuality in space and time,"[27] while the Christian gospel appeared to be stating the immediateness of God's presence within it, in the person of Jesus Christ. It was this basic conflict over the appropriateness of a dualistic epistemological framework that set the terms of the debate between Arius and Athanasius.

The figure of Athanasius has a special place of distinction in Torrance's theology. Not only the subject of various chapters and articles, he is also named by Torrance as his favorite theologian.[28] It is an admiration that is based in large part upon Athanasius's role in the Arian controversy and his articulation of what is the most important concept in the church's contention with the problem of dualism. In his essay "The Hermeneutics of Athanasius,"[29] Torrance gives an account of the forces present in Athanasius's intellectual and spiritual formation in order to give some sense of the influences that helped him accomplish that feat. With the city of Alexandria and its vibrant theological and philosophical tradition providing the backdrop, Torrance suggests three influences that provided Athanasius with the tools necessary for his later achievement. The first was the influence of Philo and his use of the *logos*, a marriage of biblical language with contemporary philosophy. The second was the apostolic tradition, which was traced back from the bishop's seat to St. Mark, and was reinforced by the presence of a number of Jewish Christians who had fled Jerusalem after the destruction of the Second Temple.[30] And finally there was the influence of Alexandria, the site of a growing scientific community that did not proceed deductively from preestablished axioms but instead allowed the object of study to determine the questioning and ultimate conclusions. Torrance sees this particular influence evident in Athanasius's willingness to allow the language he used to describe God to be shaped by God himself.[31]

---

[27]Torrance, *Trinitarian Faith*, 47.
[28]Myk Habets, *Theology in Transposition: A Constructive Appraisal of T. F. Torrance* (Minneapolis: Fortress, 2013), 13n32.
[29]Torrance, "The Hermeneutics of Athanasius," in *Divine Meaning: Studies in Patristic Hermeneutics* (Edinburgh: T&T Clark, 1995), 229-288.
[30]Torrance, "Athanasius: A Study in the Foundations of Classical Theology," in *Theology in Reconciliation: Essays Towards Evangelical and Catholic Unity in East and West* (Eugene, OR: Wipf & Stock, 1996), 215-216.
[31]Torrance, "Athanasius: A Study in the Foundations of Classical Theology," 216-217.

The effect of these influences is evident in Athanasius's departure from contemporary traditions that subordinate the identity of the Son to the doctrine of the Logos.[32] According to Torrance, Philo's understanding of the Logos had the effect of sealing off God's being from the sensible world, placing knowledge of the Logos only on the intelligible side of the separation. This "Philonic and Neo-Platonic" understanding of God meant that in theological speech, one was "forced to speak of God as finally beyond being and knowing."[33] Thus while Alexandrian Logos theology attempted to address the problem of dualism, it did so by reinforcing its basic assumptions. Athanasius reclaimed the biblical conception of a God who had real relation to his creation in and through its created structures. Rather than accepting this dualistic framework, Athanasius made the term Logos malleable so that the revelation of Jesus Christ exerted its own inner logic upon this term and thus transformed the word into something it had previously not been understood to mean, simultaneously breaking down this dualistic framework.

Athanasius went beyond Philo and even Origen in his new description of the Logos. Whereas previously the concept of the Logos indicated something that was detached from God, an external construct that in some sense mediated his relation to the world, Athanasius coined the term *enousious logos*. In this innovation within the Alexandrian tradition, the Logos is something that is of God's own being. In the article "Theological Realism," Torrance comments on this theological construct, "This word . . . is not some 'word' detached from God, but *enousious logos*, who eternally inheres in the being of God even when incarnate and addressed to us on earth and in time."[34] In describing the Logos in such a way, Athanasius made it clear that the relation between God and the Logos was an internal relation which offered real epistemic access to who God is. The importance of this reformulation of the Logos is all the more important in view of the debate with the Arians in which Athanasius found himself locked. It is in the context of that controversy that Athanasius's Logos-theology helped forge his own articulation of the *homoousios*.

---

[32] Torrance, "Hermeneutics of Athanasius," 229
[33] Torrance, "Athanasius: A Study in the Foundations of Classical Theology," 182.
[34] Torrance, "Theological Realism," 188.

The Arian controversy. The Arian controversy is popularly described as a battle between two opposing figures that was resolved at a single ecumenical council. Recent scholarship[35] has complicated and even undone those tidy categories that Torrance himself shared, but it is nonetheless helpful to provide a brief description of his understanding of the conflict in order to summarize what amounts to his "theology of retrieval." Arius, a presbyter in Athanasius's own home of Alexandria, became embroiled in a dispute with the bishop of Alexandria, Alexander. Arius sensed in Alexander's theology confusion about the status of Jesus the Son of God in his relation to the Father. He perceived that Alexander failed to distinguish properly the difference in status between the Father and the Son. As tension around this disagreement began to build and other churches, bishops, and eventually Emperor Constantine became involved, the nature of the disagreement became more and more clear. At the Council of Nicaea, a creed was forged in order to settle the dispute, and it included the crucial qualifier *homoousion* to describe the Father's relation to the Son.

There are two things that must be noted about Torrance's understanding of the Arian controversy. First, Torrance believes that the controversy was fundamentally an epistemological conflict between the message of the gospel and an intellectual framework that precluded the implications of this message. In Torrance's narration, Arius operated within an epistemological and cosmological dualism that came from Hellenistic philosophy and culture. Because of this dualistic framework, it was impossible to penetrate the separation between the sensible and intelligible realms. Because of this, the ascription of the title "Son of God" to Jesus could indicate many things with respect to Jesus' status, but it could never indicate a relation of real

---

[35] Ayres's landmark study, *Nicaea and its Legacy*, has corrected many misconceptions about the nature of the Arian controversy. Some of Ayres's conclusions—Athanasius's attribution of beliefs to Arius that he did not hold and the inconclusive nature of the Nicene Council in 325 CE among others—can be viewed as a helpful corrective to aspects of Torrance's account without affecting the fundamental insights Torrance draws from the controversy. Indeed, Torrance appears to have an implicit awareness of one of Ayres's central claims: that the debate centered around the relation between God and the Word, rather than whether Jesus was divine or human. See Torrance's account of the "internal relation" of the Father and Son below. For responses to Ayres, including his handling of Athanasius, see the reviews by Paul Molnar, "Was Barth a Pro-Nicene Theologian? Reflections on Nicaea and its Legacy," *Scottish Journal of Theology* 64 (2011): 347-359; and Khaled Anatolios, "Yes and No: Reflections on Lewis Ayres, Nicaea and its Legacy," *Harvard Theological Review* 100.2 (2007): 153-158.

identity; "Son" did not mean "fully God." It was also impossible for God to be active in the created world: "Bringing to the Gospel an epistemological and cosmological dualism derived from Hellenic culture, Arius and his followers had taught that while Christ may be called 'the Son of God,' a sharp line must be drawn between his being and nature and that of the Father. . . . As ontologically separate from God Jesus Christ is finally no more than a transient image of the eternal and unknowable God."[36]

Second, Torrance understands that the decisions one makes about this epistemological conflict are crucial to the nature of theological speech. If the Son is merely on the creature side of the Creator/creature distinction, then nothing can be said with confidence about the nature of God. This is a point that Torrance makes in multiple places in his corpus and understands to be particularly important for modern theology after Friedrich Schleiermacher: "This way of understanding Christ, not from a oneness with God in his own eternal being and nature, and thus uncontrolled by any objective reality in God himself, meant that the Arians could only think of him in detachable symbols or myths governed by their own subjective modes of thought."[37] Torrance's description of the Arian controversy is strikingly similar to his narration of the problems of modern theology: "The radical detachment or disjunction between God and this world, and the ultimate separation between the Father and his own Logos, not only meant that the Arians were thrown back upon themselves, obsessed with their own self-understanding and humanly thought-up ideas, but implied a doctrine of God as ultimately irrational or deprived of his own Logos."[38]

It is in this light that Torrance views Athanasius's achievement in the exposition of the *homoousion*. Athanasius places his reformulated Alexandrian Logos theology within the context of the *homoousion* of the Nicene Creed, which means that the knowledge we have of Jesus Christ is internal to who God is, not external. In Athanasius's own words, "And so, since they are one, and the Godhead itself is one, the same things are said of the Son, which are said of the Father."[39] Because the Logos who became incarnate is the *enousios*

---

[36]Torrance, "The Legacy of Karl Barth," in *Karl Barth: Biblical and Evangelical Theologian* (Edinburgh: T&T Clark, 1990), 167-168.
[37]Torrance, "Legacy of Karl Barth," 168.
[38]Torrance, "Athanasius: A Study in the Foundations of Classical Theology," 225.
[39]Contra *Arianos* III.4. Quoted in "Athanasius: A Study in the Foundations of Classical Theology," 227.

logos who is of God's being, through Jesus Christ real knowledge of God is possible. The epistemological dualism between God and humanity is not impenetrable: God can and does make himself known to his creation. And because this happened in Jesus Christ, genuine theological speech is possible: "Through the word made flesh, we human beings with our created minds are enabled . . . to know and think of God in such a way that our knowledge and thought of him repose upon his divine reality."[40] It is on this backdrop of epistemological dualism that Torrance understands the significance of Athanasius's accomplishment in the Arian controversy.

By understanding Torrance's reading of this moment in church history, we can understand how his historical theology shapes his own constructive trinitarian proposal. The evangelical passion that always attends the *homoousion* in his writings and centrality of the concept for his doctrine of the Trinity is rooted in the convictions that Torrance gleaned first from the Arian controversy. Thus this statement from the chapter "Three Persons, One Being" in *The Christian Doctrine of God* is representative of his wider trinitarian reflection: "The pivotal issue here, as we have already seen in our discussion of the *homoousion*, is the identity . . . between God and the revelation of himself and of his activity in Jesus Christ and what he really is in himself in his own ever-living and dynamic Being."[41] With respect to his doctrine of God, the *homoousion* is almost always for Torrance "the pivotal issue."

This guiding conviction allows us to understand the shape of Torrance's doctrine of God. When speaking of God's internal life, Torrance's instinct is always to demonstrate the unity among the persons of the Trinity. The central terms that Torrance uses in his doctrine of God, therefore, all point to that end: *homoousion*, perichoresis, and onto-relations.[42] The distinctions between processions and missions that can be found in Augustine,[43]

---

[40] Torrance, "Athanasius: A Study in the Foundations of Classical Theology," 239.
[41] Torrance, *Christian Doctrine of God*, 143.
[42] See, for instance, Torrance, *Christian Doctrine of God*, 155-159. For a discussion of Torrance's concept of "onto-relations," see Gary W. Deddo, "The Importance of the Personal in the Onto-relational Theology of Thomas F. Torrance," in *T&T Clark Handbook of Thomas F. Torrance*, ed. Paul D. Molnar and Myk Habets (London, New York: T&T Clark, 2020), 143-160.
[43] Augustine, *The Trinity*, 2nd ed., trans. Edmund Hill (Hyde Park, NY: New City Press, 2017).

Thomas,[44] and others are less useful to him apart from his ecumenical work with the Orthodox Church around the filioque. As we shall demonstrate, for Torrance the driving concern of his doctrine of God is to demonstrate that God is truly known in the person of the Son.

Key moment two: The reclamation of the homoousios in the Reformation. Torrance's narration of the victory of Nicaea, its interpretation and defense by Athanasius, and the later confirmation of its decisions in Constantinople in the year 381, are a high watermark in his history of doctrine. But the tides of history go out as well as come in, and in Torrance's account of church history it was followed by a period of time where some aspects of the truth were lost as the philosophical procrustean bed of dualism malformed theology once again. It is not the case that the church returned to precisely the same Arian heresies that had already been dealt with definitively at Nicaea. Instead, aspects of Athanasius's insights were obscured as the church's history continued to unfold. It would not be until the time of the Reformation that those important and fundamental truths would be fully recovered. And Torrance once again gives the conflict with dualism a central place in this history. Over and against the "impersonal philosophical theology of the mediaeval schoolmen,"[45] Reformation theology would emphasize a real encounter with the living Word, who is met in Jesus Christ and the witness to him in the Scriptures.

The Reformation and the "homoousion of reconciliation." When Torrance published his 1964 article on "The Roman Doctrine of Grace," he saw signs of promise in the Roman Catholic Church's embrace of biblical theology. But while he is quite willing to speak hopefully of the prospects of the Roman Catholic Church, he is equally critical of the tradition's past. In particular, Torrance is concerned with how dualism has affected the church's understanding of reconciliation and how those old struggles resurface again.

Torrance sees in the Augustinian heritage of the Roman Catholic Church a latent dualism that has deleterious effects on the concept of grace. In his estimation, Augustine operated with the same assumption of a radical,

---

[44]See the excellent description and analysis in Giles Emery, *The Trinitarian Theology of St Thomas Aquinas*, trans. Francesca Murphy (Oxford: Oxford University Press), especially chapters four and fifteen.

[45]Torrance, "The Roman Doctrine of Grace and Reformed Theology," in *Theology in Reconstruction* (Eugene, OR: Wipf & Stock, 1996), 181.

dualistic separation between the *mundus intelligibilis* and the *mundus unintelligibilis* that is latent in the Neoplatonism of his thought.[46] Standing on the shoulders of the Nicene and Constantinopolitan Councils, Augustine was too sophisticated of a theologian to return to an Arian position. And yet there were still traces of the same kind of dualism that afflicted the Arians. Thus while Augustine could straightforwardly affirm aspects of Nicene christology, Torrance sees a dualism in his thought that creates a separation between the Word and God "in terms of a distinction between the 'internal mental Word,' or 'vision' in the Mind of God, which as Word is 'formable but not yet formed,' and 'the external Word' which assumed finite form as Word in the proper sense."[47] "Even St Augustine could echo the view of Origen that the historical Christ and the historical Gospel were 'shadow' compared to the 'reality' of the eternal Truth in God."[48]

Having unknowingly imported this unnecessary radical dualism in his theology, Augustine nonetheless understood that he must address its implications. According to Torrance, this is done through his doctrine of the church, where Augustine ingeniously established the church on both sides of the dualistic divide. The church functions as the bridge between the sensible world of passing things and the eternal world of divine realities. The church, therefore, is the realm where Christians must seek divine grace: "As the mystical Body of Christ the Church is full of grace and truth, indwelt by the Spirit of Christ and illumined by his eternal Light and therefore informed with his Mind. It is therefore within the Church where the fulness of divine grace and truth dwells that we may be enlightened and saved."[49]

As Roman Catholic tradition continued to develop, the identification of the doctrine of the church with the doctrine of grace also continued. This development unfolded in two complementary ways. On the one hand, the church was understood to be continuous with the incarnation as the place

---

[46]The thesis, popular in Torrance's day, that Neoplatonism exercised a controlling and distorting influence on Augustine's theology has since been overturned. For a concise account of the complicated relationship between Augustine and the Platonism of his day, see Lewis Ayres, *Augustine and the Trinity* (Cambridge: Cambridge University Press, 2010), 13-20.

[47]Torrance, "Karl Barth and the Latin Heresy," in *Karl Barth, Biblical and Evangelical Theologian*, 222.

[48]Torrance, "Roman Doctrine of Grace," 175.

[49]Torrance, "Roman Doctrine of Grace," 175.

where nature and grace converge.[50] This localized the work of grace in the institution of the church in such a way that grace was understood as a "power actualized and embodied in the structured life of the Church on earth."[51] On the other hand, the church's place within Roman culture meant that there was a preoccupation with controlling the "ways and means" of grace: "Grace came to be considered within the orbit of ways and means, as something that required to be dispensed and controlled through institutional structures."[52]

According to Torrance, it was this kind of understanding of grace and of church that the Reformers confronted during the Reformation. While Torrance praises Thomas Aquinas and affirms the evangelical nature of his theology as it sought to remain faithful to the gospel within the terms he was given to work with, the dualist Trojan horse had already entered the gates.[53] Thus at the time of the Reformation, the Roman church's doctrine of grace could be said to have made grace "something to be rationally defined and administered under the control of the Church."[54] All of this is to be traced to the epistemological and cosmological dualism that was imported through Augustine's theology and which found expression in his doctrine of the Church.

The presence of this dualism created friction with the Reformers as they began to rearticulate the doctrine of grace. The Reformers sensed a gap between the church's description and administration of grace and the doctrine of God. Augustine had attempted to close this gap by way of his ecclesiology, but the fundamental separation remained. According to Torrance, the Reformers deployed the same insight that was grasped at Nicaea, the *homoousion* as the concept that overcomes the problem of dualism: "It is the same teaching [the *homoousion*], according to Reformed theology, that must be applied to the grace of God, for what God communicates to us in his grace is none other than himself. The Gift and the Giver are one."[55] By rejecting the presuppositions of dualism and reinserting the concept of *homoousion* into theology in the doctrine of grace, the proper relation was

---

[50] Torrance, "Roman Doctrine of Grace," 178.
[51] Torrance, "Roman Doctrine of Grace," 176.
[52] Torrance, "Roman Doctrine of Grace," 172.
[53] Torrance, "Roman Doctrine of Grace," 176.
[54] Torrance, "Roman Doctrine of Grace," 179.
[55] Torrance, "Roman Doctrine of Grace," 182.

restored. What Athanasius had grasped in the fourth century was laid hold of by the Reformers in the sixteenth century.

In the same way that detaching the identity of Jesus Christ the Son from God damages and distorts the evangelical message, detaching the *work* of the Son from God has a deleterious effect upon grace. The rejection of this dualism is one of the great legacies of the teaching of the Reformers. Thus, Torrance writes,

> Grace is not something that can be detached from God and made to inhere in creaturely being as 'created grace'; nor is it something that can be proliferated in many forms; nor is it something that we can have more or less of, as if grace could be construed in quantitative terms. . . . Grace is whole and indivisible because it is identical with the personal self-giving of God to us in his Son. It is identical with Jesus.[56]

Thus, at this second key juncture in church history, it is the specter of dualism that is confronted.

Again, we see just how significant the *homoousion* is for Torrance's dogmatic project and thus why it has such a central place in his doctrine of God. In establishing the proper relation between persons of the Trinity, the *homoousion* secures not only the epistemic foundations of revelation but also the effectiveness of the saving work of Christ. Torrance understands the Reformation to be the moment in history that reminds the church of this truth: "We believe that if the Lord God himself had not actually come among us and become one with us and acted for us in the life and work of Jesus Christ, the Gospel of the Love of God, the Grace of our Lord Jesus Christ and the Communion of the Holy Spirit, would be utterly wanting of any divine validity in its message of reconciliation, salvation, and redemption."[57]

Key moment three: Karl Barth as the "theologian of the homoousion." In Torrance's analysis the controversies of the fourth century and of the sixteenth century are at root the same: "The struggle of Nicaea and the Reformation was for the same fundamental truth: what God is toward us in Jesus Christ and in the Holy Spirit he is inherently and eternally in himself as the one living God."[58] As the previous analysis of Torrance's argument

---

[56]Torrance, "Roman Doctrine of Grace," 182-83.
[57]Torrance, *Christian Doctrine of God*, 142.
[58]Torrance, "Legacy of Karl Barth," 166.

demonstrates, at both junctures in church history this insight came into conflict and eventually overcame the problem of dualism. But according to Torrance, it was not long before dualism returned and once again infiltrated the theology of the Western church. It was the great achievement of Torrance's *Doktorvater* and mentor, Karl Barth, to articulate the gospel in such a way that it was not imprisoned within the strictures of dualism.

In Torrance's view, one of the great achievements of Karl Barth's theology is his synthesis of the two great insights of Nicaea and the Reformation. Barth's theological and philosophical context was dominated by the same dualistic framework that the Arians had assumed and that was also latent in Western Augustinianism. Philosophically, Descartes, Hume, and Kant furthered the presupposition of the radical separation between the sensible and intelligible worlds, though each had their own strategy for resolving (or even simply accepting) the gap between the two. In Protestant theology, what resulted were two distinct and seemingly opposing traditions—liberal Neo-Protestantism and Protestant Scholasticism. The former attempted to bridge the dualist divide by proposing a correspondence between the divine and the "subjective structures in man's religious self-consciousness."[59] Having assumed that the rationality of the Word of God could not cross the sensible-intelligible chasm, the Neo-Protestant tradition tried to preserve God's communication by locating it in the religious self-understanding of the individual or the community. The Protestant scholastics, on the other hand, responded to this epistemological quandary by resorting to a nominalist system, described by Torrance as "a closed system of doctrinal propositions formalized in such a way that they were equated with the divine truths they were intended to express."[60]

As Torrance narrates Barth's theology in his collection of essays, *Karl Barth: Biblical and Evangelical Theologian*, Barth found in his own work of historical theology the resources to address this radical dualism. As he investigated the Nicene and Reformation controversies, Barth recognized the same theological principle in play: "Twice over, [Barth] claimed, the Church had been compelled to contend for the supreme truth that revelation

---

[59] Torrance, "Karl Barth and the Latin Heresy," 224.
[60] Torrance, "Karl Barth and the Latin Heresy," 225. For a rejoinder to the thesis that Protestant scholasticism was inherently nominalist, see Richard A. Muller, "Not Scotist: Understandings of Being, Univocity, and Analogy in Early-Modern Reformed Thought," *Reformation and Renaissance Review* 14.2 (2012): 127–150.

properly understood is God himself, for just as God is of and through himself, so he may be known only on the free ground of his own being, out of and through himself alone."[61] What Barth then did was take the key insights of the *homoousion* that were worked out in these two controversies and unite them for his own dogmatic project. For Torrance, the *homoousion* is a central hermeneutic for understanding the *Church Dogmatics*. He writes,

> This is how, I believe, his *Church Dogmatics* must be assessed: in respect of his determination to think through the bearing upon our understanding of divine revelation and grace of the supreme truth that the incarnate and risen Jesus Christ is one in being and act with God the Father, and thus to draw out the far-reaching implications of the inner logic of the Gospel brought to light in the formulation of the *homoousion* for the whole range of the Church's preaching and teaching.[62]

At this third key juncture in Torrance's reading of church history, the *homoousion* is the key to confronting the invidious influence of dualism.

Torrance's reading of church history provides a fascinating and revealing window into the central concerns that drive his theology and, thus, his doctrine of God. Torrance understood the perennial enemy of the church to be a dualist epistemology and cosmology that seals off humanity from God, preventing real knowledge of the triune Lord and distancing humanity from his saving action in Jesus Christ. While the story that Torrance tells of Western theology is not without significant problems,[63] it is effective in

---

[61]Torrance, "Legacy of Karl Barth," 165.

[62]Torrance, "Legacy of Karl Barth," 166. This quote can be understood as a kind of summary *in nuce* of Torrance's own positive doctrine of God. The integral aspects are all present: the reference to the term *homoousion*, the centrality of Act and Being, and the application of these concepts to the particular doctrinal loci of revelation and reconciliation.

[63]As we have already noted and shall see later on in this work, the scholarship of Ayres, Muller and others presents a significant challenge to Torrance's reading of Nicaea, Augustine, and Calvin. The more one presses into the details of church history, the more readily one can see that the insights and lessons of each moment are to varying degrees more complicated than Torrance describes. (It is also telling that Barth himself moved beyond the initial insights of the 1934 essay "Revelation," that apparently inspired Torrance's work, and on to a more nuanced engagement with the tradition.) There are many things that can be said about Torrance's historical theology in light of more recent scholarship, but it is important to note that his body of work represents one of the first English-speaking Protestant attempts at a theology of retrieval. If we cannot ultimately agree with some of Torrance's conclusions, we can also note with gratitude both his attempt and the way in which he has helped to establish a movement in the English-speaking world that continues to bear fruit.

helping us to understand Torrance himself. And in so doing, we can now understand and describe the evangelical impetus of his theology and the resulting implications for Torrance's doctrine of God.

As we turn to that task, we should note how Torrance's historical theology has introduced the key insight that shapes his doctrine of God. According to Torrance, Nicaea, the Protestant Reformation, and the theology of Karl Barth each demonstrate the centrality of the *homoousion* for the church's proclamation of the gospel in light of the challenge of dualism. We will not be surprised to find that this reality has a determinative role in Torrance's own constructive doctrine of God.

Torrance's Doctrine of God: A Response to Dualism

***The* homoousion *and the Holy Spirit*.** Torrance believes the *homoousion* was such a crucial concept because of his conviction that it was essential for the church's understanding and proclamation of the gospel in light of the perennial issue of dualism. His decision to make *homoousion* the central descriptive term for the relation of the Father and the Son reflects how significant Torrance understands the dangers of dualism to be. And the explanatory power of the *homoousion* leads him to utilize it elsewhere in his doctrine of God. Before considering Torrance's doctrine of God in full, we must first understand how the *homoousion* is deployed in the Holy Spirit's relation to the Father and the Son.

As we might expect, Torrance's argument about the use of the *homoousion* with respect to the Holy Spirit runs through his historical theology. In Torrance's narration of the doctrinal controversies of the fourth century, the identity and status of the Son was closely related to the identity and status of the Spirit. Those theologians who argued for a Nicene understanding of the Son's identity made the same argument for the Spirit.[64] Athanasius, again prominent for Torrance, laid the foundational arguments: "Athanasius developed the doctrine of the Spirit from the essential relation to the one God and his undivided coactivity with the Father and the Son, and specifically from his inherence in the being of the eternal Son."[65] Torrance understands this coactivity to be the driving force behind the early church's eventual

---

[64]Torrance, *Trinitarian Faith*, 200.
[65]Torrance, *Trinitarian Faith*, 201.

acknowledgement of the Holy Spirit as a coequal in divinity with the Father and the Son. In the same way that acknowledging God's being and act in the person of Jesus leads to the confession of the *homoousion*, so it becomes necessary to make the same argument with the Holy Spirit.[66] "It became clear that the truth and effectiveness of the Gospel rest not only on the oneness in being and agency between the incarnate Son and God the Father but on the oneness in being and agency between the Spirit and both the Son and the Father."[67]

The importance of this relationship of coactivity of the Spirit with the Father and the Son is demonstrated in the epistemological link between the Spirit and the Son. In Athanasius's letters *Ad Serapionem*, a seminal text in Torrance's account of the development of the doctrine, his pneumatology unfolds from an understanding that knowledge of the Son is only possible in and through the Holy Spirit. To know the Son in his true identity as the Son who reveals the Father, the work of the Spirit is required. Thus, Torrance states, "It is only in the Spirit that we may . . . know the Son, and know that he is antecedently and eternally in himself in God what he is toward us in revelation and redemption."[68]

This conclusion about the Spirit's coactivity with the Son (and thus the Father) means that the Spirit is understood first and foremost in his *internal relations* with the Father and the Son: "Precisely because the Spirit *is* the Spirit of the Father and of the Son, Athanasius developed the doctrine of the Spirit from his essential relation to the one God and his undivided coactivity with the Father and the Son, and specifically from his inherence in the being of the eternal Son."[69] For Torrance this Athanasian insight is foundational and becomes a significant part of his own pneumatological proposal. In this way Torrance is following Athanasius as he applies the concept of *homoousios* to the Holy Spirit.

It is important to note that Torrance's argument for the *homoousion* of the Holy Spirit with the Father and the Son contains many of the same elements

---

[66] "Once the Spirit has been implicated in the Son's work and has been presented as completing that work, then all the arguments that have been used to link Father and Son can be used of the Spirit. Athanasius' concern here is a fundamentally soteriological one." Lewis Ayres, *Nicaea and its Legacy*, 212.
[67] Torrance, *Trinitarian Faith*, 200.
[68] Torrance, "Spiritus Creator: A Consideration of the Teaching of St Athanasius and St Basil," in *Theology in Reconstruction* (Eugene, OR: Wipf & Stock, 1996), 215.
[69] Torrance, *Trinitarian Faith*, 201.

of his argument for the *homoousion* of the Son with the Father. The fourth century Fathers and the sixteenth century Reformers are given a prominent place (though the argument for the latter operates on a more general level than that which he provides for the former).[70] Perhaps most significantly, Torrance's description of the Holy Spirit is once again accompanied by concerns about dualism. Here, Torrance lays blame for confusion about the identity of the Spirit at the feet of Origen, who held to an "axiomatic assumption of the *chorismos* [separation] between the intelligible and sensible worlds."[71] Nicaea's rejection of this cosmology was accompanied by "the very different biblical distinction between the Creator and the creature, and the freedom of the Creator to be present and active in his creation."[72] The church's eventual articulation of the person of the Holy Spirit involved in part a rejection of a cosmology at odds with Scripture.

The dualistic concerns that inform Torrance's pneumatology are emphatically epistemological. In a way similar to the *homoousion* between the Father and the Son, the *homoousion* of the Holy Spirit serves to secure trustworthy knowledge of God: "It is . . . only through staunch support of the *homoousion* . . . that there can be prevented a dissolution of the work of Christ into timeless events, and a dissolution of the operation of the Spirit into timeless processes."[73] Torrance is concerned that the pneumatology can all too easily be enlisted into institutional or "religious" projects: "There has been a marked failure to distinguish the Holy Spirit from the spirit of the Church or the spirit of religious man, that is, from the self-consciousness of the Church or the self-consciousness of the believer."[74] Thus throughout his work Torrance understands the *homoousion* of the Holy Spirit to give the church the objectivity it requires in its knowledge of God. This objectivity is grounded in the person of Jesus Christ, who, in distinction from the Spirit, comes to humanity "within the conditions and structures of our earthly existence and knowledge."[75] The Spirit, as *homoousion* with the Father and

---

[70] "The extent to which the Reformation had to recall the Western Church to the centrality of Christ is the measure of its departure from the *homoousion* of the Spirit." Torrance, "Relevance of the Doctrine of the Spirit," 230.
[71] Torrance, "*Spiritus Creator*," 211.
[72] Torrance, "*Spiritus Creator*," 211.
[73] Torrance, "Relevance of the Doctrine of the Spirit," 230.
[74] Torrance, "Relevance of the Doctrine of the Spirit," 231.
[75] Torrance, *Trinitarian Faith*, 203.

the Son, operates in unity with the revelation of Jesus Christ to secure knowledge of God: "It is on that ground, the same ground where we know the Father through the Son, that we may also know the Spirit, for it is in the Spirit sent to us by the Father through the Son that knowledge of God is mediated and actualised within us."[76]

Torrance is at pains to distinguish this objectivity from a different kind that might attempt to work within the constraints of dualism: "This is not a divine objectivity that stands behind some radical dichotomy between the objectifiable and the non-objectifiable, between the given and the non-given (in relation to which we can only have a feeling of absolute dependence)."[77] Rather, this is an objectivity determined by the *homoousion* of the Son Jesus Christ with the Father, "an objectivity that meets us in the particularity of Jesus Christ where God has really given himself to us within the structures of our intra-mundane and intra-personal relationships."[78] And by properly understanding the Spirit as *homoousion* with the Father and the Son, "we are not allowed to confound the objective reality of God with our own subjective states, or to resolve it away as the symbolic counterpart of our human concerns."[79] Thus again we see the way Torrance's use of the *homoousion*, in connection with his pneumatology, mitigates the problem of dualism.

Torrance's Doctrine of God: Theological, Realistic Objectivity

A brief summary of Torrance's doctrine of God is helpful at this juncture in our engagement with his thought. First, and as we have already demonstrated, *homoousion* is the central, controlling concept of God's triune life. This is not only true for the relation between the Father and the Son, but indeed for each person of the Trinity in their relations with one another. The *homoousion* is so crucial because it reflects the logic of Scripture's witness about the identity of the Son and the reality of salvation. Thus Torrance writes about the concept, "It expressed the fact that what God is 'toward us' and 'in the midst of us' in and through the Word made flesh, he really is in

---

[76]Torrance, *Trinitarian Faith*, 203.
[77]Torrance, "Relevance of the Doctrine of the Spirit," 234.
[78]Torrance, "Relevance of the Doctrine of the Spirit," 234.
[79]Torrance, "Relevance of the Doctrine of the Spirit," 235.

himself; that he is in the internal relations of his transcendent being the very same Father, Son and Holy Spirit that he is in his revealing and saving activity in time and space toward mankind."[80] The importance of this term relativizes the use of other classical language about God's life such as procession, generation, or spiration. It is the *homoousion*, more than any other, that provides the framework for understanding God's immanent relations and his triunity.

Two other terms—one classical and the other a neologism—fill out the language of Torrance's doctrine of God. *Perichoresis* is the first concept, and in many ways, it is Torrance's way of applying the insights of the *homoousion* to God's triune identity. Whereas *homoousion* indicates the identity and distinction between two persons of the Trinity, *perichoresis* demonstrates the Trinity's unity and the distinctions of the Father, Son and Spirit. Thus Torrance defines *perichoresis* as "the truth that no divine Person is he [sic] who he truly is, even in his distinctive otherness, apart from relation to the other two in their mutual containing or interpenetrating of one another in such a way that each Person is in himself whole God of whole God."[81] *Perichoresis* demonstrates how the persons of the Trinity can neither be isolated from one another nor can they be collapsed into one another: "While it helps to clarify the circularity of our belief in the Trinity through belief in his Unity, and our belief in his Unity through belief in his Trinity, it does not dissolve the distinctions between the three divine Persons unipersonally into the one Being of God."[82] That same identity-in-distinction balance that is preserved by the *homoousion* is also preserved by *perichoresis*.

The second additional concept that is central to Torrance's doctrine of God is *onto-relation*. For Torrance, onto-relation is a term that indicates what it means for us to speak of God's *hypostases* and his *ousia*. In brief, onto-relations means that "the relations between the divine persons belong to what they are as Persons—they are constitutive onto-relations."[83] When we speak of God's being, our language should be shaped by the reality of God's triune life and not abstracted through the improper

---

[80]Torrance, *Trinitarian Faith*, 130.
[81]Torrance, *Christian Doctrine of God*, 174.
[82]Torrance, *Christian Doctrine of God*, 175.
[83]Torrance, *Christian Doctrine of God*, 157.

application of otherwise helpful philosophical language. For Torrance this means that God's inner life "is to be understood as essentially *personal, dynamic, and relational Being*."[84] These two terms—*perichoresis* and onto-relations—provide helpful context for understanding how Torrance's doctrine of God is understood in its entirety. But at the same time, it is clear that it is the *homoousion* that is the keystone concept for his trinitarian theology.

Torrance's use of *homoousion* as a foundational concept in his doctrine of God has a number of implications for understanding the shape of his thought. Stephen R. Holmes has suggested that for Torrance the concept functions similarly to how the doctrine of divine simplicity did for the Cappadocians.[85] Jason Radcliff proposes that Torrance uses the *homoousion* as a way of reconstructing the Solus Christus of the Reformation.[86] And Paul Molnar states that in Torrance's theology, "the *homoousion* was seen as the main point of Christian orthodoxy and godliness because . . . to reject it meant to reject the message of salvation which was the content of the Gospel message."[87] Each of these statements gives a helpful perspective on how the concept functions within Torrance's thought. But within the argument that we have made about Torrance's prevailing concern with dualism and its downstream effect on the shape of his theology, another argument can be made about the importance of the *homoousion* in Torrance's thought. In order to present this argument, we must examine one of the formative influences on Torrance's thought: Karl Barth.

Torrance had already encountered Barth's theology while studying at New College. Upon entering New College, his mother gave him a copy of Barth's *Credo*.[88] And he soon was a part of a conflict in the Edinburgh University Christian Union which centered on the difference between Barth's

---

[84]Torrance, *Christian Doctrine of God*, 124.
[85]Stephen R. Holmes, "Response: In Praise of Being Criticized," in *The Holy Trinity Revisited: Essays in Response to Stephen R. Holmes*, ed. Thomas A. Noble and Jason S. Sexton (Milton Keynes: Paternoster, 2015), 152. Holmes, who admits that he is "painting in very broad brushstrokes," does not expand upon this proposal in great detail, though he has hesitations about putting the *homoousion* to this kind of theological work.
[86]Radcliff, *Thomas F. Torrance and the Church Fathers*, 67.
[87]Molnar, *Thomas F. Torrance: Theologian of the Trinity*, 58.
[88]McGrath, *Thomas F. Torrance*, 25.

theology and traditional Calvinism.[89] Most significantly, Torrance encountered Barth through H. R. Mackintosh, the chair of systematic theology at New College, who as early as 1926 began to give attention to Barth and was increasingly influenced by his theology until his death in 1936.[90] It is largely because of Mackintosh's influence that Torrance chose to study with Barth in Basel after graduating from New College.

When Torrance arrived in Basel to begin his studies, Barth was lecturing on the material that would make up II/1 of the *Church Dogmatics*.[91] The influence of this material, which contains some of the central aspects of Barth's doctrine of God, is evident in Torrance's thought. Torrance later described his encounter with this material, stating, "I still believe that the *Gotteslehre* of *Church Dogmatics* II/1 and 2 is the high point of Barth's *Dogmatics*. What I have in mind is the epistemology of II/1, which must be read along with Barth's work on St. Anselm . . . ; in particular, his doctrine of God as Being-in-his-Act and Act-in-his-Being."[92] In this statement we find the fundamental conceptual framework that Torrance would integrate into his own theological project, and indeed into his understanding of the *homoousion*: the concepts of God's act and being.

In the material covered in II/1, Barth explores the grounds of theology's knowledge of God. Here he is concerned to distinguish proper knowledge of God from knowledge that is abstract or determined by alien elements that have been smuggled into the theological task. Thus, Barth states, "The act of God's revelation . . . carries with it the fact that man, as a sinner who of himself can only take wrong roads, is called back from all his own attempts to answer the question of true being, and is bound to the answer to the question given by God Himself."[93] The epistemological quandary of humanity's sinfulness and the limits of creaturely reason drive Barth to articulate a unique formulation of knowledge of God: "Barth has no confidence in the theological strategy which handles the term 'God' as if it could be understood without reference to a particular identity

---

[89] McGrath, *Thomas F. Torrance*, 25.
[90] McGrath, *Thomas F. Torrance*, 32-33.
[91] Torrance, "My Interaction with Karl Barth," in *How Karl Barth Changed My Mind*, ed. Donald K. McKim (Grand Rapids, MI: Eerdmans, 1986), 54.
[92] Torrance, "My Interaction with Karl Barth," 54.
[93] Karl Barth, *Church Dogmatics* II/1, ed. Geoffrey W. Bromiley and Thomas F. Torrance (Edinburgh: T&T Clark, 1957), 262.

(that enacted in the drama of creation and reconciliation summed up in Jesus Christ). What theology seeks to unearth is thus the sheer 'this-ness,' the irreducible specificity, of the one indicated in the Christian confession."[94]

Barth's answer is to state that God's being can only be known in his acts: "Every statement of what God is, and explanation of how God is, must always state and explain what and who He is in His act and decision."[95] By understanding God's being in and through the concrete act as understood in Scripture and centrally through the person of Jesus Christ, Barth secures theological knowledge upon its only trustworthy foundation. In so doing, Barth's aim is to exclude distorting criteria: "We are dealing with the being of God: but with regard to the being of God, the word 'event' or 'act' is final, and cannot be surpassed."[96] "If we keep this clearly in mind, if all our thoughts are always grasped by God's action, because in it we have to do with God's being, we may be sure that they cannot err, and become either openly or secretly thoughts about ourselves."[97]

This methodological decision by Barth, often called "actualism" or "actualistic ontology,"[98] had a profound impact upon Torrance, and the influence is evident in his theology. Significantly, Torrance understands Barth to be dealing here with the same insight that is contained in the *homoousion* as understood in Torrance's narration of the Nicene and Reformation periods. According to Torrance,

> Barth showed . . . the credal *homoousios to Patri* clearly implied a oneness in agency as well as in being between Jesus Christ and God the Father. It was the genius of Karl Barth that he should combine in one both forms of this evangelical principle, thus bringing together the Greek Patristic emphasis upon

---

[94]John Webster, *Karl Barth* (London: Continuum, 2004), 83.
[95]Barth, *CD* II/1, 272.
[96]Barth, *CD* II/1, 263.
[97]Barth, *CD* II/1, 272.
[98]For further explanation, see the description given by George Hunsinger in *How to Read Karl Barth: The Shape of His Theology* (Oxford: Oxford University Press, 1991), 30-32. Alan Torrance notes some of the dangers in utilizing this term as a description of Barth's thought: "It is not Barth's concern or intention to seek to universalise an actualistic concept of being. His emphasis on the *a posteriori* nature theological articulation precludes this kind of ontological agenda." Alan Torrance, *Persons in Communion: Trinitarian Description and Human Participation* (Edinburgh: T&T Clark, 1996), 32n57.

the being of God in his saving acts and the Reformation emphasis upon the act of God in his being revealed to us through Christ and in the Spirit.[99]

Such a statement may only give us Torrance's sometimes quite idiosyncratic understanding of the Fathers, the Reformers, and Barth[100] (rather than the Fathers, the Reformers, or perhaps even Barth themselves), but in so doing it is quite helpful in understanding Torrance himself.

For Torrance the *homoousion*, as understood through the doctrinal matrix supplied by Barth's actualism, gives the church the resources to speak with confidence and energy about God and his saving action. John Webster notes how Barth's argument in *Church Dogmatics* II/1 provides a robust "theological realism" for Torrance so that "attention to ontology provides a means of resisting subjective reduction to affective or moral discourse."[101] While agreeing with the thrust of Webster's argument, we might substitute "dualistic modes of thought that separate God from creation" as the more fundamental object of Torrance's resistance. We would also add the term "objective" to the otherwise fitting description of Torrance's project.[102] It is nonetheless true that Torrance's doctrine of God—particularly his use of the *homoousion* and the concepts of act and being—is constructed in order to emphasize a particular account of knowledge about God and his activity that is in broad agreement with Webster's suggestion.[103] Thus Torrance says,

---

[99]Torrance, "Legacy of Karl Barth," 175. This is a statement Torrance repeats at various points. See "My Interaction with Karl Barth," 54.

[100]See, for example, the criticisms of Richard A. Muller in "The Barth Legacy: New Athanasius or Origen Redivivus? A Response to T. F. Torrance," *The Thomist* 54.4 (1990): 673-704.

[101]John Webster, translator's introduction to *God's Being Is in Becoming: The Trinitarian Being of God in the Theology of Karl Barth*, by Eberhard Jüngel (Edinburgh: T&T Clark, 2001), xx.

[102]Katherine Sonderegger has noted the limited usefulness of describing the break of Barth, Torrance, et al. from liberal Protestantism as simply a move toward mere "realism":

> The problem, often misdiagnosed in criticism of modern theology, is not irrealism—not certainly in the aim or structure of Schleiermacher-inspired theology. There truly is a key, and it in fact unlocks the door.... Barth was well aware of this fact, and his brusque rejection of Emil Brunner's denunciation of Schleiermacher as a 'mystic' is built on that insight. God is real, and really given in pious awareness, just as the world is, really given to and knit up in the interplay of freedom and dependence that human creatures bring to the net of nature and its relations. The problem that Barth spies in all this is that the Reality of God is measured by and conformed to the strictures of creaturely awareness. (Katherine Sonderegger, *Systematic Theology: The Doctrine of God*, vol. 1 [Minneapolis: Fortress, 2015], 117).

[103]Torrance's account of realism takes on a different shape than that of Barth's. For Torrance the "givenness" of the knowledge of God is constrained by his adaptation of Michael Polanyi and the *kataphysic* nature of proper knowledge, but in a way that emphasizes the objectivity of realism more emphatically than in Barth. Barth, in contrast, was more guarded about the extent to

> The doctrine of the *homoousion* was as decisive as it was revolutionary: it expressed the evangelical truth that what God is toward us and has freely done for us in his love and grace, and continues to do in the midst of us through His Word and Spirit, he really is in himself, and that he really is in the internal relations and personal properties of his transcendent Being as the Holy Trinity the very same Father, Son, and Holy Spirit, that he is in his revealing and saving activity in time and space toward mankind, and ever will be.[104]

Trustworthy knowledge of God is available, and it is available in the act of God toward humanity, understood in the *homoousion*.

This objectively realist impulse in Torrance's theology helps us to understand the place of one of the more striking original elements in Torrance's theology: the stratified structure of knowledge. In two of his later works on the doctrine of the Trinity, *The Ground and Grammar of Theology*[105] and *The Christian Doctrine of God*, Torrance introduces into Christian theology this concept, which was first used by Albert Einstein in his essay "Physics and Reality." In his appropriation of Einstein, Torrance delineates three interconnected levels of knowledge: the evangelical/doxological level, the theological level and the higher theological and scientific level.

The initial level of knowledge is the "evangelical and doxological level," "the level of our day-to-day worship and meeting with God in response to the proclamation of the Gospel and the interpretation of the Holy Scriptures within the fellowship of the Church."[106] At this level, the focus is on direct apprehension and intuitive appropriation in the light of the Church's kerygma and *didache*. All theological knowledge begins from this common foundation, a foundation Torrance identifies with the encounter with God that takes place in the worshipping life of the local church. In this "incipient

---

which realist knowledge could be understood to be "given" and thus spoke of the need for an idealist element in his account of human knowing in a way that Torrance did not. See Barth's "Fate and Idea in Theology," in *The Way of Theology in Karl Barth: Essays and Comments*, ed. Stephen W. Sykes (Eugene, OR: Wipf & Stock, 1986), 25-61. (I am grateful to Martin Westerholm for pointing out this article and for his assistance in understanding this difference between Torrance and Barth.) Bruce McCormack gives an excellent summary of these issues in "Beyond Nonfoundational and Postmodern Readings of Barth: Critically Realistic Dialectical Theology," in *Orthodox and Modern: Studies in the Theology of Karl Barth* (Grand Rapids, MI: Baker Academic, 2008), 109-113, 157-165.

[104] Torrance, *Christian Doctrine of God*, 130.
[105] Torrance, *Ground and Grammar of Theology*, 156-173.
[106] Torrance, *Ground and Grammar of Theology*, 156.

theology," Torrance says that, "Our minds apprehend this evangelical Trinity intuitively, and as a whole, without engaging in analytical or logical process of thought, which we are constrained though faith in Christ to relate to the Mystery of God's inmost Life and Being."[107]

As this first level of experience is reflected upon, the second level of knowledge, the "theological level," is formed. Torrance identifies this level of reflection with the economic Trinity. In light of reflection upon the first level of knowledge, intellectual tools are developed to form appropriate patterns of thought and speech that accurately describe the first level. For Christian theology, this means the development of the doctrine of the Trinity and a coherent articulation of his works *ad extra*: "As we direct our inquiries into the field of evangelical and doxological experience, we reflect on the fact that God reveals his one Being to us as God the Father, God the Son, and God the Holy Spirit, in a three-fold *self*-giving in which revelatory and ontological factors are indivisibly integrated."[108] At this level, Torrance says, "we are concerned with the Act of God in his Being," that is to say, the economic Trinity.[109]

The *homoousion* is unsurprisingly, again, crucial in Torrance's articulation of how the movement from the first to the second level of theological knowledge is possible. While the term is, like other theological concepts, alien to the biblical idiom, it is not an abstraction but a faithful representation of Scripture's meaning: "The *homoousios* here represents a faithful distillation of the fundamental sense of the New Testament Scriptures in many statements about the unique relation between the incarnate Son and the Father in order to describe it in as definite and precise a sense as possible."[110] More importantly, this movement does not leave behind the first level of "evangelical and doxological" knowledge, but instead moves deeper into it. In his description of Torrance's understanding of the stratification of knowledge, Benjamin Meyers writes, "We have therefore moved not away from the level of concrete experience but deeper into that level, by uncovering the patterns and structures which gave rise to our experience in the first place."[111]

---

[107]Torrance, *Christian Doctrine of God*, 89.
[108]Torrance, *Christian Doctrine of God*, 92.
[109]Torrance, *Ground and Grammar*, 157.
[110]Torrance, *Christian Doctrine of God*, 94.
[111]Benjamin Myers, "The Stratification of Knowledge in the Thought of T. F. Torrance," *Scottish Journal of Theology* 61.1 (2008): 9.

There is finally the third level of knowledge, the "higher theological level." The movement to this level from the second level is a movement from our reflection upon the economic Trinity to our reflection upon the immanent Trinity. Here the theologian moves "from the level of economic trinitarian relations in all that God is toward us in his self-revealing and self-giving activity to the level in which we discern the trinitarian relations immanent in God himself which lie behind, and are the ground of the relations of, the Economic Trinity."[112] Once again the *homoousion* is of great significance, though in a different way than as was evident in the movement from the first to the second level. Here the concept allows our knowledge of God to be pressed beyond the level of the economic Trinity to the immanent Trinity in a way that affirms the fundamental continuity between the two ("the Being of God in His Act"). But in moving to this third level, the *homoousion* requires a "critical edge" in order that human speech about God's immanent life will be appropriately reverent and reticent, a point which we will explore in greater detail below. At this level, the *homoousion* "stands for the basic insight deriving from God's self-communication to us, that what God is toward us in his saving economic activity in space and time through Christ and the Holy Spirit, he is antecedently and inherently in himself."[113]

The force of Torrance's understanding of the stratified nature of knowledge, funded in large part by the concept of the *homoousion* and the theological categories of act and being, is to make clear the way in which "evangelical and doxological" knowledge is in fact a knowledge of who God is in his immanent life: "This means that our evangelical experience of God in Christ is not somehow truncated so that it finally falls short of God, but is grounded in the very Being of God himself; it means that our knowing of God is not somehow refracted or turned back on itself in its ultimate reference to God, but that it actually terminates on the Reality of God."[114] Again Torrance demonstrates the significance of theological objective realism for his theology, as well as the way in which the crucial elements of his thought work toward this end.

Epistemological and soteriological realism. Before we draw Torrance's doctrine of God into a comparison with another recent attempt to utilize

---

[112]Torrance, *Ground and Grammar*, 158.
[113]Torrance, *Christian Doctrine of God*, 99.
[114]Torrance, *Christian Doctrine of God*, 99.

resources drawn from the doctrine of God—in order to address contemporary issues related to the church's proclamation of the gospel and mission to the world—there is more to be said about this theological objective realism. We examined at the beginning of this chapter how, as in the case of the Arian and Reformation controversies and in the theology of Karl Barth, Torrance understands the church to have recovered key insights of the *homoousion* with respect to revelation and reconciliation (or, as elsewhere in Torrance's parlance, "being" and "act" respectively). In connection to his discussion of these moments in the church's life and also at other junctions in his thought, Torrance details aspects of his theological objective realism as it unfolds in his understanding of the knowledge of God and of salvation. To these descriptions we now turn.

Internal knowledge of God's being. Torrance's realist description of the knowledge of God is composed of an emphatic affirmation of our knowledge of who God is *in se* with an element of apophaticism. The emphasis of his account is clearly with the former: in Jesus Christ and the Holy Spirit, humanity has been given real knowledge of God. This is unsurprising in light of Torrance's understanding of the stratified nature of theological knowledge and the way that allows the knower to move freely and transparently from our experience of God in worship and prayer to an understanding of who God is in his immanent life. Here as elsewhere, the *homoousion* provides the fundamental insight: "The *homoousios to Patri* was revolutionary and decisive: it expressed the fact that what God is 'toward us' and 'in the midst of us' in and through the Word made flesh, he really is in Himself; that he is in the internal relations of his transcendent being the very same Father, Son and Holy Spirit that he is in his revealing and saving activity in time and space toward mankind."[115]

Understanding the *homoousion* as the indicator of "*oneness in being* between the incarnate Son and the Father"[116] provides Torrance an objective point of reference that establishes an epistemological realism about the immanent divine life: "The knowledge which God thus gives us of himself in his incarnate Son is from a centre in his own being, where all our human understanding and conceiving of him may be governed and tested in

---

[115]Torrance, *Trinitarian Faith*, 130 (emphasis original).
[116]Torrance, *Trinitarian Faith*, 49.

accordance with his divine nature."[117] Because of this, Torrance can describe the life of the immanent Trinity as more fundamental than what we might say about God is in his economic activity. For instance, Torrance makes a great deal of the statement of Athanasius that, "it would be more godly and true to signify God from the Son and call him Father, than to name him from his works and call him Unoriginate."[118] Jesus Christ reveals who God is *in se*. The kind of knowledge that stops with God's economic activity only gives "external" knowledge of God: "When we seek to know God from his created works . . . we do not know him as Father, but only of him as Maker, and are no better off than the Greeks."[119] If in our attempt to understand who God is we operate only on the creature side of the Creator/creature distinction, we will find that there is an arbitrary character to our speech about him. Without an anchor in God's own nature, knowledge of God is ultimately a speculative venture. But because the *homoousion* is understood to describe the presence of the incarnate Son on the created side of the distinction, then this meaningful and real divine presence generates the possibility of true speech about the nature of God as Father, Son, and Holy Spirit.

Torrance counterbalances these claims to objectivity and knowledge of God in his internal relations with an element of apophaticism. While Torrance can see no other place to ground knowledge of God except in the person of the incarnate Son Jesus Christ, he is at the same time cognizant of the dangers associated with advancing this argument. Because of this, Torrance states that in the movement from the economic Trinity to the immanent Trinity (and in the aforementioned movement from the second level of knowledge to the third level of knowledge), there is "a need for a real measure of *apophatic theology* grounded in the *homoousion*."[120] This apophaticism is not to be understood as privileging the negative over the positive, for that would ultimately undo Torrance's understanding of the achievement of the *homoousion*: "Apophatic knowledge of that kind implies that the economic condescension of God in revelation and salvation is only of a temporary or transient nature, one 'by way of reserve' or 'economy' and

---

[117]Torrance, *Trinitarian Faith*, 52.
[118]Quoted in Torrance, *Trinitarian Faith*, 76.
[119]Torrance, *Trinitarian Faith*, 52.
[120]Torrance, "Toward an Ecumenical Consensus on the Trinity," in *Trinitarian Perspectives: Toward Doctrinal Agreement* (Edinburgh: T&T Clark, 1994), 85.

not one identical finally with the abiding reality of God."[121] Rather, this apophaticism is instead rooted in what Torrance calls the "positive ineffability" of God. Torrance describes this as the "positive ineffability of God who in making himself known through the Son and in the Spirit reveals that he infinitely transcends the grasp of our minds."[122]

Thus, Torrance understands the *homoousion* to broker knowledge of God in such a way that a proper distinction between the economic and immanent Trinity is maintained:

> The *homoousion* is found to have a critical significance in regard to what may and what may not be read back from God's revealing and saving activity in history to what he is antecedently, eternal and inherently in himself... so that a significant distinction and delimitation between the economic Trinity and the ontological Trinity must be recognised as well as their essential oneness.[123]

Torrance is clear that the implementation of the "critical edge" required in applying the *homoousion* is not a straightforward process: "The situation is rather more difficult in theology than in natural science, for due to our deep-rooted sin and selfishness we are alienated from God in our minds, and need to be reconciled to him."[124] The objectivity that is needed to purge human knowledge from anthropomorphic descriptions of God requires a repentant posture of thinking: "A repentant rethinking of what we have already claimed to know and a profound reorganisation of our consciousness are required of us in knowing God."[125]

This repentant rethinking is secured by Torrance in the Holy Spirit's activity toward humanity. The Son is the objective center of humanity's knowledge of God because in the incarnation he is present and available to human knowing. Thus Torrance will describe the incarnation as taking place "within the structured objectivities of our created world in such a way that an epistemic bridge is established in Christ between man and God that is grounded in the Being of God and anchored in the being of man."[126] Alone this would seemingly leave humanity in a relationship with God mediated

---

[121] Torrance, "Toward an Ecumenical Consensus," 85.
[122] Torrance, "Toward an Ecumenical Consensus," 87.
[123] Torrance, *Christian Doctrine of God*, 97 (emphasis added).
[124] Torrance, *Christian Doctrine of God*, 99-100.
[125] Torrance, *Christian Doctrine of God*, 100.
[126] Torrance, *Christian Doctrine of God*, 100-101.

only through creaturely forms. But the Holy Spirit, though always operating in unity with the Son, is not similarly constrained: "The Holy Spirit is God of God but not man of man, so that our knowledge of the Holy Spirit rests directly on the ultimate objectivity of God as God, unmediated by the secondary objectivities of space and time, and it rests only indirectly on those objectivities in relation to the Son with whom he is of one being as he is with the Father."[127] The Spirit's work, always inseparable from the Son, thus allows humanity to move beyond an anthropomorphic understanding of the immanent Trinity.[128] "Through the oneness of the Son and the Spirit the imaging of God in Jesus the incarnate Son or the Word made flesh is *signitive*, not mimetic. Thus the creaturely images naturally latent in the forms of thought and speech employed by divine revelation to us are made to refer transparently or in a diaphanous way to God without being projected into his divine Nature."[129]

Therefore, for Torrance, the *homoousion* establishes the possibility of objective realist knowledge about who God is within his own internal relations. But as the Christian moves deeper into the knowledge of God's ineffable being, the *homoousion* acquires a "critical edge" so that human knowing acquires a proper apophaticism as it seeks trustworthy knowledge of God "in his internal intelligible personal relations."[130]

Identity between God and his gracious acts. Torrance's soteriological realism is constructed in response to his perception of the dualisms within certain forms of catholic ecclesiology and builds upon his understanding of the insights of the Reformation and the theology of Karl Barth. Torrance's critique and his accompanying proposal correspond with his epistemological concerns; whereas there he wishes to affirm "God's Act-in-His-Being," here the concern is "God's Being-in-His-Act." Crucial to an account

---

[127] Torrance, *Christian Doctrine of God*, 101.
[128] Muller's critique of Torrance's use of the *homoousion* as undermining divine transcendence here misses the mark. See Muller, "New Athanasius or Origen Redivivus?," 699-700.
[129] Muller, "New Athanasius or Origen Redivivus?," 699-700. See the similar argument made in "The Epistemological Relevance of the Holy Spirit" in *God and Rationality* (London: Oxford University Press, 1971), 166-167: "Thus by letting our thinking obediently follow the way God Himself has taken in Jesus Christ we allow the basic forms of theological truth to come to view. That happens, however, only as in the Spirit the being and nature of God is brought to bear upon us so that we think under the compulsion of His Reality. That is the activity of the Holy Spirit whom Jesus spoke of in this connection as the Spirit of Truth" (167).
[130] Torrance, *Christian Doctrine of God*, 102.

of salvation for Torrance is the affirmation that "the divine Giver and the divine Gift are one and the same."[131]

On the one hand, Torrance's use of *homoousion* at this juncture is unsurprising. Radcliff's description of Torrance's thought is apt: "The famous dictum 'all roads lead to Rome' could be inverted and applied to the Torrancian-Athanasian *homoousion*: all roads depart from, go through, and lead back to the *homoousion*."[132] But on the other hand, the application of the *homoousion* is also strikingly curious. As a work of history, Muller is correct here in that Torrance's application of *homoousion* directly to soteriology is not how it was used in the Nicene period.[133] *Homoousion*, though not without extensive soteriological consequences, was a term used to establish the identity of the Son with the Father, and was not in its original context utilized in the ways that Torrance pressed it to use. But this does not prevent us from engaging with Torrance and exploring how, despite his lexical innovation, he appears to be moving within the bounds of creedal orthodoxy broadly construed. What, then, does Torrance intend in the application of his "imaginative Reformed-evangelical reconstruction" of the *homoousion* to soteriology?[134]

This question finds its answer in the analysis of his *Doktorvater* that Torrance gives in "Karl Barth and the Latin Heresy." The "Latin Heresy," as Torrance understands it, represents "the Western habit of thinking in abstractive *formal relations*."[135] These formal, or external relations, are the inevitable endgame of the dualistic frameworks that Torrance finds in Augustine, Descartes, Newton, and Kant.[136] As we have already noted while discussing Torrance's interpretation of Barth in a different context, the great achievement

---

[131] Torrance, "Preaching Christ Today," 20.

[132] Radcliff, *Thomas F. Torrance and the Church Fathers*, 68.

[133] Muller, "New Athanasius or Origen Redivivus?," 690. The divergence between Muller and Torrance with respect to the nature of the task of historical theology is particularly evident here. For a "critical appreciation" of Torrance's historical theology, see Radcliff, *Thomas F. Torrance and the Church Fathers*. The best assessment of the characteristics of pro-Nicene theology remains Lewis Ayres, *Nicaea and its Legacy: An Approach to Fourth-Century Trinitarian Theology* (Oxford: Oxford University Press, 2004).

[134] This term is utilized by Radcliff in his assessment of Torrance and his proposal for how Torrance's theology can be critically appreciated and adopted. See in particular Radcliff, "Conclusion: An Assessment and Proposed Adoption of Torrance," in *Thomas F. Torrance and the Church Fathers*, 182-199.

[135] Torrance, "Karl Barth and the Latin Heresy," 215.

[136] Torrance, "Karl Barth and the Latin Heresy," 215.

of Karl Barth with respect to the "Latin Heresy" is found in his recovery and integration of the principles of Nicaea and the Reformation. Barth's greatness as a theologian is to be found in large part "with the place which Barth, like Athanasius, gave to *internal relations* in the coherent structure of Christian theology, and of the way in which he exposed and rejected the habit of thinking in terms of *external relations* which had come to characterise so much of Western theology."[137]

The latter half of Torrance's essay focuses upon the soteriological implications of Barth's recovery of the fundamental insight of the *homoousion*. Just as he argued with respect to the knowledge of God, Torrance proposes a realist understanding of salvation: salvation is a present reality in Jesus Christ. He writes, "Reconciliation is not just a truth which God has made known to us; it is what God has done and accomplished for us. . . . How could God actually reveal and give *himself* to us across the chasm, not only of our creaturely distance but of our sinful alienation from him, except through a movement of atoning reconciliation?"[138] For Barth, and also for Torrance, to understand the *homoousion* properly is to state that Jesus Christ *is* salvation. Salvation is an act that is accomplished in his person and it is a reality that is completed within him.

Torrance provides a full description of the objective and, therefore, realist nature of the salvation obtained in Jesus Christ throughout his work. While space does not allow us to describe in detail all that Torrance says, a general sense of his understanding is given in "Karl Barth and the Latin Heresy." The emphasis upon internal relations is obtained by the explicit connection between the incarnation and the atonement. A merely forensic account of salvation, while understood as a part of Torrance's understanding of the atonement, fails to grasp the implications of the incarnation. This is because in the incarnation, Jesus Christ is at work in humanity accomplishing the work of salvation throughout his earthly career: "There took place in Christ as Mediator an agonizing union between God the Judge and man under judgment in a continuous movement of atoning reconciliation running throughout all his obedient and sinless life and passion into the resurrection and ascension."[139]

---

[137]Torrance, "Karl Barth and the Latin Heresy," 217.
[138]Torrance, "Karl Barth and the Latin Heresy," 227.
[139]Torrance, "Karl Barth and the Latin Heresy," 230.

That initial emphasis is then filled out with greater specificity in Torrance's belief that Jesus Christ assumed fallen humanity. Over and against an external account of Jesus' work, Torrance argues for the "total substitution" of humanity by Jesus Christ: "The Latin heresy operates with a form of autonomous reason which has not been allowed to come under the judgment of the Cross, in which Christ wholly took our place, substituting himself for us in mind as well as in body."[140]

This understanding of Christ's work is present in Torrance's thought from the very beginning of his theological career on to his final writings. In his doctoral dissertation, *The Doctrine of Grace in the Apostolic Fathers*, written under Barth, Torrance is already attentive to this issue. Torrance's dissertation is a sustained criticism of a series of pre-Nicene theologians for their inability to grasp the full truth of the New Testament concept of grace and to lapse instead into what Torrance believes to be sub-Christian conceptions of the Pauline understanding of *charis*. In the introduction to the study he writes, "The real content of the word [*charis*] is ... the person of Jesus Christ. Grace is the transcendent Christ in gracious and forgiving and enabling motion."[141] This conviction would remain with Torrance for the entirety of his life; it is an insight that secures the objective nature of salvation.

Torrance is here concerned about any slippage or separation between the person of Jesus Christ, his gift of grace, and its objective and accomplished reality. Because salvation is nothing less than that which is established and realized in the incarnate Son, grace is never to be conceptually separated from the person of Jesus: "The Gift and the Giver are one. Grace is not something that can be detached from God and made to inhere in creaturely being as 'created grace'; nor is it something that can be proliferated in many forms."[142] In his interpretation of the sixteenth-century Roman Catholic understanding of grace, Torrance argues that it runs against the grain of the New Testament to position the church as an intermediary between God's gracious generosity to sinners and the sinner who seeks forgiveness. Whenever this separation occurs, the church has overstepped its place in the economy of grace, usurping the place that belongs properly only to Jesus:

---

[140]Torrance, "Karl Barth and the Latin Heresy," 236.
[141]Torrance, *The Doctrine of Grace in the Apostolic Fathers* (Eugene, OR: Wipf & Stock, 1996), 32.
[142]Torrance, "Roman Doctrine of Grace and Reformed Theology," 182-183.

"The grace of God given to us in Christ is not some kind of gift that can be detached from Christ, for in his grace it is Christ himself who is given to us. . . . It is impossible to think of grace or of the Spirit as endowments bequeathed by Christ to the church to be administered under the authority of the church."[143] For Torrance, Christian dogmatics must preserve the objectivity of the doctrine of grace.

DUALISM, THE *HOMOOUSION*, AND THE CHURCH'S MISSION

This chapter began with an examination of the significant aspects of Torrance's historical theology. As we followed his narration of church history, we noted the significant concern Torrance had with the problem of dualism. Torrance understands dualism in its epistemological and cosmological forms to have had a deleterious effect upon the church's understanding and proclamation of the gospel. According to Torrance, at three key moments in the church's history—the Arian controversy, the Protestant Reformation, and the theology of Karl Barth—this dualistic framework was identified and overcome through the insights of the *homoousion*. While Torrance's narration of the church's theological tradition may contain questionable elements when considered by its own, it merits close examination because of how significant historical theology is for Torrance's own positive construction of his doctrine of God. Indeed, the apparently disproportionate emphasis Torrance places on dualism throughout his historical theology only makes clearer how significant of a problem Torrance considers it to be. In light of this study of Torrance's historical theology, it is clear that Torrance's doctrine of God, and the fundamental place of the *homoousion* within it, is shaped in large part by his concerns about dualism and how it inhibits the church's proclamation and ministry of the gospel. In particular, the *homoousion*, understood via the conceptual framework of Barth's "Act and Being," functions to ground the theological objective realism that the church requires in its knowledge of God and his work in a world that would otherwise obscure this through its tendency toward dualism.

It can be argued that Torrance's doctrine of God is in one sense representative of what Maarten Wisse has in a different context called the "*functionalization*

---

[143]Torrance, *Preaching Christ Today*, 20.

of the idea of God as Trinity."¹⁴⁴ Torrance's description of the Trinity is handled in such a way as to emphasize how the doctrine confronts and overcomes the distinctly modern problem of dualism. While this "functionalization" is not undertaken intentionally, it is nonetheless the case that the conceptual framework of Torrance's trinitarian theology is shaped to confront this issue. At the same time, Torrance's extensive historical theology and his engagement with the primary texts of the Nicene and Reformation traditions serve as a kind of anaphylactic, preventing modern concerns from encroaching so far that they subsume his doctrine of God into a peculiarly modern shape. Torrance's doctrine of God, while in one sense quite certainly a "creative reconstruction" of the tradition he engages with, it is at the same time a "catholic" project in the sense Torrance intended it to be.¹⁴⁵

Indeed, the argument can be made that Torrance's understanding of the doctrine of God is a unique and significant contribution to the church's resources in its understanding and proclamation of the gospel, not least with respect to its theological realism. While Torrance does not utilize the language of processions and missions in his doctrine of God, the *homoousios* functions in much the same way as the classical tradition has deployed these ideas. The missions reveal the processions; there is continuity between God's life *ad intra* and *ad extra*. What Michael Allen has said elsewhere about the relation of the doctrine of God to the doctrine of justification could similarly be said of Torrance's understanding of the doctrine of God to the church's understanding of mission: "The justifying work of the triune God, then, is not accidental or arbitrary. God does not simply

---

[144] Maarten Wisse, *Trinitarian Theology Beyond Participation: Augustine's* De Trinitate *and Contemporary Theology* (London: T&T Clark, 2011), 5. Wisse continues (though the argument is overstated with respect to Torrance), "If the idea or dogma of the Trinity is a mere mystery, or a mere equivalent to the name of God, it is hard to draw implications from the dogma to every single locus of systematic theology. Hence, if the doctrine of the Trinity is to become the *Rahmentheorie* for systematic theology, the content of this type of theology needs to be comprehensible or rationally perspicuous. This is precisely the case in contemporary Trinitarian theology. It is characteristic of this type of theology to develop the doctrine of the Trinity in a highly functionalized way" (5).

[145] Thus, while Stephen R. Holmes parts ways with Torrance's distinctive use of the *homoousion*, he nonetheless maintains that "Torrance offers a doctrine of the Trinity that is in visible continuity with the classical doctrine." Holmes, "In Praise of Being Criticized," 152.

happen to go this route or take this course fortuitously. God's missions express the divine processions. In other words, the course of God's economy expresses the very character of God."[146]

Torrance's Doctrine of God *in conversation with John Flett's* The Witness of God. The distinctive contribution to the church's proclamation and understanding of the gospel that is Torrance's doctrine of God is clarified when we draw it into comparison with another recent proposal, that of John Flett in his recent book *The Witness of God: The Trinity,* Missio Dei, *Karl Barth, and the Nature of Christian Community*. In this book, Flett advances a particular reading of Barth's theology so as to argue for the necessity of the church's missional nature from its prior ground in God's being. For the purposes of this comparison, we will not attempt to adjudicate the appropriateness of Flett's reading of Barth and his doctrine of God. Instead, we will describe Flett's proposal and then compare it with the doctrine of God that we find in Torrance. This comparison will be fruitful not only because of the similar departure points of the two approaches but also because of the divergences that emerge from the two proposals.

Writing out of a deep concern for the witness of the church in the West, Flett's diagnosis is that the church's missiological ills are the result of a fundamental misunderstanding about the nature of the church. Flett's argument in *The Witness of God* seeks to trace these ecclesiological and missiological problems to an origin in the doctrine of God: "The problem of the church's relationship to the world is consequent on treating God's own mission into the world as a second step alongside who he is in himself. With God's movement into his economy ancillary to his being, so the church's own corresponding missionary relationship with the world is ancillary to her being."[147] The descriptor *ancillary* is crucial. That it is possible to give an account of the church in which the church's mission is secondary is, for Flett, indicative of a serious dogmatic error. The church's malaise is to be traced to a "breach in the being and act of the church, with deleterious

---

[146]R. Michael Allen, *Justification and the Gospel: Understanding the Contexts and Controversies* (Grand Rapids, MI: Baker Academic, 2013), 21.
[147]Flett, *Witness of God*, 3.

consequences for accounts of the nature of Christian community and witness. The community becomes one focused in on herself."[148]

It is difficult to overstate the appropriateness and urgency of Flett's diagnosis. His concerns are reflective of the wider "missional church" movement; the church in the West has far and wide lacked, or at the very least failed to apply, the theological resources necessary to face the challenges of the collapse of Christendom and the advance of secularism. Thus Darrell Guder can accurately write, "The obvious fact is that what we once regarded as Christendom is now a post-Constantinian, post-Christendom, and even post-Christian mission stands in bold contrast today with the apparent lethargy of established church traditions in addressing their new situation both creatively and faithfully."[149] Flett's identification of a church in which mission is a fundamentally ancillary (as opposed to primary) activity is representative of the kind of problem that the missional church movement is correct to engage with, and the attempt to provide a properly theological, rather than pragmatic, response is to be commended. But with respect to the central component of his argument, there is reason to question the particular solution that Flett proposes in *The Witness of God*.

Flett's answer to this problematic conception of the church is to trace the error to its origin in the doctrine of God: "The question of the grounding and consequent form of mission is, first, a question of who *God* is in himself. God is a missionary God because his deliberate acting in the apostolic movement toward humanity is not a second step alongside—and thus in distinction to—his perfect divine being."[150] The description of God's "movement toward humanity" in the incarnation as a kind of "second step" in God's immanent life is the source of the church's missional confusion. God can be conceived in his perfections in a way that is not determined by the mission of the incarnate Son: "While the economy epistemically reveals God to be three in one, God's *movement* into the economy cannot be itself ontologically determinative."[151] And this, according to Flett, is precisely the problem: "If it is possible to so define God's true being

---

[148]Flett, *Witness of God*, 195.
[149]Darrell Guder, "From Sending to Being Sent," in *Missional Church: A Vision for the Sending of the Church in North America*, ed. Darrell L. Guder (Grand Rapids, MI: Eerdmans, 1998), 7.
[150]Flett, *Witness of God*, 197.
[151]Flett, *Witness of God*, 199.

apart from his economy, then his *coming* in the economy, though it forms as a parallel to God's eternal nature, occurs in contest with his being. . . . In himself, God remains the almighty Lord, but in his becoming human he lives at some distance from his being."[152] Flett identifies this "distance" as precisely what must be overcome if the church is to reclaim fully its fundamentally missional identity.

While attempting to close this perceived "breach" and "distance" between God's being and his act in Jesus Christ, Flett states at the same time his desire and intention to preserve a proper distinction between the Creator and the creature: "God is in himself distinct from his creation. His connection, as such, occurs not via a simple extension, or abrogation, of his being. Nor does his movement in creation result from some contingency external to God's own life as though his being required some addition to become complete."[153] But while arguing this on the one hand, Flett also wishes to maintain that there is no "second movement" of creation or election in God's immanent life, because it is precisely this that introduces the distance into God's being: "This language of a first and second movement in the life of God tends to be formulated in terms of logical and consequential order. God's perfection attaches to the first movement in such a way that the second movement proceeds out of the first."[154] There, God is understood to exist in this first movement in the perfect and complete life of the Holy Trinity, and only then can the "second movement" be conceived. But as one's doctrine of God ultimately unfolds into ecclesiology, "This has acute consequences for the missionary nature of the church, as indicated by the general absence of mission from dogmatic treatments of God's connection with his creation and from the concomitant ecclesiologies. In other words, one can develop full accounts of the church without reference to her missionary being."[155]

Flett's answer is to collapse these first and second movements into a single movement in which being and act are identified with one another, without remainder. This decision is grounded upon Flett's reading of Barth's doctrine

---

[152]Flett, *Witness of God*, 199.
[153]Flett, *Witness of God*, 202.
[154]Flett, *Witness of God*, 205.
[155]Flett, *Witness of God*, 205.

of election, which Barth formulated so as to avoid the speculative implications of the *logos asarkos*.[156] Flett takes this same insight and utilizes it so as to eliminate any conception of a "second movement" in God's life: "God's *movement* into the economy belongs to his being for all eternity. It is not alongside who God is; rather, it is the very plenitude of God's own life that is capable of including the human in such a way that this inclusion is God's own self-realization."[157] The emphasis is to be placed on the determinate place given to the mission of the Son in God's immanent life: "Grounding mission in the Trinity means grounding his movement into the world in his being from and to all eternity."[158] It is thus that Flett argues, "The church is a missionary community because the God she worships is missionary."[159]

And yet while we wish to affirm the missional identity of the church community, we cannot follow him in the theological remedy he proposes. The language that Flett finds so troubling in the doctrine of God—language of "distance" or of a "second movement"—and which he wishes to jettison so as to secure the church's missionary nature is language that is theologically important and which protects the truths of God's freedom and the gracious nature of God's action by providing a proper distinction between the economic Trinity and the immanent Trinity. While language of "distance" may be troubling and perhaps other language would be more appropriate, the purpose of this kind of speech is to maintain a proper distinction between God and creatures thus to affirm the unnecessary, gratuitous nature of grace. Talk of a "second movement" is not used in order to introduce a "breach" in God's own being, but is rather used in a qualified sense, once again in order to affirm that God's loving movement toward his creation is free and unconstrained. When Flett describes God's movement into the economy as a part of God's "self-realization" without accompanying language that affirms God's freedom, it would seem as if incarnation has become a necessity in an improper way. Moreover, Flett's fundamental decision to ground God's immanent life in the economic mission—not

---

[156] An influential, although controversial (in its implications), description of this has been given in Bruce McCormack's "Grace and Being," in *The Cambridge Companion to Karl Barth*, ed. John Webster (Cambridge: Cambridge University Press, 2000), 92-110.

[157] Flett, *Witness of God*, 208 (emphasis original).

[158] Flett, *Witness of God*, 200.

[159] Flett, *Witness of God*, 208.

merely as a revelation of the internal processions, but as constitutive of God's own being—is equally problematic.

Torrance's account of the doctrine of God provides a conceptual framework that protects against these kinds of errors in three significant ways. First, Torrance utilizes the language of time—in a very qualified sense—to God's immanent life as a way of distinguishing God's *ad intra* and *ad extra* life. The context of Torrance's application of this concept is within a discussion of God's unchangeableness, which Torrance further describes as "the constancy of his self-living, self-moving and self-affirming personal Being."[160] While this description makes it clear that Torrance wishes to avoid introducing a kind of voluntarism into his doctrine of God, he nonetheless introduces the language of "moment" and "time" into God's life as a way of speaking of God's freedom in his relation to creation. The language of time is utilized in a qualified sense, as Torrance explains: "We must think of the constancy of God which is his unchanging eternal Life as characterised by *time*, not of course our kind of time which is the time of finite created being with beginning and end, and past, present and future, but God's kind of time which is the time of his eternal Life without beginning and end."[161]

This language is combined with Torrance's use of the descriptors of "direction" and "fulfillment" when describing God's purpose in his dealings with creation. *Direction* refers to the constancy of God's character as it is revealed in his works *ad extra*, and *fulfillment* is meant to refer not to God's "self-realization" within creation but instead to God's unswerving faithfulness to his purpose. When this is understood in coordination with Torrance's qualified use of "time" in God's immanent life, he can thus state, "There is a purpose of love and so a definite direction in God's eternal Life, marked by distinct *moments* in it such as that before and after the creation or before and after the incarnation, in which it moves toward the divinely determined fulfillment revealed in Jesus Christ."[162] And it is this language of "moments" (performing a similar function to that of a "second movement") that provides Torrance with the proper distinction between

---

[160]Torrance, *Christian Doctrine of God*, 240.
[161]Torrance, *Christian Doctrine of God*, 241.
[162]Torrance, *Christian Doctrine of God*, 241-242.

the immanent and economic Trinity, while at the same time maintaining their fundamental continuity.[163]

> The fact that in the incarnation God became man without ceasing to be God, [sic] tells us that his nature is characterised by both repose and movement, and that his eternal Being is also a divine Becoming. This does not mean that God ever becomes other than he eternally is or that he passes over from becoming into something else, but rather that he continues unceasingly to be what he always is and ever will be in the living movement of his eternal Being.[164]

Commenting on this theme in Torrance's writing, Paul Molnar describes Torrance as having stated that, "God can do something new, new even for himself because he is a living God and because, without any dependence on history and created time, he himself has his own eternal time."[165]

Second for Torrance, the doctrine of election has a specific and much more modest place than in Flett's proposal. For Flett, election is a determination of God's own being which then determines the church's being: "The event of election in which the missionary determination of God determines the human missionary correspondence remains the event of election."[166] In contrast, for Torrance election does not determine God's being but rather is something like a "secondary movement" that is grounded upon God's immanent life (as opposed to grounding that life). Thus Torrance states, "Election rests on the relation of love between the Father and the Son, and election is the *prothesis*, the setting forth, the projection of that love in Christ the beloved Son of God, through whom we are adopted into Christ's eternal relation of sonship in love to the Father."[167] Torrance has a relatively modest doctrine of election for a Reformed theologian,[168] and he understands the doctrine as a way of describing the constancy of God's dealings

---

[163] For an exploration of how these decisions may put Torrance's doctrine of God in tension with other aspects of classical theism, see James E. Dolezal, *All That Is In God: Evangelical Theology and the Challenge of Classical Theism* (Grand Rapids, MI: Reformation Heritage Books, 2017), 79-104 and particularly 101n58.
[164] Torrance, *Christian Doctrine of God*, 242.
[165] Paul D. Molnar, *Faith, Freedom and the Spirit: The Economic Trinity in Barth, Torrance and Contemporary Theology* (Downers Grove, IL: IVP Academic, 2015), 211.
[166] Flett, *Witness of God*, 213.
[167] Torrance, *Incarnation: The Person and Life of Christ* (Downers Grove, IL: IVP Academic, 2008), 178.
[168] This is true both in comparison to Reformation and Reformed Orthodox figures such as John Calvin and Francis Turretin, as well as Barth, for whom election is central to the doctrine of God. In contrast, Torrance is much more restrained in his use of the doctrine of election.

with humanity while attempting to avoid any abstraction from the person of Jesus Christ: "The twofold significance of *prothesis* means that our salvation in Christ does not rest upon any eternal hinterground in the will of God that is not identical with the foreground in the actual person of the incarnate Son, Jesus Christ."[169] Thus while Torrance clearly wishes to distinguish his own position from other, more traditional species of the Reformed tradition, he at the same time does not push the doctrine of election into God's immanent life in the same way as his *Doktorvater* Barth did. Commenting on this aspect of Torrance's thought, Molnar states that "Torrance carefully stresses that what is completed in God's movement toward us is not the fulfillment of the divine being, but the fulfillment of the divine love in its purposes for us."[170]

Third, and perhaps most basically, Torrance's approach rejects the fundamental analogy Flett draws between God's being and act and the church's being and act. This decision, which drives the heart of Flett's proposal, hangs too much on an equivalency that Torrance (and perhaps even Barth) would find more appropriate to build upon christology and the two natures of the person of Jesus Christ (a point that we will explore in chapters three and four). Thus, Torrance writes, "The incomparable God is not to be understood on the analogy of our finite creaturely human being with whom word, act, and person are different from another. With us word is different from act."[171] Torrance's description of the church, and the analogy that will drive that description, is built on what he understands to be the firm foundation of christology.

Conclusion

In this chapter we have explored T. F. Torrance's doctrine of God by examining it in a different register than that of other studies of a similar type. Guided by Torrance's own self-understanding of his calling as an "intellectual evangelist" of Western culture, his continued involvement in the life of the church while teaching at New College and later while Moderator of the Church of Scotland, and his desire to fulfill his pastoral and missionary

---

[169] Torrance, *Incarnation*, 179.
[170] Molnar, *Faith, Freedom and the Spirit*, 202.
[171] Torrance, *Christian Doctrine of God*, 236.

calling through academic theology, we have studied the central elements of Torrance's trinitarian theology with an eye trained to the missional impulses and implications of his thought. As we followed Torrance's historical theology, which has a significant relationship to Torrance's own constructive work, we noted the influence of the dualisms that Torrance perceives to run through history and their corrosive effect on the church's proclamation of the gospel. Torrance's concern about dualism leads him to privilege a particular understanding of the *homoousion* as a central aspect of the doctrine of God. This construction of the *homoousion* is combined with the conceptual framework of act and being that Torrance learned from Karl Barth. In light of this analysis of his theology, we have argued that Torrance's trinitarian theology is best understood in light of his desire to secure a theological realism through his doctrine of God that will provide a firm doctrinal foundation for the church's understanding and proclamation of the gospel in Western intellectual culture.

Having provided a description of this element of Torrance's theology, we then compared Torrance's doctrine of God with another, more recent proposal—that of John Flett—to draw missional implications from the doctrine of God. In examining Flett's *The Witness of God*, we noted how Flett seeks to make mission an essential part of the church's nature by attempting to ground God's immanent life in his *ad extra* missions. The comparison with Flett was fruitful in that it makes clear what Torrance's doctrine of God does not do: attempt to ground mission fundamentally in God's immanent life. As we saw, Torrance's doctrine of God resists this kind of proposal, as this would fail to provide a proper distinction between the immanent Trinity and the economic Trinity. God moves, ineluctably, into the economy in the incarnation of Jesus Christ, in that he is faithful and constant to who he is *in se*. But this movement does not in any sense ground who he is *in se*. While Torrance does understand mission to be an essential aspect of the nature of the church, he believes that this concept is better grounded elsewhere in Christian doctrine.

For Torrance, christology is the doctrinal locus that provides the material ground for understanding the church and its mission. While Torrance is often known as a "theologian of the Trinity," his christology is no less a part of the unique contribution that he has made to systematic theology.

Torrance's christology is a creative synthesis of biblical and Reformed theology—a synthesis that, as we shall later see, is one part of the foundation that Torrance lays for the church's participation in the mission that is crucial to its existence. It is to that doctrine, and Torrance's description of it, that we now turn.

2

The Lord of Mission

THE THREEFOLD OFFICE AND ASCENSION OF JESUS CHRIST

IN THE FINAL CHAPTER OF *Space, Time and Resurrection*, Torrance asks the reader to join him on what he calls a "thought-experiment." Let us imagine, Torrance says, that we send back in time a modern reporter and give him the assignment of investigating and documenting the life of Jesus of Nazareth from the time of his baptism by John the Baptist until his resurrection from the tomb. Over the course of these three years, this reporter spends his time following Jesus throughout his ministry:

> Above all he studies Jesus himself, in his treatment of the common people, his encounter with the authorities, his behaviour in the synagogue and in the temple, his arguments with lawyers, his conflict with the priests, his exposure of the hypocrites, his association with outcasts, his treatment of Samaritans and aliens, his compassion for the poor, the sick, the crippled and the blind, his welcome to little children.[1]

Throughout this inquiry, the reporter's task is "to penetrate into the inner intention of Jesus in an attempt to understand him from within his own life and mission."[2]

This task, Torrance continues, proves to be difficult for our reporter. As the reporter's task continues and more information is gathered, the reporter

---

[1] Thomas F. Torrance, *Space, Time and Resurrection* (London: T&T Clark, 2019), 161-162.
[2] Torrance, *Space, Time and Resurrection*, 162.

himself grows more and more puzzled. Jesus' wondrous miracles, his plainly evident authority in dealings with other religious authorities, his remarkable insight into persons he encounters—all of these escape the categories and profiles that the reporter has imported into his task. This bafflement is not reducible to any one aspect of Jesus' person:

> In the last analysis . . . what baffles our reporter is Jesus himself. He does not seem to fit into any conceivable mould; he breaks through every ordinary conceptual system; he resists being subsumed in any general scheme of things or even being brought into a connected relation with other understandable possibilities and conditions, for his nature somehow transcends all the criteria that he can think of on the basis of hitherto recorded experience.[3]

Our reporter cannot assimilate Jesus into his world; he must instead submit himself and every conceptual apparatus to Jesus.

Torrance's "thought-experiment" illustrates the place of christology within his thought and why at this juncture in our study we must devote ourselves to an examination of Torrance's christology. It is in the person of Jesus Christ that our preconceptions about reality are confronted and reconstructed. It is the person of Jesus Christ who requires the reschematization of our minds as his holiness and reality press upon us. Thus, for Torrance, the question of the identity of the church and the nature of its mission is only answerable with reference to the identity of Jesus Christ.

In this chapter we will focus our examination of Torrance's christology upon two loci. First, we shall examine Torrance's understanding of how Jesus Christ, the one mediator between God and humanity, accomplishes the act of atonement. As a theologian within the Reformed tradition, Torrance utilizes a familiar concept: Christ's threefold office, the *munus triplex*. We choose this aspect of Torrance's christology because he identifies it as the determinative framework through which we are also to understand the church's participation in Christ's ministry: "The mission of the whole Church as the Body of Christ on earth and in history is called through the Spirit, as it were, into contrapuntal relation to the heavenly ministry of Christ, King, Priest and Prophet."[4] In order to understand the church's

---

[3]Torrance, *Space, Time and Resurrection*, 163.
[4]Torrance, *Space, Time and Resurrection*, 122.

mission and ministry we will need to understand the foundation it is built upon, and so we must first explore this doctrine. Second, we will examine Torrance's doctrine of the ascension. Torrance devotes significant space within his work to this event, and he does so because it determines his understanding of the nature of Jesus' presence until his return, and thus the nature of the time and space that the church inhabits now. In exploring these two loci, we are aligning ourselves with the methodology displayed in Torrance's "thought-experiment." It is through christology that we are given the tools to understand the church and its mission.

THE *MUNUS TRIPLEX* IN TORRANCE'S CHRISTOLOGY

The threefold office in Reformed theology. The concept of the threefold office is integral to Torrance's understanding of the person of Jesus Christ and his mediation of salvation.[5] Torrance's use of the doctrine of the *munus triplex* is an example of the kind of theological methodology Torrance employs throughout his work: it is a concept built upon early church tradition, rooted in the Reformed expression of the faith, and informed by biblical-theological categories. Torrance notes that the threefold office was first important to Justin Martyr, John Chrysostom, Cyril of Alexandria, and Aquinas before John Calvin provided the standard formulation of the term.[6] He then correlates the distinctions of the threefold office to what he understands to be the three primary biblical categories for understanding redemption.[7] This integrative methodology is typical of Torrance; he constantly sought to draw upon and connect biblical theology and catholic tradition in his scholarship.

But the reasons for Torrance's appeal to the *munus triplex* cannot be reduced simply to the biblical-catholic nature of his theology. Within Reformed christology, the threefold office is a part of the tradition's reasoning about the nature of Christ's mediation of redemption. As the concept ties together Jesus' person and his work, it provides clarity about the nature of

---

[5]Throughout this discussion we will use the singular "office" to describe both the threefold office that Christ fulfills and also each of the individual offices that comprise it. Properly speaking, there is only a single, threefold office that Christ takes up, but during the course of this discussion we will at times refer to each particular aspect as an office as well.

[6]Torrance, *Atonement: The Person and Work of Christ* (Downers Grove, IL: IVP Academic, 2009), 59.

[7]Torrance, *Atonement*, 59.

Jesus' identity and what benefits his work has won for the church, in contrast to the abstract accounts of Christ's mediation, which preceded Calvin's development of the term. Some historical background to Calvin's development of the *munus triplex* is helpful here: Calvin's immediate interlocutors in the 1559 *Institutes* are Roman Catholics for whom (Calvin claims) Christ's titles are deployed "without understanding their purpose and use."[8] He in turn proposes that Christ's threefold office be utilized "in order that faith may find a firm basis for salvation in Christ, and thus rest in him."[9] The threefold office is, for Calvin, a way to give close attention to Scripture's narration of Christ's identity as he takes up and fulfills the Old Testament history. Thus Richard Muller states, "In describing the work of Christ as a threefold office, Calvin presses upon us the historical continuity of the covenants, the historical dynamic of salvation from promise to fulfillment, and the historical nexus of the divine saving causality toward which the entire economy of salvation points."[10] Calvin's discussion of the threefold office in the 1559 *Institutes* takes place in the course of his discussion of the person of the mediator and in this way sets the course for the tradition of Reformed theology.

In the same way, for Torrance the *munus triplex* provides a way to delineate the nature of the redemption Christ has established by following the logic of the biblical narrative[11] and allowing biblical themes to control the description of Christ's mediation of salvation. In what follows, we will provide a description of Torrance's understanding of the *munus triplex* and the shape of each of the aspects of the office before noting what is distinct about his account. In order to illuminate the uniqueness of Torrance's account, we have chosen John Calvin as the chief point of comparison for Torrance's account of the *munus triplex*. Although he is only one of a larger number of Reformed theologians to utilize the *munus triplex*, including Francis Turretin, Herman Bavinck, and Karl Barth, Calvin nonetheless

---

[8]John Calvin, *Institutes of the Christian Religion*, ed. John T. McNeill, trans. Ford Lewis Battles (Louisville, KY: Westminster John Knox, 1960), 494.

[9]Calvin, *Institutes*, 494.

[10]Richard A. Muller, *Christ and the Decree: Christology and Predestination in Reformed Theology from Calvin to Perkins* (Grand Rapids, MI: Baker Academic, 1986), 33.

[11]Calvin's use of the *munus triplex* was compelling to Karl Barth for much the same reason. Phil Butin notes how the threefold office is integral to the narrative shape of Barth's christology in vol. IV of the *Church Dogmatics*. Butin, "Two Early Reformed Catechisms, the Threefold Office, and the Shape of Karl Barth's Christology," *Scottish Journal of Theology* 44.2 (1991): 195-214.

provides a helpful point of reference not only because of his place at the genesis of the Reformed tradition's understanding of the threefold office but also because of Torrance's own extensive professed reliance upon Calvin. In chapters four and five we will return to the description provided here as we understand the implications of the *munus triplex* for Torrance's missional ecclesiology, an ecclesiology which, as we shall see in chapter three, is built upon a christological foundation. Our present task, however, is the exposition of Torrance's understanding of the *munus triplex*.

Torrance's biblical-theological foundation of the threefold office. Before examining Torrance's understanding of the particular offices of prophet, priest, and king, we must first note how Torrance understands these offices to be embedded within Scripture's narration of the act of atonement. Torrance's substantial treatments of the *munus triplex* in *Atonement* and *The School of Faith* are formally preceded and materially established by his understanding of the biblical grammar of the work of Christ.[12] For Torrance, the central descriptive idea in the New Testament for understanding Christ's atoning work is the concept of redemption: "In his 'word' about giving his life as a ransom Jesus makes quite central the concept of redemption and the price of redemption, *lutron*."[13] Torrance also uses redemption in a more specific way as a subset of his understanding of atonement alongside the categories of justification and reconciliation, but he generally understands redemption to be synonymous with atonement.[14]

Torrance's identification of redemption as the central New Testament concept for understanding the atonement leads him to investigate its Old Testament context. He notes three Hebrew terms in the Old Testament that "are all regarded as building together one conception of redemption."[15] These three terms are *padah*, *kipper*, and *goel*. While Torrance is indebted to the

---

[12]Torrance, *The School of Faith: The Catechisms of the Reformed Church* (Eugene, OR: Wipf & Stock, 1996), lxxxvii-xcv; Torrance, *Atonement*, 61-72.
[13]Torrance, *Atonement*, 26.
[14]"Redemption is used in the New Testament in a general comprehensive sense to speak of the great act of our salvation through justification, expiation, and reconciliation in Christ. . . . But redemption also has a more specific sense in the New Testament, one in which it speaks of God's saving act in Christ as reaching out from grace, *charis*, to glory, *doxa*." Torrance, *Atonement*, 171.
[15]Torrance, *Atonement*, 27.

Theological Dictionary of the New Testament,[16] it appears that the conclusions that he draws about the usage of these biblical concepts as they connect to the *munus triplex* and his overarching understanding of redemption are largely his own. Here, we will engage with each of the three terms he uses in turn so as to better understand how these concepts coordinate with his understanding of the *munus triplex*.

Padah. Torrance states that *padah* comprehends the "dramatic aspect of atonement,"[17] and it "speak[s] of redemption with emphasis upon the cost of redemption and the nature of the redeeming act rather than upon the nature of the redeemer."[18] While there are cultic and liturgical uses of the term, particularly in connection to the substitutionary nature of redemption,[19] the primary use of *padah* is in relation to Israel's redemption out of Egypt. Torrance extrapolates from this event a number of points of theological significance. First, it leads him to an understanding of biblical redemption, which is both "out of the judgement of God and out of an alien and repressive power."[20] Torrance notes that the exodus event is a deliverance from the oppressive hand of Pharaoh as well as a deliverance from the angel of death sent by God: "Somehow redemption out of the power of evil oppression is only possible through redemption from the judgment of God and redemption into a covenant bond with God."[21]

Torrance connects the concept of redemption, which *padah* describes, to a cluster of similar deliverance themes in the New Testament. First he identifies in the synoptic Gospels a resonance with "the breaking in of the kingdom upon those bound in sin, bringing them release and freedom."[22] Second, in the Pauline corpus, Torrance sees a parallel in how the law is understood to function within the history of salvation, and in particular

---

[16]His dependence upon the *Theological Dictionary of the New Testament* is observed in the footnotes of the first chapter of *Royal Priesthood: A Theology of Ordained Ministry* (Edinburgh: T&T Clark, 1993). There we see its usefulness for him in his description of the priestly office, though Torrance goes considerably beyond what is found in the articles he cites. See Torrance, *Royal Priesthood*, 1n1-2.

[17]Torrance, *School of Faith*, lxxxvii.

[18]Torrance, *Atonement*, 27.

[19]Torrance, *Atonement*, 28.

[20]Torrance, *Atonement*, 29 (emphasis added).

[21]Torrance, *Atonement*, 29.

[22]Torrance, *Atonement*, 29.

"the law as it is used by sin . . . for the powers of evil use its accusations against the sinner to bind them all the more in the slavery of sin."[23] Third, Torrance sees deliverance in the New Testament to be tied closely to improper exercise of the *exousia* (authority), which God has delegated to human authorities. Here the application of the *padah* concept to the New Testament means that "the Gospels think of the incarnation as the invasion of the mighty Son of God into our domain where evil has come to exercise its sway, in order to break its bonds and deliver us from its captivity."[24] Through Jesus Christ and the deliverance he accomplishes, humanity is freed from the oppression of the unjust exercise of *exousia* in fallen creation.

Holiness is the means of deliverance that corresponds to *padah*: "By his very holiness and perfect obedience sin had no power over him, and it was therefore as the holy one in entire fulfillment of the holy will of God that he invaded the domain of evil and redeemed us out of the powers of darkness by his holy life and his holy submission to the Father's will even unto the death of the cross."[25] Torrance further states that in his redemption of humanity, Jesus Christ not only frees humanity from enslavement to evil powers but also destroys these same powers (an argument made from the fact that the Greek verb from which redemption is derived, *luo*, can mean either "to loose" or "to destroy"). Thus, for Torrance, the grounding of the New Testament conception of redemption upon the Old Testament concept of *padah* yields a fundamentally "dramatic" picture of redemption that is the result of a powerful act of grace and power and which delivers humanity from the power of sin.

Kipper. In contrast to *padah*, which emphasizes the redemption from sin's power, *kipper* has to do with "redemption as the actual wiping out of sin and of guilt, and so of effecting propitiation between man and God."[26] Torrance is here emphasizing an understanding of redemption as "an expiatory sacrifice for sin made in the offering of Christ's life for our life in obedience to the divine Will and Mercy."[27] Torrance develops this concept from the root of *kipper*, which means "to cover sin or nullify through the offering of a

---

[23]Torrance, *Atonement*, 30.
[24]Torrance, *Atonement*, 31.
[25]Torrance, *Atonement*, 32.
[26]Torrance, *Atonement*, 33.
[27]Torrance, *School of Faith*, lxxxvii.

propitiatory gift, and so to conciliate."[28] Throughout his description of *kipper*, Torrance is careful to affirm that God is the subject, and not the object, of this action.

Torrance locates *kipper* within a cultic and forensic context as it related to Israel's life and worship. He notes that for Israel, there was no separation between law and cult, or moral and religious categories. In the same way that both existed within a unity, so also *kipper* was applied to both the cultic and forensic aspects of Israel's life. Torrance points to the importance of holding both the cultic and the forensic elements of redemption together, in contrast to the modern tendency to introduce a false dichotomy between "the physical and the spiritual, the dramatic and the ethical, the cultic and the forensic."[29] If this separation is upheld, the fullness and unity of the New Testament vision for atonement disintegrates.

Torrance also emphasizes how *kipper* is a part of a covenant understanding of God's relation to humanity. The cultic-forensic categories that Torrance addresses in his discussion of *kipper* provide the shape of this covenant relationship. Because the covenant is the framework for Israel's relationship with God, the disobedience of the people of God causes a rupture in that relationship. *Kipper* redemption describes how God restores that relationship in the face of human disobedience. Here God "provides in his own mercy and initiative, ways and means of reconciliation, of wiping out offences, of canceling the effects of sin, of re-establishing true relations with himself."[30] Torrance calls this conception of redemption "the *cultic-forensic* aspect of atonement . . . the priestly and judicial work of propitiation though sacrifice."[31]

Goel. The final term Torrance identifies as a part of the Old Testament concept of redemption is *goel*. This term, often known as the idea of kinsman-redemption, focuses on the redeemer and his relation to the redeemed. Whereas *padah* focuses on the dramatic nature of the act of redemption and *kipper* on the nature of the expiatory sacrifice, *goel* emphasizes the person of the redeemer: "The *goel* acts in virtue of their position

---

[28]Torrance, *Atonement*, 34.
[29]Torrance, *Atonement*, 36.
[30]Torrance, *Atonement*, 38.
[31]Torrance, *School of Faith*, lxxxviii.

and relation to the person who is in need through forfeiture of their right or through bondage, and the *goel* redeems them by rightfully claiming the person's cause as their very own, standing in for them and taking their burdens upon their own self, since they are unable to do it for themselves."[32]

Boaz is the most recognizable example of the *goel* in the Old Testament. In Ruth, we see how Boaz redeems Ruth out of her helpless condition and into full membership of the people of God. The term is also applied to God in his relation to his people at various places in the Old Testament. In the New Testament, the same understanding of the *goel* is found in the person of Jesus and the unique relation he has to humanity through the incarnation: "The primary fact that stares us in the face is the incarnation itself, the fact that the Son of God has become bone of our bone and flesh of our flesh, so that we are bone of his bone and flesh of his flesh."[33]

Just as with *padah* and *kipper*, Torrance distills a particular aspect of the atonement from this idea. Alongside the dramatic and the cultic-forensic aspects of the atonement, the idea of the *goel* represents the incarnational and ontological aspect of the atonement: "It is the incarnational or ontological aspect of atonement that is uppermost, that is the relation of our salvation to the nature and constitution of the Person of the Redeemer."[34]

Torrance's account of these three aspects of the atonement ends with an argument for the importance of maintaining the unity of the three concepts. When held in isolation, or when only two are emphasized, the atonement becomes dislocated from its biblical basis and the fully orbed picture of redemption in the New Testament is lost. But before he draws to a close his discussion of the Old Testament background to redemption, Torrance notes the correlation of *padah*, *kipper*, and *goel* to the distinctions of the threefold office of Christ. Jesus Christ the prophet correlates to the *goel* aspect of redemption, for he is "the Word made flesh, as He who brings the Word of the Father to bear upon man in his darkness and sin, but also as He who from within our darkness and alienation bears the Word before God."[35] Jesus Christ the priest corresponds to the *kipper* aspect of redemption, for

---

[32] Torrance, *Atonement*, 45.
[33] Torrance, *Atonement*, 48.
[34] Torrance, *School of Faith*, lxxxviii.
[35] Torrance, *School of Faith*, lxxxxix.

"through the expiatory blood of Christ God draws near to man in mercy and forgiveness and draws man near to Himself in an unbreakable union of love and communion."[36] And Jesus Christ the king corresponds to the *padah* aspect of redemption, describing how "the Redeemer as a mighty Prince leads captivity captive and opens up an entirely new situation in which the old order is annulled and a new order of freedom in the Spirit is ushered in."[37]

It is important to note that, for Torrance, it is fundamentally the Old Testament language of redemption that provides the background that grounds the threefold office. His instincts at this juncture are broadly Reformed in the way he utilizes the language and imagery of Scripture and its narration of God's gracious dealings with humanity so that they provide formal structure and material content to christology.[38] But the claim that these three specific Old Testament terms provide the material content for the *munus triplex* is a notable variation from Calvin and the wider Reformed tradition, which typically chose to found the threefold office on the fact that each of the offices of prophet, priest, and king was given through anointing, and that Jesus Christ—literally "Jesus the Anointed One"—summed up all of the roles in himself. Other Reformed accounts of the *munus triplex* were also tied much more closely with the historical covenant structure of God's relation to humanity. Torrance notes the connection of the threefold office to the Messiah's anointing,[39] and there are elements of covenant theology within his understanding of the *munus triplex*, but his account is different in how the biblical categories of *padah, kipper,* and *goel* provide the material content for his later discussion of the threefold office in *Atonement* and *The School of Faith*.

Torrance's organization of the munus triplex. The architectonic of Torrance's account of the threefold office offers two interesting departures from similar treatments within his Reformed tradition. As we move toward his treatment of the different aspects of the office, it is important to draw

---

[36]Torrance, *School of Faith*, xc-xci.
[37]Torrance, *School of Faith*, xciv.
[38]Thus, Stephen Edmondson describes Calvin's christological method in this way: "We are first to consider how God, who is the author of history and of the scriptural texts which record it, administers God's relationship with the world and with God's Church in particular. From there we are to draw images, concepts, and the dynamic that give form to how we speak of Christ." Edmondson, *Calvin's Christology* (Cambridge: Cambridge University Press, 2004), 40.
[39]Torrance, *Atonement*, 59.

attention to these features of Torrance's thought because of how these descriptions affect Christ's continuing mediatorial role. These two features are Torrance's understanding of the relation between the prophetic and priestly aspects of Christ's office and his understanding of the proper ordering of the aspects of the office.

As we have just seen throughout his work, Torrance is keen to integrate traditional theological categories with recent work in biblical theology. This integrative desire is also displayed in his understanding of the relation between the prophetic and priestly offices. Upon closer inspection we find that for Torrance, the *munus triplex* is in another sense a *munus duplex*, with the prophetic office subsidiary to the priestly office and only arising distinctly in response to events in Israel's history.

Torrance's fullest treatment of the priestly/prophetic relation is found in his volume on ordained ministry, *Royal Priesthood*, though he makes the same argument elsewhere.[40] The Old Testament priesthood, Torrance states, is determined by its relation to the Word of God and its location in Israel's cultic life.[41] "All that the priest does, all liturgical action, answers to the Word given to the priest who bears that Word and mediates it to man, and only in relation to that primary function does he have the other functions of oblation and sacrifice."[42] Within the framework of the centrality of the Word, the priesthood has a double character. On the one hand, the priesthood mediates God's Word. On the other hand, the priesthood witnesses to God's will. This double character is seen in the first members of the priesthood, Moses and Aaron. Moses demonstrates the former aspect of the priesthood: "In this supreme relation to God's Word, Moses is priest *par excellence*, whose mediatorial functions are seen as he pleads with God for Israel's forgiveness . . . or as upon Horeb he intercedes for Israel in her battle."[43] "Over and against" and also "in secondary status" to the Mosaic priesthood, Aaron manifests the latter aspect of the priesthood. The

---

[40] Torrance, *Atonement*, 20-21, 63-67.
[41] This is an insight that Torrance draws from the *Theological Dictionary of the New Testament*'s entry on the priesthood: "The first traces of the priesthood in the earliest sources make it plain that originally the primary function of the priest is the delivery of oracles rather than sacrifice." Gottlob Schrenk, "ἱερός," in *Theological Dictionary of the New Testament*, ed. Gerhard Kittel, trans. Geoffrey W. Bromiley, vol. 3 (Grand Rapids, MI: Eerdmans, 1965), 260.
[42] Torrance, *Royal Priesthood*, 1.
[43] Torrance, *Royal Priesthood*, 3-4.

Aaronic priesthood witnesses to the primary Mosaic priesthood and its once-and-for-all character: "Aaron is regarded as the liturgical priest who carries out in continual cultic witness the actual mediation that came through Moses."[44] Thus Torrance presents the basic structure of the priesthood, with the Mosaic, mediatorial aspect primary and the Aaronic, witnessing aspect secondary.

As the Old Testament narrative continues to unfold, tension and conflict develop between the two aspects of the priesthood. In particular, the Aaronic priesthood seeks independence from the Mosaic priesthood and its secondary status. Torrance cites as evidence for this Aaron's culpability in the golden calf incident and Aaron and Miriam's challenge to the uniqueness of Moses in Numbers 12. Both of these events demonstrate that despite the attempt to establish independence, Aaron's priesthood does in fact properly depend upon the mediation of Moses. But it also represents a more fundamental tendency in the human heart, "the temptation to escape from direct meeting or encounter with the living God. . . . The Old Testament tells us that sin is so deeply ingrained in man that he seeks to erect the divine ordinances of worship into priestly ritual efficient in itself."[45]

The conflict between the two aspects of the priesthood continues as the biblical narrative progresses. As the Aaronic aspect of priesthood continued to seek independence from the Mosaic aspect, God sent prophets in order to call Israel back to proper worship and the full vision of the priestly office. Torrance notes that most of the Old Testament prophets are themselves members of the priesthood and out of that office protest the distortion of Israel's worshipping life. Finally, though, prophets arose who had no relation to the priesthood, which is itself a sign of judgment against the institution: "When the priesthood became very corrupt, God raised up prophets like Amos who had no relation to the priesthood and who came voicing the word of God in criticism of cultic performances."[46]

After the exile, the reorientation of Israel's worship led to a corresponding change in priesthood. Torrance understands Ezra to demonstrate the rehabilitation of the Word and liturgical aspects of the priesthood into two new,

---

[44]Torrance, *Royal Priesthood*, 4.
[45]Torrance, *Royal Priesthood*, 5.
[46]Torrance, *Atonement*, 64.

combined forms: "liturgised law and legalised liturgy."[47] This new form of the priesthood, and the accompanying emergence of scribes in Israel, is for Torrance a negative development: "Law and liturgy go hand in hand, but in such a way that they are made self-sufficient and independent, liturgised Scripture and legalised priestcraft. Here there is no room for the prophet, the direct intervention of the charismatic word, for the Word of God is made of none effect by the traditions of men."[48] This development is the culmination of Israel's will for independence from God's Word and demonstrates Israel's inability to avail itself of its means of grace and also of the necessity of the incarnation: "Without the priestly mediation of the Word of God and its dynamic intervention in the life of Israel, Israel is delivered over to God-forsakenness, hardened by sin in the very use of the ordinances of grace."[49]

Thus, while Torrance will employ the *munus triplex* throughout his understanding of Christ's mediatorial work, he understands the *munus duplex* to be the basic framework of Scripture. This is not a complete innovation within the Reformed tradition; Torrance demonstrates that his position is to some extent in agreement with Calvin,[50] although by the 1545 version of the *Institutes*, Calvin had fully embraced the *munus triplex* over the *munus duplex*.[51] Torrance's drawing together of the prophetic and priestly aspects is noteworthy, though. This decision, combined with the coordination of the prophetic office with the *goel* (incarnational) aspect of redemption, gives Torrance's understanding of the prophetic aspect a different shape than the majority of Reformed accounts of the prophetic office. Whereas Calvin and others will identify the prophetic office with either the church's preaching and teaching or in some connection to Jesus' continuing revelatory work, Torrance primarily (but not exclusively) emphasizes Jesus'

---

[47]Torrance, *Royal Priesthood*, 7.
[48]Torrance, *Royal Priesthood*, 7.
[49]Torrance, *Royal Priesthood*, 7.
[50]Torrance, *Atonement*, 59. This argument was made in its fullest form by J. F. Jansen (*Calvin's Doctrine of the Work of Christ* [London: James Clarke, 1956]), and although Torrance never cites Jansen, it is likely he was aware of this study. Jansen's argument for the priority of the twofold office has been criticized by Stephen Edmondson (*Calvin's Christology* [Cambridge: Cambridge University Press, 2004], 160-167). See also Alan J. Torrance, "Reclaiming the Continuing Priesthood of Christ: Implications and Challenges," in *Christology Ancient and Modern: Explorations in Constructive Dogmatics*, ed. Oliver Crisp and Fred Sanders (Grand Rapids, MI: Zondervan, 2013), 188.
[51]A. Torrance, "Reclaiming the Continuing Priesthood of Christ," 188.

representative humanity: "Christ is prophet as the Word become flesh, the Son who declares the Father become man. . . . Christ comes as our *goel-redeemer* in word and act, as our advocate who not only gives an account for us to God but stands in for us, taking our cause completely upon himself."[52] Calvin's description from the 1559 *Institutes* is broadly representative of the later Reformed tradition. In contrast to Torrance, he understands the prophetic office in relation to the church's preaching: "[Christ] received anointing, not only for himself that he might carry out the office of teaching, but for his whole body that the power of the Spirit might be present in the continuing preaching of the gospel."[53] In our examination of Torrance's understanding of the *munus triplex*, we will attempt to grasp the reasons behind his decision to provide a different description of the prophetic office and to evaluate the resultant effects.

The other aspect of Torrance's understanding of the *munus triplex* that we must note before turning to his understanding of the doctrine itself is his ordering of the threefold office. Most accounts of the *munus triplex* begin with an account of the prophetic, then move to the priestly work, and then finally describe the kingly aspect. This ordering is understood to follow the chronology of Jesus' life. The life, teaching, and ministry of Jesus is identified with the prophetic work, his death upon the cross and resurrection correspond to the priestly work, and the ascension inaugurates his kingly reign.[54] While Torrance follows this ordering initially, he notes the need to change the order in light of the ascension: "As we consider the threefold office within the period inaugurated by the ascension, it is evidently with another order that we have to work: King, Priest, and Prophet."[55] This reordering of the threefold office will not need to be discussed in the present investigation of Christ's threefold office, but when we discuss the church's participation in the threefold ministry of Christ in chapters four and five, we will need to examine this new ordering. But first we must look to the nature of Jesus' redemptive work before the ascension, and thus to the ordering of prophet, priest, and king.

---

[52]Torrance, *Atonement*, 61.
[53]Calvin, *Institutes*, 496.
[54]Notable exceptions are, interestingly, Calvin (prophet-king-priest, although here the formal organization of the material seems to be of little importance) and Karl Barth (priest-king-prophet).
[55]Torrance, *Space, Time and Resurrection*, 106.

The *Munus Triplex*

Giving a full description of Torrance's understanding of the *munus triplex* is not without some difficulty. To begin with, Torrance's description of Jesus' work as prophet, priest and king is found in various places in his work and often deployed in arguments and contexts that serve varying purposes. For example, in *Atonement* Torrance begins with the aforementioned biblical categories of redemption (*padah*, *kipper*, and *goel*), and then correlates these with the aspects of the threefold office before moving on to a discussion of the nature of the atonement that rarely explicitly references these categories even as they serve as the foundation for what follows. But the lack of formal organization does not preclude Torrance's consistent affirmation of the material importance of the doctrine for understanding Christ's work.

The challenge is increased by the fact that Torrance often alternates between the *munus triplex* and the *munus duplex*. Whereas in works such as *The School of Faith* he straightforwardly adheres to the threefold office, elsewhere he appears to understand the prophetic aspect to be basically subordinate to the priestly aspect. Thus, while Torrance understands the emergence of a distinct prophetic tradition in Scripture to be necessary in the course of the biblical narrative, he will in some places state that the priestly and prophetic are reintegrated in the person of Jesus Christ as he takes up and fulfills Israel's form of life. In this way, Torrance can write, on the one hand, that in Jesus "the *two* aspects of the priesthood are combined and fulfilled. Jesus Christ compromised in Himself both God's saving action toward man, and man's perfect obedience toward God."[56] And yet in the very next paragraph he refers to the *munus triplex*, stating that Jesus is "the Messiah, the Anointed One, Prophet, Priest, and King in One."[57] Additionally, when describing the Mosaic aspect of the priesthood, Torrance at times appears to be describing aspects of Christ's person and work that are understood elsewhere simply as his prophetic work. We can surmise that Torrance saw no intractable contradiction between these two variations on Christ's person and work because of the ease with which he can move from one to the other. But our account of the threefold office will need to be mindful of the sometimes blurry distinctions that accompany Torrance's

---

[56]Torrance, *Royal Priesthood*, 7 (emphasis added).
[57]Torrance, *Royal Priesthood*, 8.

understanding of the relation between the priestly and the prophetic aspects. With these guides in mind, let us now turn to the larger task and seek to unpack and evaluate the logic of Torrance's understanding of the person and work of Jesus Christ as it relates to the *munus triplex*. This will enable us to present the portrait of Christ's office that is found throughout Torrance's work.

The prophetic office. From the perspective of the narrative of Jesus' redemptive work leading up to the ascension, Torrance considers the prophetic office first. Thus Torrance can say of the entirety of the lectures that make up *Incarnation: The Person an Life of Christ*, "All that we have considered so far can be subsumed under the saving work of Christ as *prophet*, that is as Word made flesh, as advocate."[58] By initially identifying the ministry and teaching of Jesus with the prophetic aspect of Christ's office, Torrance follows the tradition of Reformed accounts of the *munus triplex*. Thus Calvin, whose use of the doctrine sets the trajectory for the tradition, will state, "We see that [Jesus] was anointed by the Spirit to be a herald and witness of the Father's grace. And that not in the common way—for he is distinguished from other teachers with a similar office."[59] But in other significant ways, Torrance's description of Jesus Christ's prophetic office is a unique contribution to the Reformed tradition.

Torrance offers the outline of a description of the prophetic office in his introduction to *The School of Faith*, *w*here we find the basic components of what is filled out elsewhere in his writing. Torrance states, "The *Prophetic Office* cannot be understood only in the narrow sense of His teaching, although His teaching is an essential element of His atoning work, inasmuch as revelation and reconciliation cannot for a moment be separated from one another."[60] Torrance is clearly keen to move beyond a simple identification of the office with Jesus' teaching or a simple account of the mediation of revelation. Rather, Torrance's description of the prophetic office constantly draws attention to the *person* of the incarnate Son and also to the place of revelation in the economy of reconciliation as the context that meaningfully illuminates Jesus' prophetic office. In order to emphasize the connection

---

[58]Torrance, *Atonement*, 1. Here Torrance is looking back on the lectures that compose the previous volume, *Incarnation: The Person and Life of Christ* (Downers Grove, IL: IVP Academic, 2008).
[59]Calvin, *Institutes*, 496.
[60]Torrance, *School of Faith*, lxxxix.

between reconciliation and revelation, Torrance stresses how the prophetic office serves to mediate both the relation of God to humanity *and also* the relation of humanity to God:

> The Prophetic Office refers above all to Christ's work as the Word made flesh, as He who brings the Word of the Father to bear upon man in his darkness and sin, but also as He who from within our darkness and alienation bears the Word before God. . . . He is not therefore only the Word of God to man, but the Word of man to God in perfect response and obedience, and in that two-fold capacity He is our Advocate.[61]

This runs counter to accounts of the prophetic office, which center only on the relation of God to humanity (and not also humanity to God, as we see in Torrance) in their description.

With respect to the emphasis on the person of Jesus Christ in his prophetic office, Torrance stresses how in the prophetic office we are to remember that this is the *incarnate* Son. Thus, for Torrance, the mediation of revelation that takes place in Christ's prophetic office is a revelation that takes place in and through Jesus' humanity. It is only because revelation is in and through the humanity of Jesus Christ that it is intelligible to fallen creatures:

> That is the prophetic ministry of Christ, the Word made flesh to bring God's word to man, to incarnate that Word in himself, and so to be the word of God to us in our alienation and estrangement from God—not to be for us an alien word, for then he could not touch us or find us or communicate himself to us, and then his action would be neither reconciling nor revealing action. But within our alienation he is real word of God to us in such a way that he still remains eternal Word of God, word of God addressed to man.[62]

It is only when it is understood that Jesus' prophetic ministry takes place in the person of Jesus Christ—and particularly the unity of the divine and human natures in his person—that the nature of revelation can be grasped.

Torrance also emphasizes the relation between the prophetic office and reconciliation. While it is not uncommon for Christ's prophetic office to be linked to reconciliation in some way—particularly in their relation to a

---

[61] Torrance, *School of Faith*, lxxxix.
[62] Torrance, *Incarnation*, 64.

particular aspect of sin such as blindness[63] or ignorance[64]—Torrance's conception is unique in that the prophetic office mediates the relation of humanity to God as well as God to humanity. Thus in *The School of Faith*, Torrance writes, "[Jesus] is this Advocate not because He steps in as a third party from outside, but because He is really and truly one of us, and very Man, our Kinsman, as well as really and truly one with God, and very God, God's Son. It is thus in the integration of the Prophetic Office of Christ and His incarnational union with us that the Prophetic Office is to be understood."[65] As is implicit in this description, Torrance is here drawing on the link between the prophetic office and the *goel* aspect of redemption that we have already noted. Indeed, by placing the prophetic office within the context of *goel* redemption, the emphasis of the prophetic office is in fact the mediation of the human/Godward relation in Jesus Christ: "Christ is prophet as the Word become flesh, the Son who declares the Father become man. That corresponds to the *goel* aspect of redemption and provides its ontological ground.... Christ comes to us as our *goel-redeemer* in word and act, as our advocate who not only gives an account for us to God but stands in for us, taking our cause completely upon himself."[66]

The relation between the prophetic office and reconciliation is developed further by Torrance in the connection he makes between the Mosaic aspect of the priesthood and the atonement as it is described in the Pauline epistles. We have already noted Torrance's use of the *munus duplex* and the division of the priesthood into its Mosaic and Aaronic forms. In *Atonement*, Torrance picks up this distinction again and applies it to the different "method[s] of approach" to the atonement found in Scripture. The Aaronic priesthood corresponds to the approach found in Hebrews, while the Mosaic priesthood/prophetic office corresponds to what is demonstrated by Paul in his letters: "atonement in terms of expiation and justification before the word or law of God."[67] After this programmatic statement, the prophetic/Mosaic priesthood

---

[63]See for example Emil Brunner, *The Christian Doctrine of Creation and Redemption—Dogmatics*, vol. 2 (Eugene, OR: Wipf & Stock, 2014), 275-281.
[64]Francis Turretin, *Institutes of Elenctic Theology: Eleventh Through Seventeenth Topics*, vol. 2 (Philadelphia: Presbyterian and Reformed, 1994), 397-403.
[65]Torrance, *School of Faith*, lxxxix.
[66]Torrance, *Atonement*, 61.
[67]Torrance, *Atonement*, 73.

aspect of the atonement never makes an explicit appearance in Torrance's exposition, but the same concerns that are evident elsewhere in his writing on the prophetic office are found here as well. The Pauline concept of justification has to do first with revelation and truth as they are mediated from God to humanity: "Justification is God's word and Paul speaks of it as the *revelation* of righteousness, the apocalypse of truth. Revelation of righteousness is truth."[68] But Christ's work of mediation has not just to do with the movement from God to humanity, but also from humanity to God. When Paul speaks of justification he does so "in the twofold sense—(a) of God's just condemnation of sin in which the righteousness of God is revealed and the wrath of God from heaven is revealed against all ungodliness and unrighteousness of humanity, and (b) of God's providing a righteousness from the side of humanity which perfectly and obediently acquiesces in the fulfillment of God's righteous judgment against sin."[69]

Why do we find in Torrance an emphasis that appears to be unique in comparison with other descriptions of the prophetic office within the *munus triplex*? It is certainly the case that Torrance is developing an integrated picture of the *munus triplex* and wants to avoid either isolating revelation from reconciliation or giving a rationalistic account of the prophetic office. But this alone does not provide a full account of the shape of his prophetic office. Rather, two material decisions made by Torrance exercise a powerful shaping force on the *munus propheticum*. First, the correlation of the *goel* aspect of redemption with the prophetic office leads inevitably to an occlusion of the God-human aspect of the prophetic office as it emphasizes Jesus' representative humanity. In contrast to the other two correlations Torrance makes (*kipper*/priestly and *padah*/kingly), the exegetical dogmatic basis for this link appears to be tenuous. Second, Torrance's use of the *munus duplex* leads to a blurry distinction between the priestly and prophetic office. In contrast to accounts of Christ's office that affirm a more traditional understanding of the *munus triplex*, the Mosaic and Aaronic priesthoods are in one sense two parts of a whole, and thus the prophetic and priestly aspects also overlap one another. More can be said about this when the priestly office is considered in its own right, and to this task we now turn.

---

[68] Torrance, *Atonement*, 105.
[69] Torrance, *Atonement*, 123.

The priestly office. Torrance's description of the priestly aspect of Christ's office is similar to traditional accounts of the *munus triplex* in that it centers around the act and meaning of Christ's death. At the beginning of the lectures that make up *Atonement: The Person and Work of Christ*, Torrance states, "What we are now to consider can be subsumed under the saving work of Christ as *priest*, the Son and Word of God undertaking the awful work of expiation of guilt and reconciling sinful man to communion with holy God."[70] The description Torrance gives here follows along the lines found in the final edition of Calvin's *Institutes* (though certainly some difference is evident even in these brief introductions): "An expiation must intervene in order that Christ as priest may obtain God's favor for us and appease his wrath."[71] While Torrance himself demurs from this precise language, he nevertheless understands that Christ's priesthood occupies the same fundamental place in the atonement.

In contrast to the correlation of *goel* redemption and the prophetic office, the link between the priestly office and *kipper* redemption is clear and unforced. Torrance understands *kipper* redemption to take place within the context of a covenant relationship in need of repair. In his description of this covenant relationship, Torrance is careful to maintain God's gracious character and love for his creatures. When humanity violates the covenant, God continues to uphold the covenant: "The wrath of God is God's holiness and faithfulness directed against breaches in the covenant, and it is wrath precisely because God in his love affirms Israel to be his child and gives himself in covenant mercy to be Israel's God."[72] But as the Old Testament narrative unfolds, it becomes clear that it is God's intention for the covenant to be more than a framework—it is to be written on the hearts of the people of God.[73]

This covenantal trajectory in Scripture's narrative takes place alongside a different movement: the decline of Israel's institutional priesthood. The absence of the Mosaic aspect of the priesthood in Israel's life and the subsequent failures of the prophets to call Israel back to God are fundamentally a desire to avoid an encounter with God. Instead, Israel "sought to make the

---

[70]Torrance, *Atonement*, 1.
[71]Calvin, *Institutes*, 501.
[72]Torrance, *Atonement*, 38.
[73]Torrance, *Atonement*, 43.

temple and its liturgy independent of God's intervening will as manifested through the law."[74] As we have noted above, the Old Testament narrative draws to a close with Israel having effectively sealed off its liturgical life from the living God: "Here there is no room for the prophet, for the direct intervention of the word . . . for the word of God is made of none effect by the traditions of man."[75] Thus God's intention for the covenant to be written on the hearts of the people moves forward at the same time as the contrasting movement of God's people to resist an encounter with the Word.

In taking up and fulfilling the priestly office, Jesus places the priesthood in proper relation to the Word. Torrance notes the manifold ways Scripture demonstrates this. Jesus' actions inevitably create conflict with the scribes and the priests as he reveals that both have domesticated and tried to elude the living Word: "Into the midst of mankind's estrangement from God where it is at its very worst, into the midst of their religious alienation from God resting on a perversion of both scripture and liturgy, Jesus Christ steps forth as the living Word and calls both scribe and priest to account."[76] Central to Jesus' fulfillment of the priestly office is his restoration of the Aaronic aspect of the priesthood to a proper relation to the Mosaic aspect. While Jesus' life is marked by obedience to the priestly pattern of life,[77] all of this is done in such a way that "in the midst of it all, he lived out the life of the incarnate Word and law of God, insisting on the primacy of the Word of God in forgiveness and worship."[78] In taking the Aaronic aspect of the priesthood upon himself, Jesus fulfills it by submitting it to the Mosaic aspect, the mediation of the Word of God.

Jesus' submission of the priestly office to the Word and law of God serves the greater purpose of fulfilling the covenant between God and humanity, fully restoring this relationship and writing the covenant on the heart of the

---

[74]Torrance, *Atonement*, 64.
[75]Torrance, *Atonement*, 65.
[76]Torrance, *Atonement*, 66.
[77]Torrance describes this priestly obedience in this way: "He was circumcised and had the covenant cut into his flesh. He was redeemed as a first-born son at the age of thirty-one days. At the age of twelve he fulfilled the requirements of the law in taking the yoke of the Torah upon himself and all his life he was obedient to the law, and therefore obedient to the liturgy the law prescribed. He attended the feasts, ate the passover sacrifices and lived fully the life of an Israelite with all its legal and cultic enactments." Torrance, *Atonement*, 67.
[78]Torrance, *Atonement*, 67.

people of God. Torrance outlines how Christ's priestly mediation accomplishes this restoration in four parts. First, there is Christ's priestly propitiation, which is understood in light of the *kipper* redemption that forms the Old Testament setting for atonement and the priestly office. *Kipper*—and thus propitiation—refers to "personal healing and personal reconciliation."[79] Jesus' propitiation not only begins from God's initiative to humanity but also works from the side of humanity toward God. In Jesus' priestly propitiation we see "the God who, in his holy love, judges humanity but who draws near in so doing, for he will not hold himself aloof from men and women; but he is also the man who in our place draws near to God and so submits himself to the divine judgment, offering himself in sacrifice to God."[80] The second aspect of Christ's priestly mediation is that it is a priestly penitence. In order to write the covenant on the hearts of humanity, atonement must be not a merely external event but must have to do with "the internal *at-one-ment* between God and humanity and humanity and God."[81] Jesus does this through his vicarious repentance on behalf of and in the place of humanity, which supplies for humanity the penitence required to achieve this "at-one-ment": "In his incarnation Christ not only took upon himself our physical existence from God, but in taking it into himself he at the same time healed it, sanctified it, and changed it, bending our will back to agreement with the divine will, and bringing our human mind back into agreement with the divine mind."[82]

The third aspect of Christ's priestly mediation is his "priestly prayer," wherein with his words and his life Christ "pleads with his life and life-blood for us sinners—the prayer of priestly self-sacrifice."[83] Torrance understands Christ's active obedience to be a form of prayer, "translated into his physical existence, lived out before the Father in the unspotted existence of a human life and then poured out on the cross."[84] The imagery Torrance utilizes here is drawn from Hebrews' picture of Jesus Christ as the high priest who intercedes on behalf of his people. And the fourth and final aspect of the priestly

---

[79] Torrance, *Atonement*, 68.
[80] Torrance, *Atonement*, 68–69.
[81] Torrance, *Atonement*, 68–69.
[82] Torrance, *Atonement*, 70.
[83] Torrance, *Atonement*, 71.
[84] Torrance, *Atonement*, 71.

mediation of Jesus is that of the "priesthood and sonship."[85] Torrance notes a movement from the Old Testament and its primarily juridical and propitiatory language to the incorporation of these concepts into a fundamentally filial framework. In some sense the entire concept of the priesthood is intended to be assimilated into the more basic category of sonship: "the notion of priesthood is taken out of its interim-institutional status found in the Levitical priesthood and anchored deep in the personal and family relationship between God and his people."[86]

Three points of interest emerge from the above analysis of Torrance's understanding of Christ's priestly mediation. First, as in the prophetic office, Torrance emphasizes the human-Godward movement of this mediation as well as the movement from God to humanity. Christ's priestly mediation does not just function as a result of God's initiative (though this point is important for Torrance to stress) but it also works from the side of humanity and is thus involved in an atonement that is not merely external, but internal as well. Second, Torrance's description of the priestly office functions in tandem with his account of the prophetic office. The priestly work of mediation follows logically upon the prophetic work, not only in the necessary chronological ordering of Jesus' ministry[87] but in how, in its accomplishment of the internal aspect of atonement, the priestly work takes up the material that has to do with the incarnation that Torrance understands to fall under Christ's prophetic work.[88] Moreover, there is the constant connection of the priestly and prophetic in their historical connection to the Aaronic and Mosaic aspects of the priesthood. And third, there is a curious and significant lacuna in Torrance's discussion of the priestly work of Christ. Throughout his discussion of the priestly work of Christ in *Royal Priesthood* and *Atonement*, and even in his discussion of Hebrews in the chapter of *Atonement* titled "The Priesthood of Christ," Torrance never engages with the biblical material on the priestly figure of Melchizedek. Instead, all of the discussion of the biblical background to the priesthood centers around the

---

[85]Torrance, *Atonement*, 71.
[86]Torrance, *Atonement*, 72.
[87]"And so, first of all, He steps into the place of the Prophet, and as the Word made flesh proclaims the Word of forgiveness and healing and peace, and only then in priestly obedience to the Word of God does He advance to the living and actual liturgy of atonement." Torrance, *Royal Priesthood*, 8.
[88]Torrance, *Atonement*, 1.

figures of Moses and Aaron. The lack of attention given to Christ's identity as a priest "after the order of Melchizedek," as it is discussed in Hebrews 7, is striking, and Torrance's understanding of the priestly office is undoubtedly impoverished because of his failure to address it. Not least of concern is the failure to give attention to the relationship between the royal and priestly offices that is evidenced in Hebrews. And it is to that kingly office that we now turn.

The kingly office. The kingly office is last in the initial ordering Torrance gives to the threefold office. Torrance utilizes this order because just as he identifies the prophetic and priestly offices of Christ with the life and ministry of Jesus and his atoning death, respectively, so also his kingly ministry is most clearly identified with his resurrection and ascension, and thus "it would appear to be the order determined by the mighty salvation events in the course of Jesus' life among us."[89] But while the kingly office is given the final place in the initial order Torrance gives to the description of the *munus triplex* in its relation to the other two offices, it both interpenetrates the other two offices in Jesus' earthly ministry and brings them to their fulfillment at his ascension. Thus Torrance states in *The School of Faith*, "It is under the Kingship of Christ, the Royal Son of God, that His other offices are to be understood; that is, both of them have to be seen as offices fulfilled on the supreme basis of the Royal Decision of God."[90]

Jesus' kingly office is evident in his prophetic ministry because of the importance of the kingdom of God in his teaching: "Jesus was born to be king and as he entered his public ministry he stepped forward as the king of the kingdom he proclaimed."[91] Similarly, the priestly office bears the mark of his kingly ministry: "His priestly ministry is associated mostly with his passion in which as high priest he offered himself in sacrifice for our sins and holy oblation to the Father, but even in the midst of this ministry he was king, crowned with thorns, but king because of the cross and through the cross."[92] But while the prophetic and priestly offices are only fully intelligible in the light of Jesus' kingly ministry, Jesus is not fully inaugurated into his

---

[89]Torrance, *Atonement*, 265.
[90]Torrance, *School of Faith*, xciv.
[91]Torrance, *Atonement*, 265.
[92]Torrance, *Atonement*, 265.

kingly office until the ascension: "It is with his exaltation to the throne of God and his sitting at the right hand of the Father that his kingly ministry properly began."[93] Locating the kingly office with the ascension indicates just how important Jesus' kingly ministry is for understanding the church's ministry and mission.

Despite the statement that the kingly office is "not fully inaugurated" until the ascension, Jesus' kingly work is nonetheless evident throughout his life and ministry. This is due not only to the interpenetration of the office with his prophetic and priestly work, but also to the connection Torrance draws between the kingly office and the *padah* aspect of redemption. This Old Testament concept of redemption, which is descriptive of a dramatic act of deliverance "at once out of the judgement of God and out of an alien and repressive power,"[94] provides the background and material content for the kingly office. In his descriptions of the life and ministry of Jesus, this *padah* aspect of redemption is evident in the conflict that Jesus' holy presence inevitably creates in the fallen world: "The Gospels think of the incarnation as the invasion of the mighty Son of God into our domain where evil has come to exercise its sway, in order to break its bonds and to deliver us from its captivity. That is the significance of the whole life of Jesus, particularly from his temptations immediately after his baptism to the agony of Gethsemane and Calvary."[95]

Torrance's description of Jesus' kingly ministry has as a central theme the concept of authority (or Torrance's preferred term, *exousia*). Jesus' kingly ministry is displayed when he exposes false claims to authority and reveals his own proper authority. Jesus' desert temptations are paradigmatic: "In the temptations Jesus was confronted with the *exousia* and glory of the kingdoms of this world and offered them in return for his worship of the devil—that is to say, he was offered the *exousia* and refused it categorically. He denied the devil any rightful *exousia* and he refused to avoid the way of the cross."[96] But by taking "the way of the cross" and embracing the life of a suffering servant, Jesus' true *exousia* was revealed after the resurrection: "He came

---

[93] Torrance, *Atonement*, 265.
[94] Torrance, *Atonement*, 29.
[95] Torrance, *Atonement*, 31.
[96] Torrance, *Atonement*, 31.

through the temptation and passion of his self sacrifice on the cross clothed with the power of the resurrection, *Christus victor*, Christ triumphant, endowed with all power in heaven and earth."[97]

This conflict between Jesus' *exousia* and that which only pretends to possess real authority gives Torrance's description of Jesus' kingly ministry an animated, triumphant character. Jesus is constantly exposing and overcoming evil through the simple fact of his holiness:

> When we examine the witness of the Gospels we find that this atoning and redeeming *exousia*, in both the words and acts of Jesus, comes to grips with the demonic forces entrenched in the fallen world and overcomes them. Whenever Jesus proclaimed his word, that word was an assault upon the enemies of God and whenever he acted in forgiveness and healing that act was in deliverance of men and women from enslavement to the power of Satan.[98]

There is an inevitability not only to the conflict that Jesus creates with the fallen world but also to its ultimate defeat as he overcomes it by no other means than his holy presence: "By his very holiness and perfect obedience sin had no power over him, and it was therefore as the holy one in entire fulfillment of the holy will of God that he invaded the domain of evil and redeemed us out of the power of darkness by his holy life."[99]

The triumphant and dynamic nature of Torrance's description of the kingly ministry of Christ is striking in contrast to Calvin's treatment of the same material. While Torrance draws attention to the *Christus victor* aspect of the kingly office as a present reality, Calvin understands Christ's royal work to be the ground of our perseverance in the face of present trials and conflicts. Thus, when referencing the royal Psalms 2 and 110, Calvin writes, "Thus he assures the godly of the everlasting preservation of the church, and encourages them to hope, whenever it happens to be oppressed. . . . No matter how many strong enemies plot to overthrow the church, they do not have sufficient strength to prevail over God's immutable decree by which he appointed his Son eternal King."[100] Thus there is a sense of reserve in Calvin's claims of the current experience and enjoyment of Christ's royal office.

---

[97] Torrance, *Atonement*, 31.
[98] Torrance, *Incarnation*, 236.
[99] Torrance, *Atonement*, 32.
[100] Calvin, *Institutes*, 497-498.

Whereas Calvin emphasizes Christ's *eventual* total victory and the confidence taken from it for current struggles and trials, Torrance draws attention to the *present* experience of Christ's victory and overthrow of those who would pretend to claim his throne.[101]

Torrance's account of the kingly office leads us logically to a consideration of the ascension and its place in Torrance's theology. But before moving on, we will make some closing evaluative thoughts on Torrance's understanding of the *munus triplex*.

Torrance's doctrine of the munus triplex. We have already noted the aspects of Torrance's understanding of the *munus triplex* that are unique within the Reformed tradition: the more fundamental nature of the *munus duplex*, the place of the Mosaic/Aaronic priesthood narrative, and the distinct shape of the prophetic office. These notable features to Torrance's theology beg questions that deserve answers: What factors in Torrance's theology lead him to these descriptions? And what are the effects of these material decisions?

Torrance's understanding of the *munus duplex* and the Mosaic/Aaronic aspects of the priestly office appear to spring from the insights of biblical theology contemporary to him. Torrance's indebtedness to the *Theological Dictionary of the New Testament*, and in particular the biblical history of the priesthood that he drew from there, takes him along a path that differs from traditional accounts of the threefold office and the mediator's fulfillment of the covenant.[102] Thus while Torrance's theology is shaped by the methodological concerns typical of the Reformed tradition—in particular the concern that the narrative of Scripture determines the material content of christology—the different shape of Christ's office can be traced to the divergent exegetical conclusions made by Calvin and Torrance in their reading of salvation history.

Torrance's decision to center his discussion of the prophetic and priestly offices around Moses and Aaron is a particular weakness in his presentation of the *munus triplex*. While Torrance's attention to the biblical narrative here

---

[101]Torrance's christology has this triumphal tone in no small part due to his understanding of Christ's assumption of fallen human nature. Because of this, Torrance's narration of Christ's atonement over the course of his incarnate career has more emphatically realized consequences than are readily evident in Calvin.

[102]Schrenk, "ιερος," 257-265.

is helpful, the emphasis obscures the multivalent presentation of the various ways the three offices are understood in Scripture. We have already noted how Torrance's discussion of the priestly office does not give sufficient attention to Hebrews' presentations of the king-priest Melchizedek, which is representative of Scripture's complex presentation of the relation between the offices. In their presentation of the priestly office in *Jesus Our Priest*, Gerald O'Collins and Michael Keenan Jones note the other figures in Scripture who combine the offices: "Melchizedek (priest and king); Aaron (priest, prophet, and king); Deborah (prophet and kingly judge); Solomon (king who also acted as priest); Ezekiel (priest and prophet); John the Baptist (prophet of priestly lineage); and Caiaphas (a high priest with kingly powers who, at least on one occasion, spoke prophetically)."[103] Oliver O'Donovan also provides a divergent reading of the threefold office that deals not only with specific figures but also with how the individual offices serve within the mediation of God's redemptive work (with particular attention given to their implications for political theology). O'Donovan makes similar points to Torrance with respect to the relationship between the prophetic and priestly offices,[104] but sets it within a richer and more complex reading of the Old Testament, which also includes readings of the prophetic-kingly[105] and priestly-kingly[106] relations. Torrance's construction of the *munus triplex* deserves recognition as an effort within the Reformed tradition to understand the work of redemption within the unity of the old and new covenants and by way of a close reading of the scriptural narrative. But this reading can be strengthened at places with more attention to various ways the offices are described.[107]

Torrance's description of the covenant is also important for understanding how and why his account of the *munus triplex* differs from Calvin and others in the Reformed tradition. Here again, the contrast with Calvin

---

[103]Gerald O'Collins and Michael Keenan Jones, *Jesus Our Priest: A Christian Approach to the Priesthood of Christ* (Oxford: Oxford University Press, 2010), 15.

[104]Oliver O'Donovan, *The Desire of the Nations: Rediscovering the Roots of Political Theology* (Oxford: Oxford University Press, 1996), 62-63.

[105]O'Donovan, *Desire of the Nations*, 64-66.

[106]O'Donovan, *Desire of the Nations*, 59-61.

[107]For one attempt of this project, see Robert Sherman, *King, Priest, and Prophet: A Trinitarian Theology of Atonement* (New York: T&T Clark, 2004). Sherman's attempt is hindered significantly by an attempt to link each individual office to a person of the Trinity.

is instructive. In neither Calvin's nor Torrance's work does the covenant have a dominant place in the formal organization of their theology.[108] Formal features aside, however, the concept of the covenant is still materially significant in understanding the different conclusions each figure draws and thus in our understanding Torrance's thinking on the *munus triplex* and the nature of Christ's work. For Calvin, the covenant is a concept that keeps theology's work close to the ground of the biblical text, following the contours of the redemptive narrative.[109] These same concerns are present for Torrance, and the first chapter of *Royal Priesthood* represents Torrance's integration of the narrative arc of Scripture into his christology. But covenant for Torrance is more basically a vehicle for describing the two aspects of the relationship between God and humanity in its God-humanward direction and its human-Godward direction. Thus Torrance's *The Mediation of Christ* can speak movingly and eloquently about the nature of mediation and the person of the mediator and yet never make mention of the *munus triplex*.[110] Even within a description of the purpose and unfolding of covenant within Israel's history, what Torrance provides is most fundamentally a general discussion about the relation of God to humanity and humanity to God that does not follow the narrative of the biblical text with the same consistent attention as we see in Calvin.[111]

This different account of the covenant is what gives Torrance's prophetic office its distinct shape. While both Calvin and Torrance are concerned with the shape of mediation in the relationship between God and humanity,

---

[108]For an opinion on the development of covenant theology in Calvin, see Richard A. Muller, *The Unaccommodated Calvin: Studies in the Foundation of a Theological Tradition* (Oxford: Oxford University Press, 2000), 154-155. Cf. Titus Chung, *Thomas Torrance's Mediations and Revelation* (Farnham, UK: Ashgate, 2011), 22-30, where one can note how for Torrance so little space is devoted to the concept of the covenant.

[109]Edmondson, *Calvin's Christology*, 40-88.
   This reorientation toward the covenant history bears one very specific implication for Calvin's Christology. If we accept that the title of Mediator is central to Calvin's understanding of Christ, then we must heed his order of teaching in which this title is first introduced. . . . Calvin, in other words, has replaced a theoretical discussion of this topic, attentive primarily to the theological discussion of the previous five centuries, with a Christological narration of Scripture's history as the normative framework for understanding Christology (47).

[110]Torrance, *The Mediation of Christ* (Colorado Springs, CO: Helmers & Howard, 1992).

[111]Torrance, *Mediation of Christ*, 7-23, 26-39, 56-59. See also Chung, *Thomas Torrance's Mediations and Revelation*, 22-30.

Torrance's emphasis on the dynamic of both the God-humanward and the human-Godward relation means that the prophetic office must include both of these aspects insofar as covenant serves chiefly as a category which circumscribes the God-human relationship. This emphasis undoubtedly informs Torrance's gravitation toward a *munus duplex* (as its connection of the priestly and prophetic offices is more consistent with his understanding of covenant) and his link of the *goel* aspect of redemption to the prophetic office (and the accompanying emphasis upon the human-Godward relation). Calvin, in contrast, gives a much more unilateral account of the prophetic office, even though it is enclosed within a larger account that addresses the same concerns as Torrance. Thus, in his study *Calvin's Christology*, Stephen Edmondson writes, "The prophetic office differs from the other two; Christ as priest and king accomplishes our salvation, whereas Christ as prophet interprets and proclaims this salvation."[112] Torrance, in contrast, believes that each aspect of the threefold office must necessarily include both the God-humanward and the human-Godward relation.

We can expect that Torrance's account of the prophetic office will affect his understanding of the church's participation in Christ's prophetic office and thus the nature of preaching and teaching. Our final chapters will assess the implications of Torrance's account of the prophetic, priestly, and kingly offices for the body of Christ.

THE ASCENSION

The discussion of the threefold office, and in particular Jesus' royal ministry, moves us naturally to Torrance's understanding of the ascension. The ascension, following closely after Jesus' victory over the powers of sin and death and directly preceding Jesus' assumption of his kingly seat at the right hand of the Father and the divine government that he dispenses from there, is naturally comprehended as a part of his royal office. But while the ascension may have the most immediate connection to the kingly office, for Torrance it can only be fully understood in connection to each of Christ's offices.

The ascension receives extensive treatment by Torrance, and the doctrine is crucial in the unfolding of Christ's work to the church. Torrance's work

---

[112]Edmondson, *Calvin's Christology*, 168.

on the doctrine is unique among his contemporaries. In his study of Karl Barth's understanding of the ascension, Andrew Burgess states, "Thomas Torrance has provided one of the few significant twentieth century treatments of Jesus' ascension."[113] Within the logic of Torrance's theology, it is the ascension that secures Jesus' continued mediation of his atoning activity, linking the aforementioned description of his incarnate ministry to the church's being and mission and the structure of Jesus' threefold office to the church as it participates in Jesus' ascended ministry. In what follows, we will explore Torrance's doctrine of the ascension, seeking to understand the importance of the doctrine and how it functions to link his account of Christ's mediatorial office to the time between his ascension and his final return at the *parousia*. This will be done in three parts. We will begin with the biblical framework that Torrance understands to ground the ascension. Second, we will consider the implications Torrance draws from the ascension for the relation of God to creaturely space. And third, we will seek to understand how the ascension governs Torrance's understanding of the church's relation to its time.

The biblical description of the ascension. Torrance begins his exposition of the ascension almost identically to his exposition of the atonement. He explores the biblical language used to speak of the ascension in order to shed light on the New Testament's description of the event: "Behind the biblical employment of these terms there lies a theological and cultic significance in certain contexts which lends them deeper meaning."[114] Torrance identifies four terms utilized in Scripture concerning the ascension: *anabaino, kathizo, analambano,* and *hupsoo*.[115]

Anabaino. Torrance identifies this word, often translated as "to ascend" or "to offer," as the Greek rendering of the Hebrew *alah*, a term with "powerful cultic significance."[116] Its use in Scripture is inclusive of both priestly and royal images, referring to ascending to Jerusalem and the Temple, to the offering of a sacrifice, and to enthroning a ruler. But in the light of the New Testament, these priestly and royal associations of *anabaino* are clarified and focused: "Used in these ways the term *ascension* is essentially concerned

---

[113]Andrew Burgess, *The Ascension in Karl Barth* (Hampshire, UK: Ashgate, 2004), 111.
[114]Torrance, *Space, Time and Resurrection*, 107.
[115]Here, as elsewhere, Torrance utilizes the English transliteration of the Greek words in question.
[116]Torrance, *Space, Time and Resurrection*, 107.

with the Royal Priesthood of the crucified, risen and ascended Christ, exercised from the right hand of divine power."[117]

Kathizo. Torrance deals only briefly with this term, which is commonly rendered "to sit." The same royal and priestly connotations are found here as they are with *anabaino*. When the term is found in Hebrews, the priestly imagery is displayed (one of the few references Torrance makes to Melchizedek in his work), while elsewhere the royal imagery is equally visible. In contrast to *anabaino*, however, *kathizo* deals more directly with the idea of enthronement: "It would appear that when the New Testament uses this term in connection with Christ, it is the concept of Messianic enthronement that seems to be determinative, that is, his installation in the office of the Messianic King in which he dispenses the divine mercy and peace."[118]

Analambano. While this term (often translated as "to take up") is used in various ways in the New Testament, Torrance identifies a "distinctly cultic nuance"[119] to the term, particularly as it relates to prayer and worship. In the Old Testament the term is used to describe the assumption of Elijah into heaven. By the time of the composition of the Apocrypha, it became a technical term used to describe the assumption of figures, such as Moses and Enoch. Torrance argues that in its usage in the New Testament, the meaning has expanded in such a way that it "indicates that the ascension of Christ to heaven began with his lifting up on the Cross."[120]

Hupsoo. This final word Torrance identifies in connection to the ascension ("to lift up on high") possesses the same connotations as *analambano* as it connects Christ's ascension not only to his resurrection but also his death: "It is thus made clear that the glorification of Christ begins not with his actual ascension or resurrection, but with his crucifixion and indeed with his ascent to Jerusalem and Calvary for sacrifice."[121] Thus, for Torrance, the ascension is one aspect of a greater unity that is not to be separated: "The raising up of Christ begins, paradoxically, with his crucifixion, and his ascension begins, paradoxically, with his lifting up on the Cross."[122]

---

[117] Torrance, *Space, Time and Resurrection*, 108.
[118] Torrance, *Space, Time and Resurrection*, 109.
[119] Torrance, *Space, Time and Resurrection*, 109.
[120] Torrance, *Space, Time and Resurrection*, 109.
[121] Torrance, *Space, Time and Resurrection*, 110.
[122] Torrance, *Space, Time and Resurrection*, 110.

Torrance begins his discussion of the ascension with this section on the biblical background of the event because it provides for him the needed connection between the shape of Christ's earthly ministry and its continuation after the resurrection. The royal and cultic connotations of Scripture's language of the ascension is suggestive of the continuation of the *munus duplex/triplex* that gives structure to Torrance's account of Christ's mediation. Moreover, the unity of the movement from crucifixion to resurrection to ascension pushes the shape of Christ's earthly ministry into the domain of his ministry at the right hand of the Father: "The ascension of Christ . . . is his exaltation to power and glory but *through the Cross*, certainly an exaltation from humiliation to royal majesty but through crucifixion and sacrifice, for the power and glory of the Royal Priest are bound up with his self-offering in death and resurrection."[123] Thus the description of Christ's continuing ministry will be fundamentally identical to what has already been given in the account of Christ's incarnate life in the time leading up to the resurrection, including its cruciform and sacrificial shape:

> It is ultimately in that fusion of resurrection with the ascension in one indivisible exaltation that we are to understand the continuing ministry of Christ in presenting his "many brethren" along with himself, amidst the sanctities of the new creation and in eternal glorification of the Father. It is as such that he blessed mankind by pouring out upon them his Spirit and fulfilling in them the work of God's reconciling love.[124]

Torrance's understanding of Christ's continuing ministry is therefore structured by the threefold office as it is revealed in Jesus' earthly ministry and ordered according to the priority of the ascension (king-priest-prophet). We will return to this topic in the discussion of the church's participation in Christ's ministry in chapters four and five.

Space, Time, and Ascension

Torrance's use of the ascension to point the church to Christ's ministry even after his visible departure leads to another set of issues that he must address. Specifically, how are we to understand Christ's continued presence and ministry

---

[123]Torrance, *Space, Time and Resurrection*, 111.
[124]Torrance, *Space, Time and Resurrection*, 111.

if he is no longer visibly present in the flesh? This question is even more significant to Torrance because of his attention to the problem of dualism and the accompanying tendency to dissociate God from creation. Therefore, Torrance moves from the importance of the ascension to an account of how it functions within space and time. Torrance is particularly interested in understanding how the doctrine of the ascension confronts unreflective conceptions of God's relation to space and time. We will turn first to the issue of God's relation to space before looking to the relation of God to time.[125]

The ascension and space. As we have come to expect from Torrance, he explores this question with recourse to his catholic, Reformed heritage and how that tradition handled a similar quandary, and as a resource he identifies the sixteenth-century debates about the *extra Calvinisticum*. The *extra Calvinisticum* was the site of an extended debate between the Reformed and Lutheran traditions concerning the incarnation and the nature of Jesus' humanity within the hypostatic union. Both camps wished to maintain the integrity of the union between God and humanity in the person of Jesus Christ, but John Calvin articulated the Reformed position when he maintained that the Son of God, having taken humanity into union with himself and entered fully into the conditions of human existence, continued his heavenly reign without any subtraction of his full divinity: "Patristic and Reformed theology have always claimed that the Eternal Logos did enter space and time, and yet did not cease to be what he eternally was in himself, the Creator Word in whom and through whom all things consist and by whom all things derive and continue to have their being."[126] Lutheran theologians have demurred from this claim because it seems to imply that there was some aspect of the Son of God's divinity that was not in union with Jesus' humanity (the "*extra*" of the *extra Calvinisticum*): "When Calvin said of Christ that he became man born of the Virgin's womb without leaving heaven or the government of the world, he was interpreted by Lutherans to imply that in the incarnation only part of the Word was contained in the babe of Bethlehem or wrapped in the swaddling clothes in the cradle, and that something was left 'outside.'"[127]

---

[125] As an admirer of Einstein, Torrance would no doubt resist the separation of the categories, but we will here make a distinction for heuristic purposes.

[126] Torrance, *Space, Time and Resurrection*, 124.

[127] Torrance, *Space, Time and Resurrection*, 124.

In Torrance's analysis, the reason for this response to the *extra Calvinisticum* is found in the "receptacle view of space" to which the Lutherans were unknowingly beholden. In this view, the incarnation implies "the enclosure or confinement of the Son of God in a human body."[128] By maintaining the Son's continued transcendence, even while the earthly career of the incarnate Son unfolds, there has been within the Reformed tradition an often tacit different understanding of God's relation to space. In his interpretation and development of the *extra Calvinisticum*, Torrance proposes that in thinking out the implication of the ascension of Jesus Christ the incarnate Son, we must learn to think both in terms of his divinity and his humanity: "If we are to be faithful to the nature of Christ as very God and very Man we have to let that determine our thinking . . . and say that he really and fully became man . . . and yet remained God the Creator who transcends all creaturely being in space and time."[129] Torrance calls this a "relational view of space and time" which is "differentially or variationally [sic] related to God and to man."[130] This relational view of space and time and its accompanying methodology leads Torrance to emphasize two ways in which the ascension must be thought out. First, we must think of how in the ascension the union of God and humanity that takes place in the person of Jesus Christ ascended to heaven: "In the ascension Jesus Christ ascends from man's place to God's place."[131] Second, we must think of how Christ's atoning victory has secured humanity in its space-time conditions: "By his ascension Jesus Christ has established man in man's place in time and space."[132]

The first of these two ways, the ascension of Jesus from humanity's place to God's place, requires a different understanding of space than the aforementioned receptacle theory. In Torrance's understanding, space is not to be understood as an abstract container, but instead as "open to God's own internal Being and the infinite room of his divine life."[133] Because of this definition of space, we cannot seal off creation from God or limit his action within creation: "Statements about God for Christ must not be such as to enclose them

---

[128]Torrance, *Space, Time and Incarnation* (Edinburgh: T&T Clark, 1997), 31.
[129]Torrance, *Space, Time and Resurrection*, 126.
[130]Torrance, *Space, Time and Resurrection*, 126.
[131]Torrance, *Space, Time and Resurrection*, 130.
[132]Torrance, *Space, Time and Resurrection*, 130.
[133]Torrance, *Space, Time and Resurrection*, 131-132.

within the finite limits of the conceptualities and determinations of creaturely forms of thought and speech."[134] Rather than drawing to a close God's presence to his creatures, the ascension actually enables God's presence in a different and indeed fuller way: "The ascension of Christ is thus an ascension to fill all things with himself, so that in a real sense he comes again in the Ascension. He had to go away in one mode of presence that he might come again in this mode of presence, leaving us in the mode of man's presence to man, and returning to us in the mode of God's presence to man, and thus not leaving man bereft of himself."[135] In this way we are to understand the ascension as the continuation of God's presence to his creation.

The second of these two ways, the establishment of humanity within its own space, has significant implications for the knowledge of God within Torrance's doctrinal scheme. By withdrawing from visible apprehension at the ascension, Jesus' earthly career becomes the central and normative site for our understanding of and relating to God:

> Jesus insists in making contact with us, not first directly and immediately in his risen humanity, but first and foremost through his historical involvement with us in his incarnation and crucifixion. That is to say that, by withdrawing from our sight, Christ sends us back to the historical Jesus as the covenanted place on earth and in time which God has appointed for meeting between man and himself.[136]

Torrance calls this the establishment of "man in man's place in space and time"[137] because in this way the normal conditions of human knowledge and apprehension of God are maintained: "The ascension means that we cannot know God by transcending space and time, by leaping beyond the limits of our place on earth, but only by encountering God and his saving work within space and time, within our actual physical existence."[138] Additionally, Torrance's emphasis upon the normative place of the historical Jesus for all of our knowledge of God reinforces the continuity between Jesus' earthly mediation of salvation and his continuing ministry after the ascension, for

---

[134]Torrance, *Space, Time and Resurrection*, 132.
[135]Torrance, *Space, Time and Resurrection*, 132.
[136]Torrance, *Space, Time and Resurrection*, 133.
[137]Torrance, *Space, Time and Resurrection*, 133.
[138]Torrance, *Space, Time and Resurrection*, 134; cf. *Royal Priesthood*, 58.

there is no account of Jesus' continued mediation that can be obtained apart from the pre-ascension history of his incarnate life.

These two aspects of the ascension—both the ascended Jesus' living and active ministry at the right hand of the Father and the definitive nature of the witness of the historical Jesus for our knowledge of God—can only be held together by the Holy Spirit. It is the Spirit, Torrance states, who bridges the supposed "gap" created by the ascension and who does so not independently but in relation to the historical Jesus: "Since God's place is the place where God is, it is through the Spirit that we can think of Christ as historically absent and as actually present. It is through the Spirit that things infinitely disconnected—disconnected by the 'distance' of the ascension—are nevertheless infinitely closely related."[139] Through the Spirit the ascended Jesus is present, and present through his historical life.

Torrance conceives of this relation as the intersection of two lines, one horizontal and one vertical. The horizontal line represents the history of Jesus Christ, that is, "the appointed place in which nations and ages may meet with God."[140] But this horizontal, historical relation is not sufficient. What is required is the Holy Spirit's "immediate" relation (in complement to the mediate relation via Scripture) "so that through the Spirit [Jesus] might be present, really present, although in a different way."[141] The ascension is the keystone that holds both of these elements together. By withdrawing from physical apprehension, Jesus throws us upon the testimony of his incarnate career as the covenant place of meeting with God. But the ascension also leads necessarily to the gift of the Spirit and the actualization of the apostolic witness for the church.

> With his ascension Jesus Christ also sent upon the Church and indeed upon "all flesh" his Holy Spirit so that through the Spirit he might be present, really present, although in a different way. In order to think out the relation of the Church in history to Christ we must put both these together—mediate horizontal relation through history to the historical Jesus Christ, and immediate vertical relation through the Spirit to the risen and ascended Jesus Christ. It is the former that supplies the material content, while it is the latter that supplies the immediacy of actual encounter.[142]

---

[139] Torrance, *Space, Time and Resurrection*, 135.
[140] Torrance, *Space, Time and Resurrection*, 147.
[141] Torrance, *Space, Time and Resurrection*, 147.
[142] Torrance, *Space, Time and Resurrection*, 147.

The ascension and time. The doctrine of the ascension also governs Torrance's understanding of the relation between God and time, specifically the time that takes place after his first advent and before his second. That is to say, the ascension governs Torrance's eschatology. In a chapter of *Space, Time and Resurrection* entitled "The Ascension and the *Parousia* of Christ," Torrance begins with a definition of *parousia* that, contrary to common conceptions of the term, shifts the emphasis to Christ's presence rather than his absence: "*Parousia*, normally translated as coming or advent, means coming and presence, the *real presence* of him who was, who is, and who is to come."[143] Torrance continues, "[*Parousia*] is not applied in the New Testament or in the early Church in a spiritualized sense, as if it means a presence in Spirit only. Rather does it refer to a coming-and-a-presence in the most realist and effective sense."[144]

Crucial to Torrance's emphasis upon the "realist and effective" nature of Christ's presence in the *parousia* is that Christ's resurrection and ascension does not indicate the leaving behind of his humanity. Rather, the hypostatic union of God and humanity that takes place in the person of Jesus Christ is maintained even after the resurrection and ascension: "The physicality of the incarnation, in which the Word was made flesh and in which Jesus Christ rose again in body, indicates that here we have to do with a presence in which God has bound up the life and existence of his creation with himself."[145] That God has in Jesus Christ "bound up the life and existence of his creation with himself" means that *parousia* cannot mean the absence of the Creator from his creatures. Instead his presence to the world is now determined by the life and history of Jesus Christ: "Through the resurrection the incarnate *parousia* is established and exalted as the material content of all the *parousia* of Christ from the ascension to his coming again; the presence of the historical Jesus is eternally fused into the presence of the risen Jesus and as such constitutes the one indivisible *parousia* of the ages."[146]

But while the resurrection and ascension do not imply the leaving behind of Jesus' humanity, the ascension is indicative of a different kind of presence

---

[143]Torrance, *Space, Time and Resurrection*, 143.
[144]Torrance, *Space, Time and Resurrection*, 143.
[145]Torrance, *Space, Time and Resurrection*, 143.
[146]Torrance, *Space, Time and Resurrection*, 143-144.

within the "one whole indivisible *parousia*" that extends from Christ's first advent to his second. Torrance calls this an "eschatological pause," and this "pause" allows us to speak about a first and second advent of Christ. These two advents are distinguished in their forms: the first "in great humility and abasement," and the second "in great glory and power."[147] But because Christ's *parousia* is fundamentally indivisible, the difference between Christ's first and second advent is not representative of God's presence versus his absence, but rather a difference in the manner of God's presence. Torrance references here the assessment of Calvin's eschatology he provides in the study *Kingdom and Church: A Study in the Theology of the Reformation*. It is not that Christ's kingdom will only be truly inaugurated at the time of his return. There is, properly speaking, no "reserve" to what Jesus has accomplished: "The Kingdom of Christ was fully inaugurated with his crucifixion in its condition of humiliation, and with his resurrection in triumph over the forces of darkness and evil and his ascension as Lamb of God to the throne of the Father. . . . This is the immediacy and the finality of the Kingdom of which Christ spoke as taking place in the life-time of his hearers."[148] According to Calvin, the difference between first and second advent is not the difference between two arrivals of the kingdom, but rather two "states" of the same kingdom.[149] "Biblical language leads Calvin to draw a distinction between what he calls the two conditions of the Kingdom, i.e., 'Between the present condition of the Kingdom and its future glory.'"[150]

This "present condition of the Kingdom" is the condition in which the Christian and the church exists. One of the besetting problems of the various doctrines of mission and ministry that are adopted by the church is the struggle to articulate the way in which Jesus and the Spirit remain integral to the church's work. In the absence of clarity at this juncture, doctrinal proposals will understand their task to make the absent God present[151] or

---

[147]Torrance, *Space, Time and Resurrection*, 145.
[148]Torrance, *Space, Time and Resurrection*, 146.
[149]Torrance, *Space, Time and Resurrection*, 145.
[150]Torrance, *Kingdom and Church: A Study in the Theology of the Reformation* (Eugene, OR: Wipf & Stock, 1996), 122.
[151]The language of "incarnational ministry," though immensely helpful to the church as a corrective to malformed ministry practices, often unintentionally falls prey to this. The call to "become incarnate" in the practice of ministry implicitly occludes the continued ministry of the incarnate Son at the right hand of the Father. See the charitable appraisal of this in J. Todd

retreat to pragmatic functionalism.[152] In contrast to these meek proposals, Torrance's theology unfolds from the conviction that the task of theology is, in the words of John Webster, to speak "in a manner appropriate to the fact that God is not a mute reality to be called into presence by language or practice, but the eternally creative and active Word."[153] For Torrance, this kind of speech is governed not only by the grammar of the Trinity but also by the ascension. The doctrine of the ascension determines this space and time that the church lives and moves in, where Christ is not absent but present to his creatures. The ascension is therefore, for Torrance, that which determines "the pattern of mission of the Church in history and the relation of the Church in space and time to himself."[154]

Conclusion

In this chapter we have sought to trace the shape and to understand the content of Torrance's christology. While knowledge of this particular doctrine is important for understanding the thought of almost any theologian, it is even more true when trying to comprehend Torrance. Because, as we have already seen, the *homoousion* secures for humanity real knowledge of God through the person of the incarnate Son, christology is a central, controlling element of all knowledge of God and his acts for Torrance. And this is not only true of the knowledge of God and his acts. Insofar as Jesus is the

---

Billings, *Union with Christ: Reframing Theology and Ministry for the Church* (Grand Rapids, MI: Baker Academic, 2011), 123-132.

[152] Andrew Purves's critique of the immensely influential pastoral theology of Seward Hiltner is instructive:

> The modern pastoral care movement within the North American Protestant theological academy is by and large shaped by psychological categories regarding human experience and by symbolic interpretations regarding God. A relatively comfortable synthesis results in which pastoral theology and, consequently, pastoral practice in the church have become concerned largely with questions of meaning rather than truth, acceptable functioning rather than discipleship, and a concern for self-actualization and self-realization rather than salvation. This synthesis entails the loss of transcendence, objectivity, and reality of God, and especially the loss of a christological and soteriological clarity, and the insistence today that talk of God be assigned to the realm of myth and meaning. (Andrew Purves, *Reconstructing Pastoral Theology: A Christological Foundation* [Louisville, KY: Westminster John Knox, 2004], xix-xx).

[153] John B. Webster, "'Eloquent and Radiant': The Prophetic Office of Christ and the Mission of the Church," in *Barth's Moral Theology: Human Action in Barth's Thought* (Grand Rapids, MI: Eerdmans, 1998), 125.

[154] Torrance, *Space, Time and Resurrection*, 147.

meeting place of divine action and human response, christology is also for Torrance the foundation for understanding the church's participation in the ongoing work of the ascended Christ.

As we have seen, Torrance's christology is founded upon a creative synthesis of Reformed christological categories and biblical theology. The *munus triplex* provides the formal organization for understanding the work of Christ, but it is supplemented by the material categories of the biblical theology of Torrance's day. The result is an understanding of the threefold office that is broadly consistent with the Reformed tradition but also makes unique contributions according to that biblical theology as well as other concerns that animate Torrance's thinking. In our fourth and fifth chapter, we will see just how Torrance's distinct account of the *munus triplex* affects the church's ministry and mission.

Alongside the threefold office we also examined Torrance's understanding of the vital importance of the ascension. The ascension serves as a bridge between the work of Christ that began in his earthly career and the church's subsequent participation in that work. In the ascension Jesus creates space for his work to expand—not through his absence, but through his presence at the right hand of the Father in such a way as to be present to creation in a different but no less effective way. Significantly, Jesus' bodily ascension assures us that this new presence remains determined by incarnate ministry that unfolds in the form of the *munus triplex*.

In the book of Acts, it is the ascension that marks the transition from an account that trains its eye upon the person of Jesus to an account that turns to the body of men and women who have been caught up in his life and work in such a way that they become participants in his ongoing ministry. It is at this point in this book that we make the same transition: from christology to ecclesiology.

3

The Mission of the Body of Christ

ECCLESIOLOGY, MISSION, AND THE DEPOSIT OF FAITH

⊕

As THIS STUDY HAS TRACED both the way in which T. F. Torrance's theology has been shaped by missional concerns and begun to examine the particular resources that his thought brings into the conversation, we have attempted to follow the logic of Torrance's own scientific, trinitarian theology. In correspondence to Torrance's own thought, the discussion has self-consciously attempted to resist being framed by demands that arise from contemporary sociological or ethical dilemmas. Torrance's own understanding of the church is that it is to be a place where "we learn to think from a centre in God rather than from a centre in ourselves,"[1] and it has thus been our own task to follow his methodology and the rationality that drives and motivates his own thought.

Torrance's methodology and convictions are particularly helpful when they are brought to bear upon the area of ecclesiology. Whereas it is common for many discussions of the missional nature of the church to emerge from and be defined by sociology, the logic of Torrance's theology is different. Ecclesiology emerges from the convictions about God's triune life and the nature of Jesus Christ's work and his continuing ministry. These convictions are significant in that they frame the Church and its mission in the native language of the redemptive work of Jesus Christ and the perfecting ministry of the Holy

---

[1]Thomas F. Torrance, *Atonement: The Person and Work of Christ* (Downers Grove, IL: IVP Academic, 2009), 376.

Spirit. Torrance's methodology is here similar to that which is described by John Webster in "In the Society of God," an essay that sounds a note of caution about sociological (or here ethnographic) approaches to ecclesiology:

> The church is not simply social nature but created and fallen social nature re-created by the saving missions of the Son of God and the Holy Spirit and so reconciled to God and on the way to perfection.... The church is a society that moves itself as it is moved by God. Without talk of divine movement, of the eliciting, calling, gathering, and sanctifying works of God, an ethnography of the church does not attain its object, misperceiving the motion to which its attention is to be directed, and so inhibited in understanding the creaturely movement of the communion of saints.[2]

In order to comprehend the nature of the church and its mission, we must begin with dogmatic concerns, moving forward with the conviction to submit our reflection to what Torrance calls, "the ground and grammar of theology": the activity of the persons of the Holy Trinity.

Because we have been concerned with interpreting Torrance's statements about the church's mission and its ministry within the particular theology and rationality in which they are embedded, we began our conversation about the church and its mission in the doctrine of God. We traced the shape of Torrance's doctrine of God, noting the way that it is framed in order to emphasize objective realism in a perceived culture of dualism. Next, we considered the incarnation as the center of all of our speech about the church's mission. The incarnation is the intelligible ground of all speech about God's work in the world, and so its contours—and in particular the *munus triplex* and the doctrine of the ascension—must be understood so that we do not move from the realities of redemption into abstractions. Through the threefold office, we understand the shape of redemption as Jesus enacted it in his earthly career. And through the ascension, the work that began in Jesus' earthly ministry continues, but in such a way that it can only be spoken of with reference to Jesus Christ, the incarnate Son.

Having thus represented the logic of Torrance's own theology, our focus now turns to the nature of the church's mission. We will now consider how

---

[2] John Webster, "'In the Society of God': Some Principles of Ecclesiology," *God Without Measure: Working Papers in Christian Theology*, Volume I: *God and the Works of God* (London: T&T Clark, 2016), 193.

we are to understand the nature of ecclesial witness to and participation in God's reconciling and redeeming activity within the theological grammar that Torrance has given to us. In Torrance's writings, the concept of mission is funded by two distinct but complementary concepts: the church's identity as the body of Christ and the apostolate. In this chapter, we will examine each of these concepts in turn, beginning with the conception of the church as the body of Christ, as this concept relates the church's nature as mission to Jesus *mediately* through the implications of the incarnation. We will then move to Torrance's understanding of the apostolate, which relates the church's mission *immediately* through Torrance's understanding of the concept of the "deposit of faith."

THE CHURCH AS THE BODY OF CHRIST

In order to understand how Torrance can say that mission is of such importance to the church that "her very foundations rest upon it,"[3] we must place this discussion within the context of his larger ecclesiological project. While ecclesiology has not been one of the more commented-upon aspects of Torrance's thought, the category is nonetheless a consistent area of concern throughout his theological career. From his earlier writings birthed out of his involvement in the ecumenical movement to his later work in the Orthodox-Reformed dialogue and as Moderator of the Church of Scotland, Torrance continued to think through the implications of his dogmatic work in christology and trinitarian theology for the church. As in much of Torrance's thought, the basic shape of his thought is evident early on in his career.

Torrance's ecclesiology circles around a primary scriptural image: the church as the body of Christ. The following quote reveals the rationale for his decision to privilege this metaphor:

> The New Testament certainly uses many other terms with which to speak of the Church such as people, family, temple, flock, vine, bride, etc., and all must be used to correct and modify each theory in our understanding in any full discussion; but there can be no doubt about the fact that the body is the central and all-important conception, for it is here that the Church is seen to be rooted in the love of God which has overflowed into the world and

---

[3] Torrance, "Amsterdam—The Nature and Mission of the Church," in *Conflict and Agreement in the Church: Order and Disorder*, ed. Thomas F. Torrance, vol. 1 (Eugene, OR: Wipf & Stock, 1959), 221.

embodied itself in our humanity in the Beloved Son, and to be grounded in the crucifixion and in the resurrection of His Body, so that through union with Him in Spirit and Body the Church participates in the divine nature and engages in Christ's ministry of reconciliation.[4]

The scientific structure of Torrance's theology, which draws its driving logic from the incarnation via the "theological linchpin" of the *homoousios*, locates the person of Jesus Christ at the center of the relationship between God and humanity. By privileging the body of Christ as the primary lens through which to view the church, the logic that is present in his christology —union with Christ, the importance of the ascension, and the threefold office—remains consistent in his ecclesiology. In what follows, we will trace the important themes of Torrance's "body of Christ" ecclesiology before relating them specifically in their immediate relation to the church's missional nature.

ECCLESIOLOGY: ITS CHRISTOLOGICAL ROOTS

Classical christology and biblical theology. As we have already noted, the particular rationality of Torrance's theology drives him to find christological answers as dogmatic problems present themselves. Ecclesiology is no exception; in his response to the ecumenical dialogue and disagreement of the World Council of Churches meeting in Amsterdam, Torrance writes, "What is meant, for example, by the divine nature of the Church? How are we to think of the divine and human relations in relation to each other? To that question only a Christological answer can be given."[5] And this christological answer is to be drawn from the particular resources of the Reformed and catholic tradition in which Torrance worked: the hypostatic union and its account of the relation between God and humanity in the person of Jesus Christ.

Torrance's decision to take the framework of christology as the guide for his ecclesiology is evident early in his theological career. Three early works— "Amsterdam—The Nature and Mission of the Church," "The Atonement and the Oneness of the Church," and *Royal Priesthood*—each provide a slightly different perspective on this basic insight. The three works are the fruit of Torrance's ecumenical work with the Commission on Faith and Order, and

---

[4]Torrance, *Royal Priesthood: A Theology of Ordained Ministry* (Edinburgh: T&T Clark, 1955), 29.
[5]Torrance, "Nature and Mission of the Church," 202.

in each essay Torrance's efforts to resolve particular impasses in the movement toward church unity leads him to push behind the disagreement at hand to the foundational doctrines of Christian theology. For Torrance, the cornerstone from which to build must be the doctrine of Jesus Christ: "Our major differences clearly concern the doctrine of the Church, but let us penetrate behind the divisions of the church on earth to our common faith in the one Lord. . . . From the oneness of Christ we will try to understand the unity of the Church in Him and from the unity of Christ and His Body we will seek a means of realizing that unity in the actual state of our divisions on earth."[6] Christology provides the foundation for ecclesiology.

Torrance's stated desire is to begin with the hypostatic union as the framework for ecclesiology: "It would seem that the relation between Christ and His Church, and the nature of the Church, are to be interpreted in the light of Catholic dogma of Christ, as found, for example, in the Ecumenical Councils of the Creeds and Confessions of the Churches."[7] The reasoning behind this decision comes from an analogy that can be drawn between, on the one hand, the union of the two natures in Jesus Christ and, on the other, the church's simultaneously divine and human reality. As in Jesus Christ we see a union of divinity and humanity, so in the church we see a similar conjunction of divine presence and creaturely reality. But in order to do this, Torrance believes that the classic formulations of Chalcedon must be supplemented. Torrance's christology has its foundation in classical orthodox christology, yet is also informed by the resources of biblical theology. What takes place here is of a kind with what we have already found in Torrance's synthesis of the *munus triplex* and more contemporary insights of biblical theology, only here it is applied to the hypostatic union and the relation between incarnation and atonement: "The classical terminology of the Church in its formulation of the doctrine of Christ needs qualifying and reminting in the biblical studies of our day."[8]

To this end, Torrance emphasizes what he calls the "distinct 'moments'" in Jesus' ministry, which give insight into the relation between the hypostatic

---

[6]Torrance, "The Atonement and the Oneness of the Church," in *Conflict and Agreement in the Church*, vol. 1, 238.
[7]Torrance, "Atonement and the Oneness of the Church," 238.
[8]Torrance, "Atonement and the Oneness of the Church," 239.

union and atonement, which in turn give rise to a proper doctrine the church: "Throughout the whole life and mission of Christ, hypostatic union and reconciliation, incorporation and atonement, involved each other in redemption and new creation. It is in that mutual involution that the Church is grounded as the one Body of the one Lord."[9] These moments are Jesus' baptism, the choosing of the twelve disciples, and the Last Supper Jesus shared with his disciples. Each of these events provides a window into particular facets of the life of the incarnate Son that, when taken together, give a full picture of the hypostatic union: "We must think of Christ entering upon His active ministry as true God and true Man in one Person, in a union which penetrated into our sinful humanity and created room for itself in the midst of our estrangement, at once gathering sinful man into one Body with the Saviour, opening up a new and living way into the Holiest."[10]

The first moment, Jesus' baptism, is significant because in this event we understand the hypostatic union's taking up of sinful humanity: "The first thing He did as He entered upon His active ministry was to be baptized in a crowd of sinners—that was His identification in the body of His flesh with the whole mass of sin and death."[11] The fact that this identification with humanity takes place in baptism indicates that it points proleptically to the judgment he would assume on our behalf. The second moment—the choosing of the twelve disciples—demonstrates that while his work is in continuity with the Old Testament, it also marks a closer, more intimate identification than that which had come before: "As long before Elijah had gathered together twelve stones representing the twelve tribes of Israel to build an altar for sacrifice, Jesus gathered twelve living stones . . . and built them round Himself. . . . Upon this Twelve, the reconstituted Israel, He was to build His Church, and so He formed and fashioned them into a foundation, in a profound sense, one Body with Himself."[12] As a part of this reconstitution, the disciples are drawn into the pattern of Christ's own life: "Their Baptism in the one body was worked out in self-denial and crucifixion, such that each was a member of Christ, each renounced his own name and lived in the name of Christ."[13] It

---

[9]Torrance, "Atonement and the Oneness of the Church," 241.
[10]Torrance, "Atonement and the Oneness of the Church," 240.
[11]Torrance, "Atonement and the Oneness of the Church," 241.
[12]Torrance, "Atonement and the Oneness of the Church," 241.
[13]Torrance, "Atonement and the Oneness of the Church," 241.

is not just that Christ identifies with the disciples, but the disciples are themselves drawn into the pattern of Christ's own life. The final moment, the Last Supper, signifies the marriage of both the intimacy of the relations the disciples have with their Master and also the mission that they have been given by and in him. At the Last Supper, "Jesus in covenantal action appointed the disciples a Kingdom, and they were made a royal priesthood, to sit on twelve thrones with Christ in His Kingdom, i.e., on the basis of communion in the Body and Blood of Christ, for the Son of Man gave them to eat His Body and drink His Blood, and to become one with Him."[14] The mission of the church—to be a royal priesthood of the kingdom and the nature, union, and communion with Christ—is brought together.

These distinct "moments" shape Torrance's understanding of the hypostatic union and thus provide a description of the relation between Christ and the church. Jesus' baptism is Christ's incorporation of himself into the church, and the Last Supper is the confirmation of that union and the signification of its purpose: "that the Body of sin being destroyed he might raise it again, a glorious Body in His Resurrection."[15] This narrative of Jesus' incarnation, ministry, and crucifixion are what Torrance calls the "One and the Many." But once this work draws to its end, it is then applied back to the church at the moment of Pentecost: "It was then that the hypostatic union, carried through crucifixion to its *telos* in the Risen Christ, was through the breathing of the Spirit insert into the nucleus of the Church on Easter evening, and then, after Christ's Ascension to fill all things, into the whole Church at Pentecost."[16] The church is "given to participate in the hypostatic union, in the mystery of Christ."[17] If the "One and the Many" is the doctrine of the work of Christ, ecclesiology is found in the application of this doctrine to the church, "the Many and the One": "The relation of the One to the Many carries with it and begets the relation of the Many to the One. The One and the Many is the doctrine of Christ. The Many and the One is the doctrine of the Church, the Body of Christ."[18]

---

[14]Torrance, "Atonement and the Oneness of the Church," 242.
[15]Torrance, "Atonement and the Oneness of the Church," 242.
[16]Torrance, "Atonement and the Oneness of the Church," 242.
[17]Torrance, "Atonement and the Oneness of the Church," 242.
[18]Torrance, "Atonement and the Oneness of the Church," 242.

The goal of Torrance's articulation of ecclesiology in this fashion is straightforward: he is structuring the divine and human relation that takes place within the church using the central framework of divine-human relations in Christian theology—the person of Jesus Christ, fully human and fully God. But in order to bring greater clarity to his use of christology in the domain of ecclesiology, Torrance draws on another resource from the tradition of the church's christological reflection: the *anhypostasia* and the *enhypostasia*. In the same way the *anhypostasia* and the *enhypostasia* clarify the divine and human relationship that takes place in Jesus Christ, so they also provide the proper framework for doing the same in the church.

The twin terms of the *enhypostasis* and the *anhypostasis* have a central place in the history of Christian doctrine.[19] What is of significance at this point in our study is that, for Torrance, the terms parallel the dynamics of incorporation and substitution in the work of Christ. *Anhypostasia*, here defined as the reality that "in the *assumptio carnis* [assumption of flesh] the human nature of Christ had no independent *per se* subsistence apart from ... the hypostatic union," has to do with the substitutionary nature of Christ's work. As Torrance applies the term at this juncture, the *anhypostasia* here is indicative of the fact that the atonement involves a work of divine initiative and grace, performed on behalf of humanity: "If *enhypostasia* alone were to be applied to the atonement without *anhypostasia* then atonement would have been understood as a Pelagian deed placating God by human sacrifice."[20] Torrance goes further, stating that if the hypostatic union "was *enhypostatic* and not merely *anhypostatic*, then we must give the element of concrete substitution much greater place in our understanding of atonement."[21] The *anhypostasia* is reflective of the substitutionary nature of the atonement.

Enhypostasia, the cognate to *anhypostasia*, is defined here by Torrance as the belief that "in the *assumptio carnis*, the human nature of Christ was given a real and concrete subsistence within the hypostatic union."[22] As

---

[19]See F. LeRon Shults, "A Dubious Christological Formula: From Leontius of Byzantium to Karl Barth," *Theological Studies* 57 (1996): 431-446, as well as Ivor Davidson, "Theologizing the Human Jesus: An Ancient (and Modern) Approach to Christology Reassessed," *International Journal of Systematic Theology* 3.2 (2001): 129-153.
[20]Torrance, "Atonement and the Oneness of the Church," 243.
[21]Torrance, "Atonement and the Oneness of the Church," 244.
[22]Torrance, "Atonement and the Oneness of the Church," 242.

Torrance utilizes the term here, it is reflective of the way in which the atonement *incorporates* humanity. With Christ taking up a real and fully human nature in the incarnation, his atoning work can be located within the sphere of humanity and thus applied there. Without the *enhypostasia*, "the deed of atonement would be a pure act of God over the head of man, and not an atoning act involving incorporation."[23] The twin uses of the *anhypostasia* and *enhypostasia* thus reflect the dynamics important to Torrance's understanding of the atonement. And we have already seen and shall continue to see, these dynamics remain significant as we move from Torrance's christology to his understanding of the nature and mission of the church.

From the preceding description, we can see the basic convictions that inform Torrance's relation of christology to ecclesiology. Christology is proposed as a way through the apparent ecclesiological impasse of the ecumenical movement, allowing the church to address the nature of the church as divine and human through the framework of Jesus Christ—who in the hypostatic union is the singular example of this relation and yet who also, by the Spirit, allows the church to participate in this relation. While this relation is built upon the foundation of the hypostatic union, this doctrine is also informed by contemporary biblical theology, leading to what he termed a more "dynamic" understanding in which incarnation and atonement are emphasized in their relationship to one another. Finally, Torrance utilizes the *anhypostasia/enhypostasia* distinction as an element of the hypostatic union, which has special relevance to understanding the christological shape of ecclesiology. Having thus described the foundations of Torrance's ecclesiology, we now turn to see how Torrance provides a more precise description of the relation of christology to ecclesiology.

The analogy of Christ. Torrance understands the relationship between christology and ecclesiology to be governed by what he calls "the analogy of Christ." Torrance traces this concept to one of his favorite early Christian sources, Athanasius. The basic insight, which Athanasius provided, was that "all analogies must be subordinated to, and criticized by, the unique Revelation of the Father and the Son, for it is solely from the Incarnate Son that they have their legitimate place in Christian theology and therefore it is only

---

[23]Torrance, "Atonement and the Oneness of the Church," 243.

in accordance with the analogy of Christ that they are to be applied."[24] The analogy of Christ is simply another way of stating the guiding principle of Torrance's scientific theology: true knowledge is only possible through submission to the particular object of study. Christian theology thus can only proceed by allowing its object, the God who is revealed through the person of Jesus Christ, to dictate its terms and path. And because an actual relationship has been established between God and humanity in the incarnation, we may utilize analogy—but only this analogy.

It is important to state the precise terms of the analogy that is made between Christ and the church. The analogy does not indicate a simple one-to-one correspondence between the two: "The analogy runs not 'as God and Man are related in Christ so the divine and the human are related in the Church,' but rather 'as God and Man are related in Christ so Christ and the Church are related.'"[25] The analogy of Christ is more specifically an analogy of the hypostatic union, and an analogy that describes in what way Christ is present in the church. Stating the analogy in this way allows Torrance to avoid the kind of error he finds in certain Anglican and Orthodox conceptions of the church that overstate the ontological status of the church, giving them an apparently independent being apart from Christ.[26]

Torrance names four implications that follow from the decision to allow the analogy of Christ to set the terms of ecclesiology. There is first a *logical* implication that follows from the simple fact that this conception of the relation between Christ and the church is an analogy. The use of an analogy means that the kind of relation that exists is not one of complete identity nor total difference, but instead "something of likeness and something of difference *proportionaliter.*"[27] This first implication is more of a reflection on the concept of analogy than the specific instance of analogy that exists between Christ and the church: "Apart . . . from telling us how analogical prediction should be framed, [it] tells us nothing at all, until we come to

---

[24]Torrance, "Atonement and the Oneness of the Church," 246.
[25]Torrance, "Nature and Mission of the Church," 203.
[26]"It is a failure to give this adequate thought that has often led some of the Anglican group to speak of the Church as if she were a pre-existent ontological reality, and as often led the Orthodox group to think of the Church as if there were over against the visible Church an invisible Platonic magnitude." Torrance, "Nature and Mission of the Church," 203.
[27]Torrance, "Atonement and the Oneness of the Church," 246.

the actual relationship that has been established between God and man in the Incarnation."[28]

The second implication is *christological* and concerns the framework for understanding the incarnation that has been inherited from Chalcedon. The boundaries drawn by the "without confusion" and "without separation" of Chalcedon can be used in "a secondary and cognate sense"[29] (i.e., as an analogy) in their application to the divine and human nature of the church. When applied specifically to the church, this christological implication prevents both an understanding of the church that is "Docetic" (where the divine and human dynamics of the church have become confused with one another and the church is "transubstantiated into something beyond history"[30]) and an understanding of the church that fails to account for real ontological union with Christ (and thus separates Christ and the church). The church exists in union with Christ in such a way that it can claim neither that it has become some kind of *tertium quid* nor that Christ is completely external to its life.

The third implication of the analogy of Christ is *soteriological*. Here Torrance applies the concept of the *mirifica commutatio* (wonderful exchange) —which describes the substitutionary relation between Christ and humanity—analogically to the church. Whereas the concept is usually understood to denote the wonderful exchange that took place between Christ and humanity in the atonement, Torrance here applies the concept descriptively to the church's identity and the source of its life: "The analogical relation between Christ and the Church reposes entirely upon what He has done for the Church by taking its place that it might be conformed to Him, and is maintained because Christ continues to live for the Church so that the life of the Church is to be found not in itself, but in Him."[31] The analogical relation Torrance describes is something that the church possesses by gift and not by nature. The church's identity is constituted by Christ and his substitutionary life, leading the church to look away from itself and to its Lord and head.

---

[28] Torrance, "Atonement and the Oneness of the Church," 246.
[29] Torrance, "Atonement and the Oneness of the Church," 246.
[30] Torrance, "Atonement and the Oneness of the Church," 247.
[31] Torrance, "Atonement and the Oneness of the Church," 247.

The fourth implication of the analogy of Christ is *pneumatological*. Torrance notes the importance of the Holy Spirit at key moments in Jesus' life and ministry—his conception through the Holy Spirit, the Spirit's appearance at his baptism, his self-offering to the Father through the Spirit, and his resurrection in the power of the Spirit. In emphasizing the Spirit's action in these biblical moments, Torrance draws attention to the Spirit's role of facilitating and enabling the incarnate Son's work. In the same way, there is an analogical relationship between the church and the Spirit. The Spirit works upon the church in a way that is analogical to the way that the Spirit was present to Jesus in his earthly ministry: "Through the same Spirit Christ has assumed the Church as His Body, and is free to be present in the Church and to realize the relation of the Church to Himself giving it life-unity with Him as Redeemer and Lord of its being."[32] It is the Spirit who "realizes the relation" of Christians, both corporately and individually, to Christ, incorporating them into Christ.

Alongside these four fundamental implications of the analogy of Christ, Torrance further expands upon the concept by analogically applying the *anhypostasia* and *enhypostasia* to the church's existence. We recall that Torrance states the *anhypostasia* is descriptive of the fact that Jesus' humanity has no independent existence apart from the incarnation. The same description can be applied to the church: "*Anhypostasia* would then mean that the Church as Body of Christ has no *per se* existence, no independent *hypostasis*, apart from atonement and communion through the Holy Spirit."[33] Note that the analogy is not one-to-one: the church's existence is understood by way of the bond of the Holy Spirit rather than simply by its existence in the hypostatic union.[34] Nevertheless, this use of the *anhypostasia* has clear implications for the shape of the church's life: "The only way the Church can follow [Christ] is by way of *anhypostasia*, by way of self-denial and crucifixion, by letting Christ take its place and displace its

---

[32]Torrance, "Atonement and the Oneness of the Church," 247.
[33]Torrance, "Atonement and the Oneness of the Church," 248.
[34]Myk Habets notes the absence of Spirit christology in Torrance's understanding of the union of the Son with humanity: "Unlike Calvin, Ursinus, Owen, Edwards, and Irving, nowhere so far has Torrance introduced a discussion about the role of the Holy Spirit in the incarnation nor specifically in the doctrine of Christ's sinful humanity." Myk Habets, *Theology in Transposition: A Constructive Appraisal of T. F. Torrance* (Minneapolis: Fortress, 2013), 181-182.

self-assertion."[35] The church's life is not self-contained, but is only possessed as it is received from Christ.

The analogy of the *enhypostasia* unfolds similarly. When applied simply to christology, the concept describes how there is a real and concrete subsistence of humanity within the person of Jesus Christ. When understood analogically with respect to the church, the *enhypostasia* means that "the Church is given in Christ real *hypostasis* through incorporation, and therefore concrete function in union with Him. That is why to speak of the Church as the Body of Christ is no mere figure of speech but describes an ontological reality, *enhypostatic* in Christ and wholly dependent on Him."[36] There is also a corresponding implication for the shape of the church's existence. The church lives "by way of *enhypostasia*, by way of incorporation and resurrection, by receiving from Christ the life which He has in Himself and which He gives His own."[37] This description sounds similar to that which we found in the *anhypostasia*, but here the emphasis is upon the reality of the union that the church is given in Christ.

The merit of the *an/enhypostasia* distinction for ecclesiology is demonstrated by Torrance in making sense of both the eschatological and ontological nature of the church. When only the *enhypostasia* is recognized, the church will be understood as an extension of the incarnation, to the exclusion of the "eschatological" character of its existence. By "eschatological," Torrance means the sense in which the church does not yet possess the fullness which it will only receive at Christ's second advent.[38] Alternatively, when only the *anhypostasia* is recognized, the sense in which the church currently enjoys real participation in Christ is lost. When both *anhypostasia* and *enhypostasia* are held together, then the church can be understood properly: "The ontology will speak of the miraculous preservation of the life and being of the Church through death and resurrection in Christ, and

---

[35] Torrance, "Atonement and the Oneness of the Church," 245.
[36] Torrance, "Atonement and the Oneness of the Church," 248.
[37] Torrance, "Atonement and the Oneness of the Church," 245.
[38] "The Church is conceived as an 'event' that depends strongly on the free movement of the Word and Spirit, but not so strongly on incorporation into Christ. This view also tends to foster a separation between the visible church and Christ." Stanley S. MacLean, *Resurrection, Apocalypse, and the Kingdom of Christ: The Eschatology of Thomas F. Torrance* (Eugene, OR: Wipf & Stock, 2012), 162.

eschatology will speak of the real and substantial union of the Church with the Risen, Ascended, and Advent Lord."[39]

The biblical christology Torrance has provided—the mining of the Chalcedonian tradition and the supplementation of the *anhypostasia/enhypostasia* distinction, the argument for an analogical relationship between Christ and the church—all of this leads Torrance to a particular, definitive description of the church: "the body of Christ."[40] We will now turn to how Torrance's understanding of the "body of Christ" shapes his ecclesiology and his subsequent understanding of the nature and mission of the church.

The body of Christ. Torrance finds the term "body of Christ" helpful for the project of ecclesiology because it maintains the proper balance between identity and difference that we have already seen in his use of the analogy of Christ and the *an/enhypostasia* distinction. Torrance understands that "body of Christ" is used in two distinct ways in the New Testament. These two ways reflect the tension intrinsic to the analogy of Christ: both identity and difference may be found in the relation between Christ and the church, and both of these realities must always be held together. In the first sense of "body of Christ," it signifies "*the whole Christ who includes the church* within his own fullness."[41] Here the term "body of Christ" indicates the reality of Christ's presence within the church: "In this sense Christ is the church, for he embodied himself in our humanity and as such gathers our humanity in himself into oneness with God."[42] When the term "body of Christ" is used this way in Scripture, what is emphasized is that the church finds its identity and its life only in its relation to Jesus Christ.

The other way the term "body of Christ" is used in the New Testament emphasizes the distinction between the church and Christ rather than continuity. In contrast to understanding Christ as including the church, here "body of Christ" denotes "*the body of which he is the head.*"[43] For Torrance, to speak of Christ is to speak of the church because in the hypostatic union Christ has bound himself to our humanity. However, speech about the

---

[39] Torrance, "Atonement and the Oneness of the Church," 249.
[40] Torrance's use of this term to describe the church mirrors the similar decision Barth made in IV/1 of *Church Dogmatics*, though Torrance and Barth deploy the concept in different ways.
[41] Torrance, *Atonement*, 362 (emphasis original).
[42] Torrance, *Atonement*, 362.
[43] Torrance, *Atonement*, 362.

church does not encompass speech about Christ, because he is always more than the church in his divinity: "Christ is the church, but it cannot be said that the church is Christ, for Christ is infinitely more than the church although in his grace he will not be without it."[44]

This distinction between the two ways of speaking about the "body of Christ" grants clarity to the ways in which the New Testament speaks of the body of Christ, with the latter way in particular protecting Christ's transcendency over the church and preventing a simple identification of the church with Christ as a "continuation of the Incarnation" (a phrase to which Torrance expressed strong opposition at various times). Torrance is also clear that the metaphor "body of Christ" in no sense threatens the self-sufficiency and aseity of the incarnate Son Jesus Christ: "It is important to note that [Christ's] wholeness is constituted by Christ Himself, and would in no sense be defective if He were separated from us; nevertheless it is such a wholeness that Christ will not be without us and insists upon incorporating us into it."[45] But while he is careful to distinguish between Christ and the church and to define the nature of their relation, the overwhelming force of his use of the metaphor is to point to the positive relationship between Christ and the church as the object and instrument of his redeeming activity: "The term body of Christ directs us at once to Christ himself, laying the emphasis not on the body but on Christ. Thus it does not focus attention on the church as an entity in itself or as something that exists for its own sake, but upon the church as the immediate property of Christ which he has made his very own and gathered into the most intimate relation with himself."[46]

Thus far, our study has examined the foundation of Torrance's ecclesiology. This ecclesiology, under the impetus of the ecumenical movement's struggle to articulate the church's nature, seeks firm footing in christology as the paradigmatic expression of the divine and human relations. After describing a modified Chalcedonian christology, Torrance proposes the "analogy of Christ" as the dogmatic construct that allows one to move faithfully from the doctrine of Christ ("The One and the Many") to the doctrine of the church ("The Many and the One"). Guided by the analogy of Christ,

---

[44]Torrance, *Atonement*, 362.
[45]Torrance, "Nature and Mission of the Church," 217.
[46]Torrance, "Nature and Mission of the Church," 363.

Torrance foregrounds the biblical term "the body of Christ" as the definitive description of the church. It is this term that most accurately describes the "being" of the church: the real ontological relationship that exists between Christ and the church that is to be maintained alongside the very real difference that is only bridged by Christ's gracious action through the Holy Spirit: "Through the Spirit the *being* of the church is grounded in the being of Christ—that is the ontological basis or *esse* of the church."[47] Having thus described the "being of the church" in this way, we can now progress to interpret the implications of Torrance's methodology for understanding the church's true nature—and thus the necessary relationship between the church and its mission.

The body of Christ and the mission of the church. Using the ecclesial analogy available through the analogy of Christ, Torrance advances four complementary arguments about the necessary relationship between the church and its mission. The first draws on the resources of Torrance's understanding of the missions of the persons of the Trinity, connecting the church's being and two other reciprocal categories—the church's nature and the church's mission. The second is focused on the life and ministry of the incarnate Son, taking the narrative of the suffering servant Jesus Christ as the definitive model of the church's necessarily missional existence. The third claims that the body of Christ—the church—will necessarily be found in the same places of deep need and distress where its Lord was found. And the fourth argument is based upon Torrance's reading of Ephesians, where he sees the church involved necessarily in a movement toward "fullness."

In the first argument Torrance advances, he builds on claims he makes about the being of the church. An understanding of the church's being is accompanied by an understanding of the church's nature. When we understand the church's being to be grounded in the person of Christ, we then also understand the nature of the church to be derived from the love of God in Christ. ("Nature" here is something like "the defining characteristic of its existence.") The two concepts of being and nature are inseparable, necessarily interpenetrating one another in Torrance's understanding of the church: "Through the Spirit the nature of the church derives from the love

---

[47]Torrance, *Atonement*, 373.

of God in Christ poured out upon the church. The very nature of the church is therefore *agape* which it is the life of the church to express."[48] Torrance is not describing a quality of the church's life that it should manifest given its relation to Christ as his body. Instead, he is describing a necessary entailment of the reality of the church in its union with him: "When we speak of the Church as the Body of Christ we are saying that it is given such union with Christ that it becomes a communion filled and overflowing with the divine love."[49] Because Jesus Christ is the manifestation of the love of God poured out for humanity and its salvation, to participate in Jesus Christ is necessarily to participate in the reality of that love. To be "in Christ" means necessarily to demonstrate what Torrance takes to be the defining characteristic of Jesus' life—*agape* love.

For Torrance, the two categories of being and nature do not encompass all that must be said about the church. They also interpenetrate with a third category, the church's mission: "The being and nature of the church are equally inseparable from its *mission*, that is, its sending by Christ on the mission of the love of God."[50] Here Torrance utilizes the "analogy of Christ" as expressive of the intrinsically missional nature of the church. The analogy is based upon a reading of the upper room discourse in the Gospel of John as descriptive of the divine missions. Being, nature, and mission are inseparable here "just as the sending of Christ by the Father is inseparable from his being and nature as the incarnate Son."[51] The inseparability of the Son's nature, being, and mission unfolds analogically to the church's own life: "Since the being and nature and mission of the church interpenetrate each other in the concrete life of the church, we can never think of the being and nature of the church statically, but always in terms of the divine act, the divine movement of love from God to man, and from man to God and man to fellow man in a gathering of the life of men and women into communion with the life of God."[52] This ecclesial life, Torrance says, is constituted by the divine love of the Trinity: "The interpenetration of being and mission

---

[48]Torrance, *Atonement*, 373.
[49]Torrance, *Royal Priesthood*, 29.
[50]Torrance, *Atonement*, 373.
[51]Torrance, *Atonement*, 373.
[52]Torrance, *Atonement*, 373.

constitutes the nature of the Church, so that Church *is* Church as it participates in the active operation of the divine love."[53]

Thus, for Torrance, in the same way that the love of the triune God is ecstatic in its orientation, moving the Son in his mission of redemption, this same love moves the church into the world. To participate in the communion of the Son's love is then necessarily to participate in "not the exclusive company of the privileged, but the company of men and women bound into one body with Christ and so filled with his Spirit and love that it becomes an ever-widening communion in which the church presses out in expansion towards a fullness in the love of God."[54] The aforementioned pneumatological implication of the analogy of Christ is also utilized in this argument: it is the Spirit who enables this participation—"The Spirit makes the church participate in the concrete embodiment of the love of God in the incarnate Son. . . . Love in the church is precisely its participation in the humanity of Jesus Christ for he is the love of God poured out for mankind."[55]

The second argument for mission takes as its starting point the career of the incarnate Son. In his description of Christ's ministry at this juncture, Torrance foregrounds a particular aspect of Jesus' earthly ministry: his identity as a suffering servant. Although he uses the same Scripture here as in the previous argument—"As the Father hath *sent* me, so *send* I you"—here the emphasis is distinctly different. Whereas in the argument from the divine missions, Torrance is focused upon the movement of divine love as displayed in Christ ("As the Father hath *sent* me, so *send* I you"). Here the argument advances by way of the mode of divine love as displayed in Christ ("*As* the Father hath sent me, *so* send I you"). The church's ministry is that of a suffering servant: "If the Christological conceptions we have been discussing are to be applied to the Church . . . then on the analogy of Christ we must think of the Church sent out into the world from the Cross as the Suffering Servant."[56] The church looks to the ministry of Christ as he set his own face like flint toward the cross and takes its own posture and shape from him: "The Church militant is still under the Cross and it belongs to its life

---

[53] Torrance, *Royal Priesthood*, 30. Torrance notes John 15:9 as an indication of the scriptural basis of this concept.
[54] Torrance, *Atonement*, 374.
[55] Torrance, *Atonement*, 374.
[56] Torrance, "Atonement and the Oneness of the Church," 250.

and mission to work out analogically in itself what happened in Christ for the Church, to fill up in its body that which is eschatologically in arrears of the sufferings of Christ."[57]

What Torrance wishes to draw attention to is how in particular Christ's suffering reveals a certain constraint he felt toward the cross and the reconciliation that it would bring: "Christ was anticipating the Cross and the mighty power of the divine love in Him which kept pressing Him toward the Cross, where this love would be released upon the whole world in reconciliation, was so great as almost to be unbearable."[58] As the body of Christ, Torrance argues that the church is under the same constraint as its Lord. The church "cannot contain itself—the agony of Christ is upon it. The Love of Christ shed into the Church by the Spirit must break out in the mission of redemption."[59] Torrance is careful to emphasize the dissimilarity implied in the analogy; there is nothing redemptive in the church's suffering ministry in the same way that Christ's suffering redeems: "Jesus Christ was Suffering Servant in a unique sense in which His act was an act of God."[60] Nonetheless, there can be real participation in that ministry through the church's obedience to the implications of the analogy of Christ.

A third argument based upon the analogy of Christ is found in the essay "The Mission of the Church." Here Torrance states that the church in its mission must necessarily inhabit the same kind of spaces and situations that its Lord did in his earthly ministry. Torrance begins this discussion by making another robust claim about the church's missional identity: "The Church exists in mission, living by what it proclaims, and pouring its life out in service for Christ's sake and the Gospel's."[61] The nature of that mission and service is defined by the person and work of Jesus Christ, as the analogy of Christ dictates. And, Torrance argues, Jesus Christ will be found—even now—in places of distress and need: "Until He comes again Jesus Christ is to be found wherever there is darkness in which to shine the light of God, wherever there are lost men and women to be saved, wherever there is alienation and estrangement and division, for He has made all that His very own

---

[57]Torrance, "Atonement and the Oneness of the Church," 250.
[58]Torrance, "Atonement and the Oneness of the Church," 250.
[59]Torrance, "Atonement and the Oneness of the Church," 250.
[60]Torrance, "Atonement and the Oneness of the Church," 251.
[61]Torrance, "The Mission of the Church," *Scottish Journal of Theology* 19 (1966): 140.

in order to overcome it in Himself."⁶² The force of Torrance's argument is again found in his use of the hypostatic union; namely, that this union is a union with *fallen* humanity: "What binds men to Jesus Christ is not only their humanity, but their very sin and selfishness and corruption and rebellion, for it was all that that He took upon Himself as the Lamb of God."⁶³ And if the church is to understand itself properly through the analogy of Christ via the hypostatic union, it will order its ministry and mission accordingly:

> Therefore the Church cannot share the life of Christ to the full, and cannot embody in itself the reconciliation He bestows, without fulfilling its mission to all mankind, in bearing the Gospel of reconciliation to all for whom He died, without seeking to embody in the midst of the world's division the oneness of the fellowship of reconciliation. If the Church does not do that, it calls in question its own reconciliation in Christ, it cuts the lifeline which binds it to the Saviour, it alienates itself from the Kingdom of His grace, and quenches the Holy Spirit who gives the Church its very life in God.⁶⁴

As the church's identity is found in its analogical relation to Christ, it is found as it enacts the same pattern of Christ's union with humanity.⁶⁵

In the fourth argument made for the intrinsically missional nature of the church, Torrance argues for the essentially "teleological" nature of the church. In the exegesis of the book of Ephesians, which drives many of the insights of *Royal Priesthood*, Torrance notes the relationship of the concepts *soma*

---

⁶²Torrance, "Mission of the Church," 140.
⁶³Torrance, "Mission of the Church," 140.
⁶⁴Torrance, "Mission of the Church," 140.
⁶⁵While this argument is largely undeveloped within Torrance's theology, it is worth noting that it is the closest that Torrance draws to an exemplarist christology in his work. John Webster has previously noted the difference between Barth and Torrance on precisely this account. Torrance is less comfortable with christological formulations that distract from what he sees as the fundamentally vicarious nature of Christ's work:

> Barth and Torrance part company because the latter allows little substance to the notions of covenant partnership and reciprocal agency which are deeply embedded in the structure of Barth's account. Torrance, indeed, explicitly repudiates what he calls the trapping of grace "within a reciprocity between God and man." Behind this lies a deeper incompatibility at the level of Christology: where Torrance sees the acts of Jesus as solely vicarious, Barth sees them as representative acts which are nevertheless more than simply completed events containing proleptically our involvement: they are "really an imperative" (*CD* IV/4:67). (John Webster, "The Christian in Revolt: Some Reflections on The Christian Life," in *Reckoning with Barth*, ed. Nigel Biggar [London: Mowbray, 1988], 126).

While we will cite other reasons to agree with Webster's assessment in our conclusion, the presence of this strain within Torrance's ecclesiology suggests that this incompatibility is not total.

(body) and *pleroma* (fulfillment). It is in this argument that Torrance gives one of his more definitive descriptions of the church and its mission. After appropriating Paul's use of *soma* to describe the church and emphasizing once again the pneumatological implication of the analogy of Christ,[66] Torrance proceeds to describe the church with respect to its place in God's saving economy: "As such this body becomes matched to Christ as His *vis-a-vis* in history and as the instrument of His saving purpose in the Gospel. It is the sphere where through the presence of the Spirit the salvation-events of the birth, life, death, resurrection and ascension are operative here and now within history, the sphere where within the old creation the new creation has broken in with power."[67]

This use of *soma*, Torrance states, is to be understood in connection to Paul's connected deployment of *pleroma*. In Ephesians, *pleroma* is used as a part of the description of what Christ has and will accomplish: "until we all attain to the unity of the faith and of the knowledge of the Son of God, to mature manhood, to the measure of the stature of the fullness of Christ" (4:13); "He who descended is the one who also ascended far above all the heavens, that he might fill all things" (Eph 4:10). For Torrance, *pleroma* not only describes the person of Christ, but also describes a "movement" that involves the church. Torrance sees the basis for this argument in the connection of the two concepts of *soma* and *pleroma* in Ephesians 1:22-23: "And he put all things under his feet and gave him as head over all things to the church, which is his body, the fullness of him who fills all in all." Torrance understands this passage not only to be describing the upbuilding of the church with respect to the corporate identity of its members, but also its external expansion through the proclamation of the Word and the ingathering of the newly baptized. He writes, "This body (*soma*) reaches out through the Spirit to fulfillment (*pleroma*) in a movement which takes place intensively within the body as it is rooted and grounded in love and grows up into the fulness of Christ, but which takes place extensively as well, reaching out to the ends of the earth and to the ends of the ages."[68]

---

[66]"But here on the ground of the reconciling work of Christ the Spirit forms out of our humanity a body where the old creation is opened up from within for the reception and actualization of revelation and reconciliation." Torrance, *Royal Priesthood*, 23.
[67]Torrance, *Royal Priesthood*, 23.
[68]Torrance, *Royal Priesthood*, 24.

Torrance describes this movement as "teleological."⁶⁹ This is not to say that the church's movement in the world is a movement of linear, unbroken progress. In his study of Torrance's eschatology, Stanley S. MacLean notes that for Torrance it is in fact a "'desperate struggle,' since the church bears the cross in the world. It lives as the church militant."⁷⁰ Nonetheless, the church is moved by its Lord toward its inevitable end (*telos*) of the resurrection of humanity and the redemption of creation. In the ontological union that the church has in relation to its head, Jesus Christ, who is the first fruits of the new creation, it is established in a trajectory towards the consummation of that new creation.

The catalyst for the movement of the body of Christ towards fulfillment is Pentecost. At Pentecost, Christ "sent out His Spirit upon the Church begetting it and assuming its existence in space and time into communion with His own existence in the Body which He assumed for Himself in the Incarnation, and determining its form and course in space and time in accordance with His own life and work in the Body."⁷¹ Once Jesus atones for humanity's sin in the union of the incarnate Son with fallen humanity, the Spirit is released in order that humanity might participate in God's life: "With the completion of the atonement . . . the fulness of the divine life embodied in Jesus Christ was released for the participation of men, and all who believe in Jesus Christ enter freely into that divine inheritance."⁷² The event of Pentecost, only possible at the completion of the atonement, is the sign of the Spirit's falling upon all of humanity. Torrance sees in the Acts 2 narrative not merely the reversal of the curse of Babel, but in addition to this, the beginning of the extension of the name and power of Christ to the ends of creation: "What took place intensively in Jesus Christ, within the limits of His particular historical life, then began to take place extensively, reaching out to all men in all ages in a movement as expansive as the ascension of Christ to fill all things."⁷³

At this juncture we can see yet another use of the analogy of Christ in Torrance's ecclesiology. As we've already seen in his christology, Torrance

---

⁶⁹Torrance, *Royal Priesthood*, 24.
⁷⁰MacLean, *Resurrection, Apocalypse, and the Kingdom of Christ*, 171.
⁷¹Torrance, *Royal Priesthood*, 25.
⁷²Torrance, "Mission of the Church," 132.
⁷³Torrance, "Mission of the Church," 132.

believes that Christ's relationship to the Spirit is a vicarious relationship. He assumes the Spirit on behalf of humanity: "As the Incarnate Son he received the anointing of the Spirit upon our humanity which he wore, so that upon him and through him the doors of heaven are opened and the divine blessings are poured out."[74] The same dynamic also takes place within the church in an analogical, and clearly secondary, fashion. Noting Peter's quotation of Joel's prophecy, that God would pour out his Spirit on "all flesh," Torrance argues that this reception is one that the nascent body of Christ—the disciples—undertakes on behalf of the rest of humanity. The Spirit "was poured out immediately only upon the Church, and yet through the Church it was destined for all men, for the Church is sent out on a mission to all nations teaching and baptising them in the name of the Lord, that they might too receive the promise of the Spirit and be incorporated into the One Body."[75]

This description of the event of Pentecost adds coherence and detail to Torrance's use of the *soma/pleroma* dynamic of the book of Ephesians. The Acts narrative and Paul's epistle to the Ephesians are aspects of what Torrance understands to be the story of the New Testament: the inevitable advance of the gospel and the body of Christ to their proper *telos*, the consummation of the new creation. While this advance cannot be described as linear, the church will nonetheless one day actualize and realize the fullness that is found in its head, Christ Jesus.

In summary, Torrance makes four complementary arguments for the intrinsic relationship between the church and its mission. Each is based upon a different application of the same "analogy of Christ," which understands the relationship between Christ and the church through the relationship between divinity and humanity in the hypostatic union of the person of Jesus Christ. The church properly understood will be a church that engages in mission because (1) the church is a sent church just as the Son is sent by the Father, (2) the church is constrained by its suffering mission just as Jesus Christ is constrained to be the Suffering Servant, (3) the church's analogical identity as the body of Christ is fulfilled as it relates to fallen humanity as Christ took it upon himself, and (4) the church is involved in a teleological movement toward fullness just as Christ is the one who fills all in all.

---

[74]Torrance, *Incarnation: The Person and Life of Christ* (Downers Grove, IL: IVP Academic, 2008), 125.
[75]Torrance, *Royal Priesthood*, 26.

Torrance and Newbigin: Comparing missional ecclesiologies. Torrance's ecclesiology is an original contribution, placing mission at the center of the church by way of his characteristic christocentrism. But it is worth comparing his approach alongside others so as to better understand Torrance's work and as to ascertain any weaknesses in his formulation. To accomplish this, we will compare Torrance's work with that of his contemporary Lesslie Newbigin.

A discussion of missional ecclesiology and the place of theology in the evangelism of the West would be incomplete without engaging with Newbigin, and indeed there is a remarkable similarity in the careers of the two men. Born just four years before Torrance in 1909, Newbigin was likewise significantly motivated by the advance of secularism in Western Europe. Both men had an ecclesial home in the Church of Scotland: Newbigin initially as a missionary before his work in the ecumenical movement led him to the Church of South India, and Torrance as a parish minister and later as professor at New College. The mission field was deeply formative for both men; Torrance was born to a missionary family and grew up in Chengdu, China, and similarly Newbigin's convictions were forged during his many years of work in India. And the work of Michael Polanyi affected each man profoundly: Torrance served as the executor of Polanyi's intellectual work for a time. Newbigin first read Polanyi's *Personal Knowledge* at the behest of J. H. Oldham soon after its publication in 1958,[76] and the impression the work left upon him is evident in publications such as *Proper Confidence: Faith, Doubt and Certainty in Christian Discipleship*.[77]

More importantly, Newbigin and Torrance's theological careers overlapped for some time during the fledgling days of the ecumenical movement. Both served with the World Council of Churches—in particular with the Commission on Faith and Order—and were a part of its work as it gathered in Amsterdam (1948), Lund (1952), and Evanston (1954). Torrance quotes Newbigin appreciatively in his own assessment of the Amsterdam gathering,[78] and Newbigin for his part acknowledges the assistance of Torrance for

---

[76] Geoffrey Wainwright, *Lesslie Newbigin: A Theological Life* (Oxford: Oxford University Press, 2000), 21-22.
[77] Lesslie Newbigin, *Proper Confidence: Faith, Doubt, and Certainty in Christian Discipleship* (Grand Rapids, MI: Eerdmans, 1995).
[78] Torrance, "Nature and Mission of the Church," 215.

recommendations and guidance in the preparation of the 1953 publication *The Household of God.*

The relative similarity of Newbigin's and Torrance's backgrounds and influences provides an interesting context to investigate the differences and divergences in their respective theological projects. For the purposes of this comparison, our focus will be upon their respective ecclesiologies with particular attention given to how both Newbigin and Torrance utilize a trinitarian grammar when speaking of the church's mission. How do they differ in their understanding of the work of the persons of the Trinity in the church's mission in the world? To answer that question, we turn our attention first to Newbigin.

The best place to identify the concerns that drive Newbigin's doctrine of the Trinity is in *The Relevance of Trinitarian Doctrine for Today's Mission.* This slim volume is the beginning of his reflection on the doctrine of the Trinity, which is found later in expanded form in *The Open Secret: Sketches for a Missionary Theology* and also embedded throughout *The Gospel in a Pluralist Society.* As the starting point of Newbigin's more robust reflection on the Trinity, *The Relevance of Trinitarian Doctrine* gives us the clearest sense of how the Trinity functions within Newbigin's overall thought beyond simple agreement with the historic, orthodox Christian tradition.

Newbigin's ecclesiology is framed by the question of how we can speak of the centrality of God's activity in and through the church and yet also affirm and discern his activity in a seemingly secular world. To answer this question, Newbigin turns to the doctrine of the Trinity,[79] proposing to find there the conceptual framework that can clarify the church's missionary task: "The question of the relation between what God is doing in the mission of the Church and what he is doing in the secular events of history [will not]

---

[79] It is to Newbigin's credit that he intuited this way forward and did so while the Trinity was still understood as a somewhat obscure doctrine. When *The Relevance of Trinitarian Doctrine* was published in 1963, the "trinitarian revival" had not truly begun in the English-speaking world. The volumes of Karl Barth's *Church Dogmatics* were still finding their way into English translation, and Newbigin would not read them for some time. Karl Rahner's *The Trinity* would not be published for another four years. As is typical with Newbigin's writing, he leaves us few clues to any texts that guided this decision (although Wainwright suggests that C. N. Cochrane's *Christianity and Classical Culture* was significant [Wainwright, *Lesslie Newigin: A Theological Life*, 21] and Newbigin appreciatively quotes Leonard Hodgson's *The Doctrine of the Trinity* once at the close of the book. Lesslie Newbigin, *The Relevance of Trinitarian Doctrine for Today's Mission* (Eugene, OR: Wipf & Stock, 2006), 77.

be rightly answered, except within the framework of a fully and explicitly trinitarian doctrine of God."[80] In *The Relevance of Trinitarian Doctrine for Today's Mission*, Newbigin begins by focusing on the person of the Father in the chapter, "Missions and the Shape of World History." Here he distinguishes between the history that is revealed in and around the person of Jesus Christ and "secular" world history. He proposes that the church understand God's action in history according to "God's fatherly rule of all things."[81] The "fatherly rule" controls the church's understanding of human history and its mission in the world, not a supposedly "neutral" secular history. This different history is seen clearly in Jesus, relation to his Father in the Gospels: "From first to last [Jesus] accepts the Father's ordering of events as the form in which his mission, and that of his followers, is to be fulfilled."[82] The Father's providential control of history thus guides the church as it moves through history, often in uncertainty, struggle, and suffering: "Christians do not go through the battles of history as the master race. They go through them as a servant people, looking up to the Father who is alone the Lord of history, accepting his disposition of events as the context of their obedience."[83] For Newbigin, the Father is the one who overrules history.

The christology that Newbigin presents in *The Relevance of Trinitarian Doctrine* proceeds along a similar route. Newbigin is concerned with the breaking up of Christendom and the subsequent privatization of Christian belief and action: "There is a grave danger that the Gospel may be mistaken for a mere offer of individual and private salvation. . . . How are we to understand the secularization of these areas of human life in the light of a Gospel which announces their redemption?"[84] Newbigin's answer to this question builds upon what he has already said about the Father: the Son's existence in a world of authorities, institutions, and social structures is guided providentially by the Father and thus Jesus understands himself as subject to them (in a limited sense) even as they are ultimately subjected to him. This christology provides a framework for understanding the church's relation to secular authority and power in the new secularizing era.

---

[80] Newbigin, *Relevance of Trinitarian Doctrine*, 33.
[81] Newbigin, *Relevance of Trinitarian Doctrine*, 39.
[82] Newbigin, *Relevance of Trinitarian Doctrine*, 39.
[83] Newbigin, *Relevance of Trinitarian Doctrine*, 41.
[84] Newbigin, *Relevance of Trinitarian Doctrine*, 55.

The elements of this description can be summed up in four consecutive points Newbigin makes in *The Relevance of Trinitarian Doctrine*. First, the structures of authority and power that exist are a part of God's original intention for humanity, and the church must therefore understand its own identity in relation to them and their function within God's plan for the ordering of human existence: "The Church, following her Lord, has to accept them as the framework in which her life is to be lived, acknowledging them and fulfilling the specific duties which their proper character requires. They are not subject to the Church and are not to be directly controlled by ecclesiastical power."[85] Second, these structures "have been created through Christ and for Christ."[86] But their initial created purpose has been warped by sin, and therefore they are prone to claim ultimate authority apart from their Creator and end. Third, through his submission to the powers, Christ has accomplished victory for them and ultimately secures their complete subjection, which will be realized at his advent: "His victory is complete; yet we await its completion."[87] Fourth and finally, the church lives in this in-between time bearing witness to Christ's victory and lordship through the actions and words of Christian men and women. Thus Newbigin understands Christ's obedience to provide the framework for understanding the posture of the church in a secularizing age.

Pneumatology and mission in Newbigin and Torrance. Newbigin's reflection on the persons of the Father and the Son leads us to his description of the Holy Spirit. Here he is concerned not so much with the advance of secularization, but instead with a problem peculiar to foreign missions—"the failure of missions to produce, in the measure in which the Gospel should lead us to expect, spontaneously multiplying Christian communities."[88] At the heart of his analysis is the disparity he sees between the "spiritual dependence" of the congregations resulting from the modern missionary movement on the one hand, and the vitality and multiplying energy of the New Testament churches, even in their lack of training and resources, on the other. For Newbigin, this difference is largely reducible

---

[85]Newbigin, *Relevance of Trinitarian Doctrine*, 58.
[86]Newbigin, *Relevance of Trinitarian Doctrine*, 58.
[87]Newbigin, *Relevance of Trinitarian Doctrine*, 59.
[88]Newbigin, *Relevance of Trinitarian Doctrine*, 64.

to pneumatology: "It is not too much to say that the whole 'method' of St Paul . . . rests upon this single point: that the Holy Spirit of God is himself the missionary; that his presence and blessing are recognizable by those who have the Spirit; and that where the Spirit is, there is all the power and all the wisdom and all the grace that man needs or can expect for the [sic] life in Christ."[89]

Newbigin's description of the missionary identity of the Holy Spirit is filled out in *The Open Secret*, which expands in greater detail upon the trinitarian framework first conceived of in *The Relevance of Trinitarian Doctrine*. In *The Open Secret*, Newbigin's pneumatology is informed by his exegesis of the book of Acts. Newbigin notes the centrality of the Spirit's sovereign work at each of the key moments in the first half of Acts: Pentecost, Philip's meeting with the Ethiopian eunuch, Ananias's welcoming of the blinded Saul, Peter's encounter with Cornelius, and the first mission to the Gentiles.

Newbigin draws three principles concerning the Spirit's activity in mission based on this exegesis. First, in its participation in the Spirit's mission, the church is itself changed. The story of Peter's "conversion" to full Gentile inclusion in the people of God is central here; Peter cannot help but be changed as the Spirit leads him into the encounter with Cornelius. Newbigin understands this encounter to be representative of something much more fundamental: "Mission is not just church extension. It is something more costly and more revolutionary. It is the action of the Holy Spirit who in his sovereign freedom both convicts the world (John 16:8-11) and leads the church toward the fullness of truth which it has not yet grasped (John 16:12-15)."[90] Since the Spirit's mission changes not only the world but also the church, the church must constantly remind itself of its secondary place in mission: "Because the Spirit himself is sovereign over the mission, the church can only be the attentive servant. . . . The church's witness is secondary and derivative."[91]

Newbigin's second principle is the Spirit's presence *within* the church. Newbigin notes the use of *arrabon* to describe the Spirit as a kind of "down payment": "The gift of the Spirit is related to the coming of the kingdom as cash-in-advance is related to the full settlement of an account."[92] The Spirit's

---

[89]Newbigin, *Relevance of Trinitarian Doctrine*, 66-67.
[90]Lesslie Newbigin, *The Open Secret: Sketches for a Missionary Theology* (London: SPCK, 1978), 66.
[91]Newbigin, *Open Secret*, 67-68.
[92]Newbigin, *Open Secret*, 70.

presence, and the accompanying fruit of "love, joy, and peace"[93] give the church its character as a foretaste of the consummation of God's kingdom. For Newbigin the Spirit's presence within the church community is profoundly linked to hope. The Spirit serves as the proof that God is indeed at work, giving even now what he has promised to give in full later, and this gives the church hope as it participates in God's mission: "Seen from this point of view, mission might be defined as 'hope in action.' It is the whole way of living, acting, and speaking which arises from the fact that we have already received the first installment of the promised treasure, the first fruit of the promised harvest, and can therefore work and wait with both eagerness and patience for the fullness of what God has promised for his whole creation."[94] The presence of the Spirit gives the church hope, and hope fuels the church's faithfulness in mission.

The third principle Newbigin develops from his exegesis of the New Testament is that the Spirit *precedes* the church in mission. While the Spirit is present in the life of the church, that does not mean that the Spirit is possessed by the church. Instead, the Spirit goes before the church: "It is the Holy Spirit who leads the way, opening a door here which the church must then obediently enter, kindling a flame there which the church must lovingly tend."[95] Here again the meeting of Peter and Cornelius is central for Newbigin. The Spirit works in ways that are unanticipated by the church, calling the church to follow in mission: "In ways of which we have no advance knowledge, God opens the heart of a man or woman to the gospel. The messenger ... may be a stranger, a preacher, a piece of Scripture, a dream, an answered prayer, or a deep experience of joy or sorrow, of danger or deliverance. It was not part of any missionary 'strategy' devised by the church."[96]

Newbigin's reflection on the place of the Holy Spirit in the church's mission throws into relief an aspect of Torrance's theology that we have not yet explored in full. We are already familiar with the fundamental shape of Torrance's ecclesiology and the centrality of the analogy of Christ in the church's missional identity. What place does the Holy Spirit have in the activity of mission?

---

[93]Newbigin, *Open Secret*, 70.
[94]Newbigin, *Open Secret*, 71.
[95]Newbigin, *Open Secret*, 71.
[96]Newbigin, *Open Secret*, 71-72.

At the outset, it is important to emphasize how Torrance's pneumatology is informed by his concerns about the intelligibility of the church's mission. As we saw in our first chapter, Torrance identifies dualism as a significant challenge in the church's communication of the gospel. If the problem of dualism is left unaddressed, then the church's confidence in the knowledge of God and his action in creation is crippled. Torrance's doctrine of the Spirit emphasizes the possibility of real knowledge of God and the actuality of God's presence and activity in the world. Three distinctions will help us understand how Torrance's pneumatology functions with respect to the church's mission.

First, at the center of Torrance's pneumatology is a concern to emphasize how, through the Spirit, God is at work in creation. Without a proper pneumatology, Torrance sees the possibility of two related errors when attempting to understand God's continuing activity in the world. On the one hand, the Holy Spirit is absorbed into the life of the institutional church, a fault he sees manifested particularly in certain strands of Roman Catholic theology. There he sees "a Church which through Christ's testamentary disposition to it of the Spirit is so invested with authority and endowed with grace that it fulfills its mission in history as the divine society authoritatively administering grace to all who will own obedience to its ways."[97] On the other hand, the Spirit might be identified with the "religiosity of human consciousness," an error Torrance sees within the Liberal Protestant tradition. Torrance describes this as "the notion of the Church as the community instinct with the Spirit of Christ which develops from age to age forms of life and worship in which it manifests its own rich and manifold vitality."[98]

These kinds of pneumatologies are made more plausible by what Torrance calls "the diminished belief in the transcendent power and utter Godness of the Creator Spirit," an error made plausible by the epistemological conditions of dualism. Torrance's own doctrine of the Holy Spirit is energized by his conviction that the dualistic framework can and must be overcome through an affirmation of the *homoousion* of the Spirit. This affirmation makes clear the Holy Spirit's divinity in such a way as to affirm his

---

[97]Torrance, "Come, Creator Spirit, for the Renewal of Worship and Witness," in *Theology in Reconstruction* (Eugene, OR: Wipf & Stock, 1996), 244.
[98]Torrance, "Come, Creator Spirit," 244.

power and freedom: "The first thing that must happen to us is a glad subjection to the lordly freedom and majesty of God the Holy Spirit, and a humble readiness for miraculous divine acts that transcend all human possibilities and break through the limitations of anything we can conceive."[99]

The second distinction that must be noted about Torrance's missional pneumatology is that for him, the Holy Spirit's activity is always determined in relation to the person of the Son. Torrance's use of the *homoousios* to move across the epistemological divide supposed by dualistic frameworks functions to make christology the center of our apprehension of God and his activity because there we see God and humanity united in the person of Christ, thus bridging the dualistic gap: "The way which God has taken in Jesus Christ to reveal himself and to reconcile us to himself is the way which we have to make our own in all true understanding and thinking and speaking of him."[100] Therefore reflection upon the Holy Spirit is done with reference to and under the control of christology: "Knowledge of the Spirit as well as of the Father is taken from and is controlled by knowledge of the Son. The Holy Spirit does not bring to us any independent knowledge of God, or add any new content to God's self-revelation."[101]

This understanding of the relation between the Spirit and the Son has implications for the church's mission. Because for Torrance "the doctrine of the Spirit has Christology for its content,"[102] the church as the body of Christ is understood chiefly through christology and only indirectly through pneumatology. Thus, we are to understand the church via the incarnate Son who "sent out His Spirit upon the Church begetting it and assuming its existence in space and time into communion with His own existence in the Body which He assumed for Himself in the Incarnation, and terminating its form and course in space and time in accordance with His own life and work in the Body."[103]

The third and final distinction follows from what has just been considered. Torrance's christocentric pneumatology is, via his christocentric ecclesiology,

---

[99] Torrance, "Come, Creator Spirit," 245.
[100] Torrance, "The Place of Christology in Biblical and Dogmatic Theology," *Theology in Reconstruction* (Eugene, OR: Wipf & Stock, 1996), 128.
[101] Torrance, *The Trinitarian Faith: An Evangelical Theology of the Ancient Catholic Church* (Edinburgh: T&T Clark, 1995), 203.
[102] Torrance, *Royal Priesthood*, 25.
[103] Torrance, *Royal Priesthood*, 25.

a decidedly ecclesiocentric pneumatology, because his pneumatology is controlled by his christology, in the same way that ecclesiology has a controlling influence upon his pneumatology. This subsequently frames the relationship between the Spirit and the church in mission, and the result can be seen in the kind of language Torrance uses to describe mission. The 1966 *Scottish Journal of Theology* article, "The Mission of the Church," is particularly significant here. There Torrance states, "The fact that the Spirit is sent in the Name of Christ means concretely that He operates especially wherever that name is heard and wherever people gather together under that Name, that is, within the sphere of the Church, founded by Christ."[104] The qualification "especially" is present, but it falls within the context of an overwhelmingly ecclesiocentric description of the Spirit's activity. Thus, when describing mission, the concept of the church as the body of Christ is fundamentally central to how the mission is carried out, even as the Spirit is a key role: "The Church is thus the sphere of the Kingdom of Christ and the instrument which He uses in the power of His Spirit to extend His Kingdom to the ends of the earth and the ends of the ages."[105]

The contrast between Newbigin and Torrance reveals how Torrance's ecclesiological formulation unfolds into specific commitments about the nature of the church's ministry. The way that Torrance's trinitarian grammar serves as the foundation of the Spirit's activity leads him to a doctrine of ministry that protects the church as central sphere of the Spirit's work. We can expect this to result in an understanding of the church's ministry in which the preaching of the Word and the sacraments are the central venues through which the Spirit's activity takes place, an anticipation that we will find confirmed in the following chapter. While this is in many ways a traditionally Reformed doctrine of ministry in its emphasis upon the "ordinary means of grace," it nonetheless contrasts with a number of recent missional ecclesiologies of a similar strain to Newbigin's that are primarily concerned with tracing the Spirit's activity outside of the church.[106] The resulting doctrine of ministry of these ecclesiologies revolves around identifying the work

---

[104] Torrance, "Mission of the Church," 133.
[105] Torrance, "Mission of the Church," 138.
[106] "The church is the Spirit's primary means for mission, but there are abundant examples in church history of the Spirit's work ahead of the church's missional efforts." Ross Hastings, *Missional God, Missional Church*, 304.

of the Spirit so the church may then join in with God's work. While the strengths of Torrance's position—its internal consistency, its trinitarian structure, and the way in which it guards against irresponsible speculation about the work of the Spirit—are clear, it is purchased at the cost of the external momentum that we see in Newbigin.

It is important to consider what this assessment reveals about Torrance's ecclesiology. In his recent dissertation, Albert Shepherd suggests that Torrance's ecclesiology is hampered by the "material inflation of Christology"[107] within Torrance's wider theological system. As we have seen, the main contrast between Newbigin and Torrance can be found in the way that the exclusivity of christological categories in Torrance's thought prevents the kind of pneumatological and thus ecclesiological dynamism that we find in Newbigin. Torrance's aforementioned statement that "the doctrine of the Spirit has Christology for its content,"[108] is indicative of this tendency within Torrance's thought, as is the resultant circumscription of the work of the Spirit to Christ's body, the church. To note this aspect of Torrance's ecclesiology is not to ascribe it with a fatal flaw; Torrance's use of christology within his ecclesiology not only allows him to properly coordinate divine and human relations but also coordinates the church's ministry with that of the ascended Jesus. It is, however, to note that Torrance's does not at this juncture display that kind of proportionality that would allow his theological architectonic to honor the witness of Scripture in all of its complexities, a point illuminated by the contrast with Newbigin's exegesis of the book of Acts.

We have thus far traced Torrance's ecclesiology in an effort to explain what we might be called the "mediate" cause of the church's mission. The analogy of the body of Christ is an analogy that frames the church's existence in such a way that, in its relation to Christ, it can only understand itself as being given a call to mission that reaches down to the very foundation of its being: "That is why the Church is so concerned with world-mission, for her very foundations rest upon it. She draws her life from the new humanity in Christ. She is in faith what one day she will be, and now her life-movement

---

[107] Albert Shepherd, "The Body of Christ: T. F. Torrance's Ecclesial Ontology" (PhD diss., University of Aberdeen, 2015), 294.
[108] Torrance, *Royal Priesthood*, 25.

consists in becoming what she actually is in Christ."[109] We may call this a "mediate" relationship because it describes the church's mission with respect to its ultimate source in the person of Jesus Christ. While the case Torrance makes for the "mediate" source is one that he makes in the strongest possible terms, it is not the only way he attempts to establish the church's identity and its mission. We now turn to the "immediate" catalyst for the church's mission: the deposit of faith.

THE DEPOSIT OF FAITH

The deposit of faith may at first glance appear like a curious place to locate a doctrine of mission. When he utilizes the term, Torrance is referring to a doctrinal concept that finds its source in the apostle Paul and other biblical authors and often refers to a succinct and dense summary of the Christian faith important in the early transmission of the gospel. Torrance cites Jude 3 ("the faith that was once for all delivered to the saints") and 1 Timothy 6:20 ("O Timothy, guard the deposit entrusted to you") among other passages as the biblical foundations of the deposit of faith.[110] Tracing the deposit of faith to the apostles and to the earliest Christian communities is often an important aspect of the doctrine. Within the theological tradition, the concept is usually used as a way of explaining the formation of the canon or as a defense of the integrity of the development of early Christian theology (often alongside an argument for apostolic succession). In Torrance we see elements of all of these aspects of the deposit of faith, but as we shall see, the concept is also an element of his understanding of mission. To understand this properly, we need first to understand how the deposit of faith functions in his theology broadly.

In 1983, Torrance published three essays on the deposit of faith: one giving a general orientation to the topic,[111] another addressed particularly to the context of the Church of Scotland,[112] and a last piece formulated as a part

---

[109]Torrance, "Mission of the Church," 221.
[110]Torrance, "The Deposit of Faith," *Scottish Journal of Theology* 36.1 (1983): 2. He also cites the following: 1 Timothy 4:6; 2 Timothy 1:12-14, 2:2,4, 4:3; Titus 1:9, 13; 2 Thessalonians 2:15, 3:6; Galatians 1:9, 2:2,9; 1 Corinthians 11:23, 15:3; 2 Corinthians 11:2-4; Romans 6:7 (although it is likely Torrance intended to cite 6:17); Hebrews 3:1, 4:14, 10:23.
[111]Torrance, "Deposit of Faith," 1-18.
[112]Torrance, "'The Substance of the Faith': A Clarification of the Concept in the Church of Scotland," *Scottish Journal of Theology* 36.3 (1983): 327-338.

of the dialogue with the Orthodox churches.[113] The concept is present in Torrance's early work in the ecumenical movement and the accompanying writings on ecclesiology and missiology before this point. But 1983 is significant for Torrance as he was at the time heavily involved in ecumenical dialogue with the Orthodox churches on the doctrine of the Trinity. This dialogue seems to have precipitated further reflection on the subject of the deposit of faith. Torrance describes the deposit of faith as "the original *datum* of divine Revelation in Jesus Christ and his Gospel upon which the very existence of the Church as the Body of Christ in the world depended, and which exercised a regulative force in all its witness, preaching and teaching."[114] Thus for Torrance—as for the great Christian tradition—the concept of the deposit of faith is understood to have a regulative effect on Christian teaching and catechetical instruction and historical significance in its role in the formation of the New Testament canon.[115] This importance is derived from the deposit's identity with the apostolic teaching and its own source in the teaching of Jesus Christ himself.

For Torrance, however, the term has a greater theological nuance beyond this general definition. The deposit of faith is not merely a listing of propositional truths that provide a basis for logical agreement or disagreement with other truth statements. Instead, the deposit of faith has a much deeper and direct relationship with the person of Jesus Christ: "In the last analysis 'the Deposit of Faith' ... is to be understood as the whole living Fact of Christ and his saving Acts in the indivisible unity of his Person, Word and Life, as through the Resurrection and Pentecost he fulfilled and unfolded the content of his self-revelation as Savior and Lord within his Church."[116] Thus the deposit of faith is really to be understood in two complementary ways (or as Torrance phrases it, as "spanning two levels"). In its most fundamental sense as an "informal and undefined"[117] body of knowledge, which is "identical with

---

[113] Torrance, "The Trinitarian Foundation and Character of Faith and Authority in the Church," in *Theological Dialogue Between Reformed and Orthodox Churches*, ed. Thomas F. Torrance (Edinburgh: Scottish Academic Press, 1985), 121-156. Note that the publication date is 1985 but the essay was prepared for a 1983 meeting of the Reformed-Orthodox dialogue in Geneva.

[114] Torrance, "Deposit of Faith," 1.

[115] Torrance, "Deposit of Faith," 13.

[116] Torrance, "Deposit of Faith," 2.

[117] Torrance, "Deposit of Faith," 1.

the whole saving Event of the incarnate, crucified and risen Son of God,"[118] and, in a second sense, as the resulting effect when the former sense of the deposit is received faithfully and becomes authoritative for the apostles. As recipients of the revelation of Jesus Christ, the apostles are given a significant place in the economy of revelation and the foundation of the church: "People may have access to the Deposit of Faith only in the form which, under the creative impact of the risen Lord and his Spirit, it has assumed once and for all in the Apostolic Tradition, i.e., through the Apostolic preaching and interpretation of the Gospel."[119] These two senses of the deposit of faith are inseparable, but the latter is to be understood as self-consciously and necessarily referential to the former; "it was made to point away from itself to Christ."[120] The deposit, as we receive it through the apostolic tradition, is understood in its reference to the "Fact of Christ."

What does Torrance's doctrine of the deposit of faith tell us? First, Torrance is clearly concerned that certain conceptions of the deposit—and Christian doctrine more generally—introduce a deleterious gap between theological statements and the God to whom they refer. Here as in so many places, Torrance is concerned with dualism. This is especially clear in his critique of Roman Catholic understandings of the deposit of faith: "So far as the Roman Catholic Church was concerned, the ultimate identity of the Deposit of the Faith with the Saving Event of Christ clothed with his Gospel tended to fall into the background, which had the effect of an unbalanced stress upon the embodiment of the Faith in the Church."[121] Torrance does not only subject Roman Catholics to this criticism; the "Evangelical Churches" (Protestant Churches), are just as guilty. Above all, Torrance is concerned with the creation of a system of doctrine that loses its confessional and referential quality and thus no longer points away from its second-level quality and to the first level of identity with the "whole living Fact of Christ." In conceiving of the deposit of faith in the way that he does, Torrance connects Christian doctrine to the living God in a way that avoids the kinds of dualisms and bifurcations that give him such concern.

---

[118]Torrance, "Deposit of Faith," 14.
[119]Torrance, "Deposit of Faith," 2.
[120]Torrance, "Deposit of Faith," 15.
[121]Torrance, "Deposit of Faith," 16-17.

Second, Torrance's conception of the deposit of faith describes how the church is maintained and renewed. The complementary and cognate "levels" of the deposit of faith mean that it is through this medium that the church encounters her Lord who rejuvenates and revitalizes her. Here he appeals to Irenaeus, who is in many ways the foremost theologian of the deposit: "Thus regarded the Deposit of Faith in which that living Truth is embodied in the Church is what Irenaeus in a famous passage spoke of as 'the deposit which by the Spirit of God always rejuvenates itself and rejuvenates the vessel in which it is lodged' (i.e., the Church)."[122] The deposit is "'the charismatic principle' of the Church's renewal and continuity in history";[123] a medium in which the church encounters her Lord in the power of the Spirit. It is in relation to the deposit of faith—and through it in relation to the living Lord Jesus Christ—that the church finds the source of her life and is thus renewed.

To review, Torrance's concept of the deposit of faith functions as a way of describing both the "whole living Fact of Christ" and also the reception of his person by the apostles in such a way that it has a regulative effect in the life of the church. These two levels are coordinate with one another, with the latter pointing away from itself and toward the person of Jesus Christ. Thus, the deposit of faith avoids separating its confession from its Lord and provides for the revitalization of the church's life by providing the medium for the church to encounter the source of her life in the power of the Spirit.

In order to understand the importance of the term for Torrance's understanding of mission, we must focus on a central aspect of the deposit of faith: the concept of apostolicity. A key discussion of apostolicity occurs in *Royal Priesthood*, just after Torrance finishes the exegesis that undergirds the *soma/pleroma* argument we have already examined. Here Torrance uses the language of "the Apostolic Revelation" instead of deposit of faith, but it is clear from Torrance's description of the apostolic revelation that it is ultimately the same concept:

> It is not any new revelation or any new interpretation added to it [the self-revelation of God in Jesus Christ] or put upon the object Revelation in the

---

[122]Torrance, "Deposit of Faith," 16-17.
[123]Torrance, "Deposit of Faith," 5.

historical Christ, but the actual unfolding of the Mind of the risen Lord within His Church, the *pleroma* of the incarnational Revelation through His Spirit. The apostles thus formed the definite medium in our flesh and blood where the unfolding of the Mind of Christ was met by inspired witness and translated into the language of the flesh, the medium where, as it were, the Revelation of Christ through the Spirit became earthed in the Church as the Body of Christ, became rooted in humanity.[124]

In describing the deposit of faith through the lens of the "Apostolic Revelation," the category of mission is thrown into relief. The concept provides a link between the life, ministry, and mission of the incarnate Son and the corresponding mission of the church. The apostolic revelation is the crucial link between the "mediate" grounding of mission in the analogy of Christ and its "immediate" source in the church's life. Torrance uses the language of the apostles as "hinges": "In this way the Apostles formed the *hinges* of the divine mission, where, so to speak, the vertical mission in the sending of the Son by the Father, is folded out horizontally into history at Pentecost."[125] But this hinge is fixed upon the apostles and in particular the apostolic revelation. The apostles "are the hinges between the incarnational Revelation objectively given in Christ, and the unfolding of that once for all in the mind of the Church as the Body of Christ."[126] The particular nature of the apostolic revelation is what gives shape to and provides the immediate impetus for the church's mission in the world.

Torrance's use of the concept of the apostolic revelation understands mission to be essential to the meaning of apostleship and thus to the deposit of faith.[127] There are three implications that follow from Torrance's emphasis of the apostolic nature of the deposit of faith. First, this recasting of apostleship places the concept of apostolic succession in a different light. Many traditional understandings of apostolic succession have understood the concept as a way of describing and safeguarding the church's faithfulness and true identity in the Spirit's maintenance of the continuity of bishops from the time of the apostles up to the present. But for Torrance, it is to be

---

[124]Torrance, *Royal Priesthood*, 27.
[125]Torrance, *Royal Priesthood*, 27.
[126]Torrance, *Royal Priesthood*, 28.
[127]For a similar account, see Kevin Chiarot, "T. F. Torrance and Apostolic Succession," *Participatio* 6 (2017): 131-137.

conceived of as faithfulness to the apostolic mission. Torrance writes in the essay "Amsterdam—The Nature and Mission of the Church," "That is surely the real substance of the apostolic succession, continuity in the perpetual Ministry of the Risen and Ever-Present Christ. It is by faith and witness to this Lord that the Church is preserved and constantly recreated—by the very Word of the Gospel which she proclaims."[128]

Second, Torrance's understanding of the apostolic revelation once again reinforces the intrinsic connection between the church and its mission. We have already noted that Torrance appeals to Irenaeus's description of how the deposit of faith is the means of God's renewal and rejuvenation of the church. In Torrance's earlier writings on the mission of the church, the same concept is at work in the perspective of the apostolic revelation. And here the language is much stronger—the apostolic revelation/deposit of faith does not simply rejuvenate the church; it constitutes its existence. Torrance writes,

> This then is the Church Catholic because and in so far as she lives by the apostolic Gospel through the power of the Holy Ghost she partakes of the fulness of Him who fills all things. To engage in the Mission of this Gospel belongs to the very nature and life of the Church for "the relation between Gospel and Church is not merely consequential but integral and constitutive." . . . Therefore to halt that mission, to restrict or limit the Gospel, is to sever the apostolic succession, to destroy the life-movement of the Church, to deprive her of the Holy Ghost.[129]

It is in the act of mission, an act that is in essence the foundation of the church in the apostolic revelation/deposit of faith, that the church is revitalized by the Holy Spirit and is rejuvenated in her very nature: "That is why the Church is so concerned with world-mission, for her very foundations rest upon it."[130]

The same point is made in a more muted tone by Torrance in his christology lectures given at New College. In the course of describing the four attributes of the church found in the Apostle's Creed (one, holy, catholic,

---

[128] Torrance, "Amsterdam—The Nature and Mission of the Church," in *Conflict and Agreement in the Church*, vol. 1, 214-215.
[129] Torrance, "Amsterdam—The Nature and Mission of the Church," 215.
[130] Torrance, "Amsterdam—The Nature and Mission of the Church," 221.

apostolic), Torrance comments on the apostolic nature of the church: "In the continued mission of the church going out from the apostles into history, the church is given a continued ministry, dependent on that of the apostles, through which the church in history continues to be schooled in the apostolic gospel, and continues to be obedient to it as it is transmitted through the apostolic tradition of the New Testament."[131] A church that is apostolic is a church that continues to live in accordance with its foundation upon the ministry of the apostles.[132]

Third, this apostolic revelation functions as the definitive source of the church's relationship to its head, thereby securing the analogy of Christ, which is central to Torrance's ecclesiology and his understanding of the church's mission. At the ascension, Christ withdrew his flesh from sight and thus the church cannot merely look to the vicissitudes of history to know and obey its Lord: "By ascension Christ has withdrawn Himself from the visible succession of history, and at once sends us back to the Apostolic witness to Him."[133] It must look to where Jesus reveals himself in order to locate and understand the analogy by which it understands itself. Now Christ "sends us back to the Apostolic witness to Him. . . . It is as the Church is directed back to the Apostolic witness that the ascended Christ gathers up the Church to Himself and incorporates it into Himself as His Body."[134] It is only by looking to the apostolic revelation that the church can understand its true identity as the body of Christ.

The deposit of faith—and in particular his interpretation of this concept through the lens of the apostolic revelation—serves an important role in demonstrating the intrinsic relationship between the church and its mission in Torrance's thought. The apostolic revelation serves as the "hinge" between the divine mission of the incarnate Son and the church's necessarily correspondent and subsequent mission. Through the apostolic revelation, the

---

[131]Torrance, *Atonement*, 396.
[132]Barth makes a similar argument in his section on "The Being of the Community" in IV/1 of the *Church Dogmatics*. His discussion of the church's being is framed by the four attributes of the church (one, holy, catholic, and apostolic church), noting especially the significance of the apostolic nature of the church for its mission: "As an apostolic Church the Church can never in any respect be an end in itself, but, following the existence of the apostles, it exists only as it exercises the ministry of a herald." Barth, *CD* IV/1, 724.
[133]Torrance, *Royal Priesthood*, 28.
[134]Torrance, *Royal Priesthood*, 28.

true nature of apostolic succession is understood, the necessary relationship between the church and its mission is once again emphasized, and the shape of the analogy of Christ, so important in Torrance's ecclesiology, is secured.

Torrance's use of the apostolic deposit not only demonstrates the missional logic of his ecclesiology, but is also a unique contribution to recent discussions on the nature of apostolicity. Within the ecumenical and mission movements, the nature of apostolicity remains a particularly contentious issue. In his learned and exhaustive exploration of apostolicity, John Flett traces the way in which certain uses of the concept have proven to be a stumbling block in the translation of the gospel in missionary endeavors as different cultures attempt to appropriate the message into newly formed ecclesial structures.[135] Apostolicity is in these situations defined by way of historical continuity in terms of ecclesial structure or liturgical uniformity: "Dominant accounts of apostolicity employ culture as the mode of the church's historical continuity."[136] Problems arise when an apostolicity so closely identified with aspects of the "sending" culture meets a new culture.

Flett's constructive proposal identifies apostolicity in a way that resonates with Torrance's use of the concept: "Apostolic authority is corporate and centers on the process of the Gospel's appropriation, and while the apostle has a particular task, this both derives from and shares in the community's constitution—its being in Christ Jesus in the power of the Spirit. Apostolic authority resides in the conversion of this body to Jesus Christ."[137] While Torrance's understanding of apostolicity is not attuned to the issues of cross-cultural communication in the same way as Flett and is relatively slim in its description, it is nonetheless clear that both Flett and Torrance are utilizing the concept in very similar ways. Flett's study is the most complete exploration of apostolicity that has of yet been produced, and yet he makes no mention of Torrance in his work. While Torrance's writings on this concept are easily overshadowed by his extensive work on the Trinity, the theological dialogue with science, and christology, his contribution here is an important and significant contribution to the current discussion on apostolicity and

---

[135]John G. Flett, *Apostolicity: The Ecumenical Question in World Christian Perspective* (Downers Grove, IL: IVP Academic, 2016).
[136]Flett, *Apostolicity*, 53.
[137]Flett, *Apostolicity*, 291.

its significance of ecclesiology, one that has not yet been noted and drawn into wider conversation.

Conclusion

In 1949, at the beginning of his theological career, Torrance wrote, "To restrict the Gospel would be to cut the roots of the Church from the resurrected Body of Christ, and therefore to cut the roots of the Church from humanity. It would be to sin against the Incarnation, to fight against the Cross, and to rebel against the will of God to bring all men under its redeeming power."[138] This statement amounts to a robust call for the church to rediscover its inherently missional nature. Over the next ten years as Torrance's ecclesiology developed, this same emphasis of the intrinsic connection between the church and its mission continued. The nature of the church is missional both in its "mediate" identity as it understands itself by way of the analogy of Christ and also in its "immediate" relation to the deposit of faith. What results is a formidable contribution to the many missional ecclesiologies that have been proposed as of late, providing a clear doctrinal basis for the church's missional nature that is set within a wider theological architectonic. Having described Torrance's argument, we now turn to investigate the shape of the body of Christ's ministry as it participates in the work of its ascended head, Jesus Christ.

---

[138] Flett, *Apostolicity*, 291.

4

The Ministry of the Ascended Lord

THE CHURCH'S PARTICIPATION IN CHRIST'S KINGLY OFFICE

⊕

TORRANCE'S UNDERSTANDING OF the church's mission and ministry is built upon the foundation he has already laid in his christology and in particular his discussion of the *munus triplex*. The decision to draw christology, ecclesiology, and the mediation of Christ's work together is informed by a desire to avoid two opposite but related errors. Torrance is concerned, on the one hand, with the simple identification of Christ with the church's ministry: "There can be *no relation of identity* between the ministry of the Church and the ministry of Christ."[1] The error here, which Torrance sees in the Roman Catholic Church,[2] is to make too little of a distinction between the ministry Christ exercised in the incarnation and the activity of the church: "The ministry of the Church is in no sense an extension of the ministry of Christ or a prolongation of certain of His ministerial functions.

---

[1] Thomas F. Torrance, *Royal Priesthood: A Theology of Ordained Ministry* (Edinburgh: T&T Clark, 1955), 37.

[2] An example of this criticism can be found in Torrance's concern about the concept of the *corpus mysticum* in Roman Catholic thought. While Torrance sees some promise in the work of Roman Catholic contemporaries, he nonetheless considers it to fall short of the development needed within the tradition. His thoughts on the 1943 encyclical *Mystici Corpus Christi* are demonstrative: "The encyclical rightly rejects a separation between the Church mystical and the Church juridical, but when it goes on to identify outright the mystery of the Church with the ecclesiastical institution, it provides a signal illustration of the dialectic noted [a failure to hold in proper relation divine and ecclesial action]." Torrance, *Royal Priesthood*, 62n1.

This is the view that leads to very wrong notions of Eucharistic Sacrifice as an extension of Christ's own priestly sacrifice in the Eucharist, and to wrong notions of priesthood as the prolongation of His Priesthood in the ministry."[3] The opposite error is to separate the church's ministry from Christ totally: "On the other hand, the ministry of the Church is *not another ministry* different from the ministry of Christ, or separable from it."[4] This is to distinguish too sharply between the church and its head, an ecclesiology deeply at odds with Torrance's conception of the church as the "body of Christ": "The apostolic Church does not act instead of Christ, but He is present in the Church, and though distinct from its ministry acts in and through it, making it His own."[5] By utilizing the concept of the church as the body of Christ and understanding Christ's threefold office as the framework for the church's ministry, Torrance accomplishes two things. First, he establishes the church's place within the economy of salvation revealed in Jesus Christ, utilizing the same vocabulary that he has elsewhere used in discussing the mediation of God's grace: the particular, historical shape of Christ's action in his prophetic, priestly, and kingly roles. And second, the church's mission and ministry are understood in the christological grammar that serve as the foundation of his ecclesiology: "It is now clear that, as the ministry is grounded upon the whole relation of the Church to Christ, the doctrine of the ministry must be formulated in terms of the Christological pattern."[6] The logic is straightforward, though not without distinction: from Christ to church to the church's ministry.

Alongside Torrance's christological understanding of the church and its ministry, we again see the significance of Jesus' ascension. It seems that at the end of his earthly ministry, Jesus is no longer present to the church and therefore that christological reflection—particularly on the nature of his mediatorial work as revealed in the economy—is only of limited usefulness to the church's practice of mission and ministry. But, as we have already seen in chapter two, the ascension serves to secure the continued meaning and effectiveness of Jesus' work: "The ascension means, therefore, that the risen Lord directs all our gaze back to the historical Jesus and forward to the

---

[3] Torrance, *Royal Priesthood*, 37.
[4] Torrance, *Royal Priesthood*, 37.
[5] Torrance, "Amsterdam—The Nature and Mission of the Church," in *Conflict and Agreement in the Church*, vol. 1 (Eugene, OR: Wipf & Stock, 1959), 132.
[6] Torrance, *Royal Priesthood*, 35.

coming Jesus. It directs all our gaze to the historical Jesus because it is on the ground of His Incarnation and the work of His Incarnation in atonement that the Risen Christ insists on making contact with us."[7] The ascension instructs us that "the past is fully present reality."[8] Thus the ascension invites the church to fix its attention upon the historical Jesus as the source of its own self-reflection upon its activity and, more significantly, the reality that continues to ground its life and its mission.

The event of the ascension, however, is also indicative of a slight alteration in Torrance's conception of Christ's ministry as it is framed by the *munus triplex*. When the threefold office is understood by way of the lens of chronology of the incarnate Son's earthly career, its order is prophet-priest-king. This organization of the offices coordinates with the unfolding of Jesus' mission, who ministered first through his public teaching, then through his passion and self-offering to the Father, and then finally ascended as the exalted Son so that he might reign from the right hand of the Father.[9] Thus for Torrance, the ascension is the full inauguration of Jesus into the kingly office: "It is with his ascension that Jesus Christ was fully installed in his kingly Ministry.... It is with his exaltation to the throne of God and his sitting at the right hand of God that his kingly ministry properly began."[10] In light of this reality, the aforementioned order of the offices is now reversed.[11] "It is evidently with another order that we have to work: King, Priest and Prophet."[12] This does not mean that the prophetic or priestly offices come to an end, but rather that they are by necessity transformed in their unity with the royal office as it is brought to fulfillment: "His kingly ministry is supreme from ascension to *parousia*, but within that his ministry as Priest and Prophet is no less evident than before, for it is brought to fullness in the consummation of his Kingship; the priesthood of Christ is a Royal Priesthood, and the proclamation of Christ is a Royal Proclamation."[13]

---

[7] Torrance, *Royal Priesthood*, 58.
[8] Torrance, *Royal Priesthood*, 58.
[9] Torrance, *Space, Time and Resurrection* (Edinburgh: T&T Clark, 2019), 106.
[10] Torrance, *Space, Time and Resurrection*, 106.
[11] Herman Bavinck similarly makes note of the difference between Christ's exercise of his threefold office in humiliation and his exercise of the office in exaltation. See Herman Bavinck, *Reformed Dogmatics: Sin and Salvation in Christ*, ed. John Bolt, trans. John Vriend, vol. 3 (Grand Rapids, MI: Baker Academic, 2006), 364-368, 475-482.
[12] Torrance, *Space, Time and Resurrection*, 106.
[13] Torrance, *Space, Time and Resurrection*, 106-107.

Torrance gives a description of this subtle alteration of each of the offices in his reflection upon the significance of the ascension in *Space, Time and Resurrection*. It is important to note that Torrance does not believe there is a fundamental difference between the material content of the mediation of salvation in Jesus' earthly career and after the ascension. The mission of the incarnate Son is central to Torrance's description and methodology. The difference is rather a difference of shape and emphasis, one that Torrance understands as a consequence of the completion of that earthly mission. The completion of Jesus' earthly career and the ascension create new conditions for the ongoing work of Christ: "The ascension involves the veiling of his divine majesty and power, or the holding back, from our visible and physical contact in space and time, of his unveiled majesty and power."[14] While we will return to each of these offices as they are examined in depth, it is helpful to consider them together as a way of introducing Torrance's thought here.

THE ASCENSION AND THE THREEFOLD OFFICE OF CHRIST

The kingly ministry. In light of the ascension, the kingly ministry is understood to be first. Indeed, as we have already seen, the ascension is understood as an expression of Christ's kingly work. However, this emphasis upon the royal work of Christ does not lead Torrance to give a lengthy and thick description of this office in its differentiation from the priestly and prophetic offices. The reason for this is found in the nature of the ascension event: the "veiling of the divine majesty," which is an implication of the ascension, is accompanied by a kind of veiling of the type of redemptive activity that Torrance associates with the kingly office. "The ascension of Jesus Christ to the throne of God was the enthronement of the Word made flesh. . . . It was the inauguration of His Kingdom in which 'God gave him to be head over all things to the church, which is his body' (Eph 1.22). But until the *parousia* He holds back the epiphany of Glory."[15]

While the Lord "waits to be gracious"[16] in the time after the ascension and before the final parousia, the kingly ministry of Jesus Christ is exercised by way of the priestly office: "He exercises His Kingdom only through His

---

[14]Torrance, *Space, Time and Resurrection*, 112.
[15]Torrance, *Royal Priesthood*, 61.
[16]Torrance, *Royal Priesthood*, 61.

Priesthood, bestowing His Spirit upon the Church that the proclamation of the Word of the Cross may be power of God unto salvation to all who believe."[17] Thus, for Torrance, the ascension not only secures for the church the continued ministry of Christ, but also gives concrete expression to the particular mode of that presence. Christ reigns as priest: "Even in ascension the power of God is exercised through his sacrifice, through his atoning expiation of guilt, through his priestly mediation before God."[18] It is important to note that Torrance is not emptying the post-ascension kingly office of all of its content. Christ's kingly rule does indicate the reality of the victory Jesus has accomplished, the kingdom he has established, and his continued government over the church and all of creation: "In his ascension Christ is installed as Head of the New Humanity, the Prince of the New Creation, the King of the Kingdom which he has won and established through his incarnate life and passion.... Henceforth all things are directed from the mercy-seat of God, by the enthroned and exalted Lamb, who reigns not only over the Church, but over all creation."[19] But the specific character of this rule is controlled by the priestly office until the time of Christ's second advent, at which time Christ's authority will be fully realized.[20]

The priestly ministry. The priestly office is transformed by the royal office insofar as Christ's ascension is the vindication of the singular nature of Christ's priestly work: "Here liturgical act is identical with kingly act, for what Jesus Christ does on our behalf is actually fulfilled with final power, whereas other priesthood at the very best can only symbolize it or bear witness to it."[21] But the ascension not only demonstrates that Christ has indeed carried out his priestly work; it also secures the ongoing nature of the priestly office: "The resurrection and ascension, however, do not mean that Christ's priestly office and oblation of himself are over and done with, but rather that in their once and for all completion they are taken up eternally into the life of God, and remain prevalent, efficacious, valid, or abidingly real."[22] Torrance goes on to describe the nature of that continuing priestly work of the ascended Christ in three ways.

---

[17]Torrance, *Royal Priesthood*, 61.
[18]Torrance, *Space, Time and Resurrection*, 112.
[19]Torrance, *Space, Time and Resurrection*, 112.
[20]Torrance, *Royal Priesthood*, 59-60.
[21]Torrance, *Space, Time and Resurrection*, 114.
[22]Torrance, *Space, Time and Resurrection*, 114-115.

First, Torrance notes the "endless self-oblation" of Christ. This self-oblation is Jesus' continual presentation of himself before the Father as the one who has united himself to humanity on our behalf: "He presents himself before the Father as the Redeemer who has united himself to us and has become our Brother. He represents us before the Father as those who are incorporated in him and consecrated and perfected together with him in one forever."[23] Torrance's description here, and in particular the footnoted reference to his essay, "The Paschal Mystery of Christ and the Eucharist," indicates the significance of the concept of the "vicarious humanity of Jesus" for Torrance's understanding of the ongoing work of the priestly office. The connection between Jesus' vicarious humanity and the priestly office that is implicit in Torrance's brief description of Jesus' endless self-oblation is made explicit in that essay.[24] Having taken up our humanity before the Father in the post-resurrection continuation of the hypostatic union, Christ continues to offer his completed work to the Father.

Second, Torrance describes "his eternal intercession or advocacy for us."[25] Here Torrance takes the framework supplied by the vicarious humanity of Jesus Christ and moves it from its cultic context into one that deals more concretely with the content and implications of Jesus' earthly existence. The discussion centers upon "the vicarious life of Jesus in obedience and prayer, and the fact that the whole existence of the incarnate Son was both the fulfilled intervention of God among men and the fulfilled response of men toward God, in filial obedience, faith, trust, love, worship, prayer and praise."[26] This is the application of the description of Jesus' incarnate life as a "priestly prayer" that we note in chapter two. Here, in what is no doubt a reference to his understanding of the fundamental unity of the priestly and prophetic offices, Torrance emphasizes the ontological aspect (i.e., the "*Goel-redemption*"[27] aspect) of that priestly work of prayer and intercession. The priestly work is not only substitutionary—it is also a work of representation:

---

[23]Torrance, *Space, Time and Resurrection*, 115.
[24]"The key to understanding the Eucharist is to be sought in the *vicarious humanity of Jesus, the priesthood of the incarnate Son*." Torrance, "The Paschal Mystery of Christ and the Eucharist," in *Theology in Reconciliation* (Eugene, OR: Wipf & Stock, 1996), 110 (emphasis original).
[25]Torrance, *Space, Time and Resurrection*, 115.
[26]Torrance, *Space, Time and Resurrection*, 115.
[27]Torrance, *Space, Time and Resurrection*, 116.

"Here is an Advocacy in which Christ is the eternal Leader of our prayer and intercession, in which he makes himself the true content and sole reality of the worship and prayer of man."[28] Thus, for Torrance, Christ's work of intercession and advocacy is not only done for us, but is also done in us through Christ's vicarious humanity: "As substitute as well as representative he acts in our place and offers worship and prayer which we could not offer, yet offers them in such a vicarious way that while in our stead and on our behalf they are made to issue out of our human nature to the Father as our own worship and prayer to God."[29] Torrance goes on to apply this to eucharistic worship and prayer, a discussion to which we will return later in this chapter.

Third and finally, Torrance understands the continuing priestly work of Christ to be a work of "eternal benediction." Christ's ascension was accompanied by the act of blessing his people, an act fulfilled in the gift of the Holy Spirit. This act of blessing is to be understood in light of the Old Testament and in particular Melchizedek's blessing of Abraham and the Aaronic blessing that took place on the Day of Atonement.[30] In the New Testament, Christ's high priestly blessing is demonstrated at Pentecost, which is "the content and actualization of that high priestly blessing. He ascended in order to fill all things with his presence and to bestow gifts of the Spirit upon men."[31] Thus, for Torrance, Christ's high priestly blessing is fundamentally an empowering of the church for mission. This aspect of Christ's high priestly work is also relevant to the church's worship and in particular to the Lord's Table, because for Torrance it is at the table that the church is constituted for mission: "In the ordering of the Eucharist, and for the Church at the Eucharist, special *charismata* or gifts are given. It is made clear in the twelfth chapter [of 1 Corinthians] that the Lord's Supper and the *charismata* belong inseparably together."[32] The Eucharist is significant for Torrance's understanding of the church's mission because it is at the table that, through the Spirit, the church is renewed in the reality of its union with Christ. And it is that union that gives the church its proper identity as being included in Christ's high priestly ministry: "It is through the Church's *koinonia* with

---

[28]Torrance, *Space, Time and Resurrection*, 116.
[29]Torrance, *Space, Time and Resurrection*, 117.
[30]Torrance, *Space, Time and Resurrection*, 117.
[31]Torrance, *Space, Time and Resurrection*, 118.
[32]Torrance, *Royal Priesthood*, 65.

Christ that various gifts are distributed to members of the Church which in their manifold character and working together in the one Body are made to echo the one Priesthood of Christ. The Church is thus also a 'royal priesthood' on earth through the Spirit, but a royal priesthood in a secondary sense, participating in the one Priesthood of the ascended King."[33]

Torrance's description of Christ's priestly office in light of the ascension serves to further emphasize the significance of the priestly office in his thought and its centrality within his understanding of the *munus triplex*. It receives what is easily the most extensive description of the offices. As Torrance considers Christ's continued exercise of the priestly office after the ascension, he also makes clear the connection between the priestly office and the vicarious humanity of Christ and the church's eucharistic worship. The significance of these two doctrines for Torrance's understanding of the church's ministry will be explored later in this chapter.

The prophetic ministry. Just as the ascension secures the ongoing exercise of Jesus' priestly office, it in the same way also secures the continuation of Jesus' work as expressed through the prophetic office. As we have already seen, the double mediation between God and humanity that takes place in Jesus is important to Torrance's account of the prophetic office. Jesus fulfills the prophetic office as the Word who is mediator both from God to humanity and from humanity to God: "He is Prophet in a unique sense, for he is in himself the Word he proclaims . . . Christ ascended, then, as the Word made flesh, as he is both Word from God and word from man to God. . . . It is in that identity of Word of God and Word of man that Christ's prophetic ministry is fulfilled."[34] This description of the prophetic office is connected to Torrance's unique use of *goel* redemption as the content of the prophetic ministry.

The double mediation that takes place in the prophetic office is taken up in Christ's ascension as his prophetic ministry is fulfilled at the end of his earthly career. But in light of the ascension and the full inauguration of the kingly ministry, the prophetic ministry again moves from God to humanity. What results is a kind of triple mediation: God's Word to humanity, the perfect word from humanity back to God that is Jesus' perfect obedience,

---

[33]Torrance, *Space, Time and Resurrection*, 118.
[34]Torrance, *Space, Time and Resurrection*, 119.

and finally the post-ascension mediation of that accomplished work by the Holy Spirit: "The ascension is not only the bearing of that Word [from God to humanity and from humanity to God] before the Face of the Father, but that Word accepted and honored by God, that Word fully installed in the divine Kingdom, sent back to earth through the Spirit."[35]

The ascension thus secures the ongoing significance of the prophetic office, which is exercised primarily through the church's preaching. Commenting on the description of the apostolic preaching in Mark 16:19, Torrance states, "Here we have a statement about the relation between the Church's proclamation of Christ and the activity of Christ himself in that proclamation where, through their common objective and dynamic content, the proclamation of the Gospel in the name of Christ and Christ's own proclamation are one and the same."[36] Jesus exercises his prophetic ministry in and through the church's proclamation of the kerygma of the gospel: "As the Church bears witness to him and proclaims the Gospel of salvation in his Name, he himself through the Spirit is immediately present validating that Word as his own, and communicating himself to men through it."[37] Torrance closes his description of the prophetic office with a striking picture of the importance of proclamation for the church's ongoing participation in Christ's ministry: "The Church's proclamation of the Gospel becomes thus the *scepter*, as Clement of Rome called it, through which the risen and ascended Christ rules over the nation and all history. It is by the Word of the Gospel that he rules over all things until he comes again to judge and renew his creation."[38]

For Torrance the ascension not only secures Jesus' ongoing work for the sake of the world through the church, but it also does so in such a way as to preserve the threefold shape of that work as prophet, priest and king. The distinctive mediation of salvation to the church, as understood in the unfolding narrative of Scripture and as revealed most fully in the climactic events of Jesus' earthly career, continues as the ascended Jesus exercises his ministry at the right hand of the Father. But how does the church participate

---

[35] Torrance, *Space, Time and Resurrection*, 120.
[36] Torrance, *Space, Time and Resurrection*, 119.
[37] Torrance, *Space, Time and Resurrection*, 120.
[38] Torrance, *Space, Time and Resurrection*, 120-121.

in this ministry? What shape does the church's action take in its correspondence to Jesus' ongoing work? It is to these questions that our discussion now turns.

The church's participation in Christ's ministry. As we have already seen, Torrance's description of Christ the mediator's continuing activity in the world is governed by the *munus triplex*. As Christ continues to exercise this threefold office, the church is given the gift of participation in that work as it lives and works in the time between Christ's first and second advent. There is, therefore, a corresponding threefold shape to the church's work as it participates in that threefold office. Torrance's desire to resist either overidentifying or separating Christ and the church's action in the continued mediation of salvation is crucial to his description of this ecclesial activity. Therefore, in between his account of the ascending Christ's work and the church's identity as a "Royal Priesthood," Torrance provides a description of the nature of that participation that superintends the kind of relationship that exists between Christ and his church. Before our study can move to the church's participation in the *munus triplex*, the conceptual framework that Torrance provides must be explored.

In the most general terms, Torrance construes the relationship between the church and Christ as one of service: "The Church as the Body of Christ participates in Christ's Prophetic, Priestly, and Kingly ministry by serving Him."[39] By service, Torrance is not only describing an activity ("serving") but also a more fundamental identity ("a servant"). This fundamental concept of servanthood, which Torrance repeats throughout *Royal Priesthood* and *Space, Time and Resurrection*, is chosen by Torrance for a couple of interrelated reasons. First, the term is consistent with the christological anchoring of Torrance's ecclesiology (i.e., the church as the "body of Christ"). The church only exists in relation to Jesus, and in particular to the historical Jesus, and so it is consistently thrown back upon this fundamental relation of servant to master. And because the church can only look to the historical Jesus in order to discern its proper form in the world, the particular shape of its existence is that of a suffering servant. The church is a servant to the Suffering Servant: "The form of the priesthood in the Church

---

[39]Torrance, *Royal Priesthood*, 94 (emphasis original).

derives from the Form of Christ as the Form of the Suffering Servant."[40] This sets the analogical relation that the church is to recognize and understand as the fundamental shape of its life and ministry: "The Church that is baptised into the Name of Christ and into His servant-form in this world, [sic] has to work that out analogically in its life and witness."[41]

Second, and in close relation to the first, this description corresponds to Torrance's reading of Scripture, and in particular the concept of *hypodeigma* (form or example). In the early chapters of Acts, Torrance sees a clear identification of the church as a suffering servant, beginning with the account of Stephen's martyrdom in Acts, in Philip's exposition of Isaiah 53 with the Ethiopian eunuch, and in Jesus' own identification with the suffering church ("I am Jesus, whom thou persecutest") in Paul's conversion.[42] But Torrance discerns the center of Scripture's description of the church's identity as servant to be in John 13, where Jesus washes the feet of the disciples as a demonstration of the love commandment. Torrance draws particular attention to Jesus' statement, "I have given you an example (*hypodeigma*) that ye should do as I have done unto you."[43] This, for Torrance, is the crucial term for understanding the church's relation to Christ: "Here it is made clear that while the form or *hypodeigma* of the Church's ministry derives from that of Christ, it is related to Him nevertheless in terms of the relation of a disciple to the Master, of servant to the Lord, of apostle to Christ."[44] As this previous sentence makes clear, while identifying the church as a suffering servant maintains the kind of continuity suggested by Torrance's emphasis on the church as the "body of Christ," his understanding of *hypodeigma* preserves the kind of asymmetry that Torrance is so intent to maintain in his ecclesiology. While there is a kind of identity between the church and Christ, Torrance's use of *hypodeigma* is intended to signify that this is fundamentally an asymmetrical relation.

Torrance provides an expanded description of *hypodeigma* later in *Royal Priesthood* while discussing the concept and structure of church order. The concern that drives Torrance's use of *hypodeigma* as the central term for

---

[40]Torrance, *Royal Priesthood*, 82.
[41]Torrance, *Royal Priesthood*, 84.
[42]Torrance, *Royal Priesthood*, 82-83.
[43]Torrance, *Royal Priesthood*, 85.
[44]Torrance, *Royal Priesthood*, 85.

conceiving the church's participation in Jesus' ministry becomes clear during the course of this discussion. Torrance believes that there is a tendency to allow Neo-Platonic philosophy to have an improper influence on ecclesiology.[45] The insertion of this alien philosophical framework into the biblical and ancient catholic stream of thought led the church to begin to overidentify its own human hierarchies and actions with the "celestial hierarchy" and the action of Jesus Christ. Torrance's concern here is similar to his disagreement with the idea that the church is a "continuation of the Incarnation." Torrance is concerned not only with the conflation of divine and ecclesial action, but also with the related error of elevating the ordained priesthood over and above the corporate priesthood of the entire church. This is to be rejected because it suggests a "reciprocal relation between the celestial hierarchy and the ministry of the Church on earth that . . . allows the episcopate to presume control over the Kingdom of Christ."[46] The church cannot claim to control Christ's continued presence on earth; neither can the ordained priesthood claim to control the Christ's action in and through the church.

In contrast to this perceived conflation of divine and human action, Torrance proposes the following description of divine and human action under the concept of *hypodeigma*:

> The Church as the Body of Christ participates in Christ's Prophetic, Priestly, and Kingly ministry by *serving* Him. The Church's ministry may be described as a corporate priesthood of the Many reposing substitionarily [sic] in the One Priest, the One Mediator between God and man, the Man Jesus Christ. The pattern of this relation between the priesthood of the Church and the Priesthood of Christ is to be described in terms of *hypodeigma*.[47]

Torrance then provides the following definition of *hypodeigma*: "a pattern put forward in the Church for observation, signifying a higher reality."[48]

---

[45] Although Torrance does not make the connection explicit here, it is likely that here as elsewhere he traces this corruption to Augustine, who Torrance believed was at points overinfluenced by Neo-Platonic philosophy. See, for example, Torrance, "The Roman Doctrine of Grace from the Point of View of Reformed Theology," in *Theology in Reconstruction* (Eugene, OR: Wipf & Stock, 1996), 175.

[46] Torrance, *Royal Priesthood*, 93.

[47] Torrance, *Royal Priesthood*, 94.

[48] Torrance, *Royal Priesthood*, 94.

Torrance understands *hypodeigma* to involve necessarily a rejection of any kind of Platonic construal of the relation between Christ and the church's respective priesthoods. Instead, ecclesial action is an *observable* reality that points beyond itself to Christ and his ministry.

Two pieces of exegesis are provided by Torrance as proof that this is indeed how Scripture also conceives of this relation. Torrance points first to Romans 8, where Paul speaks both of the Son's intercession at the right hand of God and also of the groaning prayers that Christians make in the Spirit. These prayers of suffering Christians are "unutterable" on earth and yet effective before the throne, which points to both the relation and to the disjunction between the church and Christ's priesthoods: "Our prayers are in no sense transcriptions in the language of earth of the heavenly liturgy around the throne of God, nevertheless they are related to that inexpressible mystery in the Spirit."[49] Torrance then turns to the book of Revelation and the glimpse of the heavenly liturgy given in that book. Torrance observes in the picture of worship in Revelation "the closest relation between the eucharistic worship of the Church on earth and the eternal intercession of Christ at the right hand of God."[50] Yet even in this "closest relation" the earthly worship is still only an echo of that which takes place in heaven: "In other words, the eucharistic sacrifice in the liturgy of the Church on earth belongs to a different dimension; it is an echo of the sacrifice of Christ made on our behalf. It is the joyful communion of those who give thanks for a sacrifice made on their behalf and who are summoned by the music of angels to an antiphonal oblation of praise and thanksgiving."[51]

This second piece of exegesis is an excellent example of how Torrance understands *hypodeigma*. There is a relation—understood here as an "echo"—between Christ and the church's ministry. But that relation is asymmetrical and is understood as participation but not as identification.[52]

---

[49]Torrance, *Royal Priesthood*, 95.
[50]Torrance, *Royal Priesthood*, 95.
[51]Torrance, *Royal Priesthood*, 96.
[52]Torrance's concerns here are echoed by John Webster: "An evangelical ecclesiology will thus have a particular concern to emphasize the asymmetry of divine and human action: God's work and the work of the church are fundamentally distinguished. But they are so distinguished, not in order to bifurcate them (which would undermine the fact that the church is indeed ingredient within the economy of God's saving purpose) but in order to accord priority to the gracious action of God, through which the church's action is ordered to its proper end in conformity with

"Through the Spirit there is a direct relation of participation, but in form and order the relation is indirect."[53] Christ is present within the church's ministry, but in such a way as to point beyond the church's ministry: "The ordered pattern of ministry is used by Christ as a mode of His Presence in the Church, and so it points beyond itself to His Real Presence."[54]

The *Munus Triplex* and the Church's Ministry

As we turn to examine Torrance's use of the *munus triplex* in his ecclesiology and doctrine of ministry, a preliminary note should be made. Torrance is consistent in stating the significance of the threefold office for the church as it participates in Christ's ongoing ministry. In the parts of Torrance's corpus that discuss the church's ministry—*Royal Priesthood* and *Space, Time and Resurrection* in particular—we find statements that affirm the significance of the particular shape of the prophetic, priestly, and kingly offices for the church. However, these statements are not followed with extensive treatments or an architectonic of the church's ministry. We do not have, for instance, the kind of systematization that can be found in Barth's use of the royal, priestly, and prophetic offices as the organizing principle of IV/1, IV/2, and IV/3 in the *Church Dogmatics*. This lacuna is no doubt due to the occasional nature of much of Torrance's writing and the fact that in his later years Torrance found himself focusing more on the doctrine of the Trinity and not the christological and ecumenical work that occupied him in his lecturing at New College and his participation in the World Council of Churches. Because of this, one of the objectives of this work is to disentangle what is actually a coherent articulation of the church's participation in the *munus triplex*. In what follows we have done precisely that, tracing Torrance's various references to the threefold nature of the ascended Christ's work throughout his extensive reflections on the Church and its ministry.

Christ's kingly ministry. As we saw in chapter two, for Torrance, the royal office of Christ can only be understood properly in its Old Testament background and in particular the term *padah*. As a descriptor of God's redemptive

---

the will of God." John Webster, "The Self-Organizing Power of the Gospel," in *Word and Church: Essays in Christian Dogmatics* (London: T&T Clark, 2006), 196.
[53]Torrance, *Royal Priesthood*, 96.
[54]Torrance, *Royal Priesthood*, 96.

activity, *padah* points forward to the "dramatic" aspect of Christ's atonement so that it can be understood through the lens of Israel's deliverance both from captivity in Egypt as well as from the improper exercise of the authority (*exousia*) God had delegated in creation. Thus for Torrance, the concept of *padah* informs Christ's royal office, providing the following description of God in his redemptive work: "It is through demolishing the usurped power of the law and the power of darkness over man that the Redeemer as a mighty Prince leads captivity captive and opens up an entirely new situation in which the old order is annulled and a new order of freedom in the Spirit is ushered in."[55] As we shall see, these twin themes of law and authority are significant in how Torrance applies Christ's ongoing kingly ministry to the church.

Torrance's reading of the New Testament and his construal of the kingly office draw a connection between the office and Christ's resurrection and ascension. The triumphant events of Jesus' victory over death and his session at the right hand of the Father are particular manifestations and indeed the culmination of a theme that runs throughout Jesus' ministry: the revelation and establishment of proper authority. As we have already seen, Torrance reads the Gospels in such a way as to highlight the way in which the incarnation confronts Satan's false authority with the authentic authority of God:

> When we examine the witness of the Gospels we find that this atoning and redeeming *exousia*, in both the words and acts of Jesus, comes to grips with the demonic forces entrenched in the fallen world and overcomes them. Whenever Jesus proclaimed his word, that word was an assault upon the enemies of God and whenever he acted in forgiveness and healing that act was in deliverance of men and women from enslavement to the power of Satan.[56]

While Jesus' earthly ministry demonstrates the kingly office in a provisional way, it is only in the ascension that the royal ministry of Christ begins in earnest. There we find Jesus gathering up all that had been already foreshadowed in his earthly career and fully assuming the kingly office: "It is with his exaltation to the throne of God and his sitting at the right hand of the Father that his kingly ministry properly began."[57]

---

[55]Torrance, *School of Faith: The Catechisms of the Reformed Church* (Eugene, OR: Wipf & Stock, 1996), lxxxvii-xcv; Torrance, *Atonement: The Person and Work of Christ* (Downers Grove, IL: IVP Academic, 2009), xciv.
[56]Torrance, *Incarnation: The Person and Life of Christ* (Downers Grove, IL: IVP Academic, 2008), 236.
[57]Torrance, *Space, Time and Resurrection*, 106.

What, then, is the shape of the ascended Jesus' kingly ministry? As we have already noted, there is a paradox at the center of Christ's royal ministry. The ascension, Torrance states, demonstrates both the revelation of Christ's power on the one hand and the veiling of that power on the other: "It is in the conjunction of grace and omnipotence that Christ ascends to the throne of God in order to fulfil his saving work and fill all things with his sovereign presence and power—yet, as we shall see, the ascension involves the veiling of his divine majesty and power, or the holding back, from our visible and physical contact in space and time, of his unveiled majesty and power."[58] This upward movement begins when Christ is lifted up on the cross.[59] And as that movement continues on through the resurrection and the ascension, it is revealed that it is here that Christ accomplishes all that is intended by his earthly ministry as his power is revealed in the incorruptible life demonstrated in his victory over the grave and his session at the right hand of the Father: "The resurrection means that the crucified Jesus is actually risen from the dead, and has broken through the limitations of our corrupt existence into which He entered for our sakes, and in doing so has redeemed our humanity from vanity and our time from illusion, establishing Himself in the fulness of His Humanity and in the fulness of His time as the reality of our humanity and the reality of our time."[60] The movement from cross to resurrection to ascension not only secures the efficacy of Christ's work, but also provides a gracious and necessary distance between humanity and the no-longer-veiled holiness of the glorified Lord: "The ascension means the establishment of the Church in history with historical structure and form, in which the time of the Church is the time of faith, not yet the time of sight, the time when the realm of *grace* is not yet dissolved by the realm of *glory*."[61] Christ's kingly office is for the time being exercised at the intersection of his accomplished victory and his gracious absence. The time between Christ's first and second advent, the time in which the ascended Christ is hidden from humanity's sight, is the time where the church extends to the world the hope of the gospel before Christ returns and the time for free decision draws to a close.

---

[58] Torrance, *Space, Time and Resurrection*, 112.
[59] "The ascension of Christ to heaven began with his lifting up on the Cross." Torrance, *Space, Time and Resurrection*, 109.
[60] Torrance, *Royal Priesthood*, 57.
[61] Torrance, *Royal Priesthood*, 59.

If Christ's kingly office is exercised within the context of his physical absence and the gracious delay of his return, and if, as we have already seen, Christ's priestly ministry is currently the fundamental avenue of his redeeming work,[62] then in what way is it possible to give a positive description of the ascended Christ's earthly ministry? The categories that we have found thus far in Torrance's discussion of the office, categories of presence and absence, of victory and yet waiting, suggest eschatology as the way forward. And this is indeed the case: throughout his work we find that Torrance's depiction of the royal office of Christ is argued for by way of his eschatology. If we understand Torrance's doctrine of "last things" we will be able to trace Christ's exercise of his royal office.

Hypostatic union, eschatology, and union with Christ. Torrance's most significant discussion of eschatology as it relates to the ministry and mission of the church is found in a chapter of *Royal Priesthood* entitled, "The Time of the Church." At the beginning of this chapter, Torrance makes a programmatic statement about his eschatology: "Eschatology properly speaking is the application of Christology to the Kingdom of Christ and to the work of the Church in history."[63] In the same way that christology serves as the control for Torrance's pneumatology and ecclesiology, so too we find it serving the same role in his eschatology.

In the same way that the *anhypostatic/enhypostatic* distinction guides his use of christology in his ecclesiology, Torrance's eschatology is guided by a cluster of christological concepts. Here the distinction between Christ's humanity and divinity, the union with Christ that is enjoyed by the church, and the application to the church of the crucifixion, resurrection, ascension, and eventual return of Christ together form the scaffolding of eschatology.

> Union with Christ means union with the Christ who rose again from the dead, who ascended to the right hand of God the Father, and who will come again; and therefore union with Him here and now carries in its heart the outreach of faith toward the resurrection of the dead and the renewal of heaven and

---

[62]"Even in the ascension the power of Christ is exercised through his sacrifice, through his atoning expiation of guilt, through his priestly mediation before God." Torrance, *Space, Time and Resurrection*, 112.
[63]Torrance, *Royal Priesthood*, 43.

earth at the Second Advent of Christ. The crucial issue in eschatology concerns the Humanity of the risen Christ, and our participation in His Humanity through Word and Sacrament in the Church.[64]

Torrance's eschatology, and thus his understanding of the application of Christ's royal office, is formulated according to these basic christological doctrines of Christ's humanity and divinity and how the church participates in Christ through union with him.

The classical doctrine of the hypostatic union governs Torrance's understanding of Christ's divine and human natures. In the incarnation, the divine Son assumes human nature in such a way as to maintain the integrity of both his divinity and his humanity. It is "a union in which divine nature and human nature are united in Christ in such a way that there is no diminishing or impairing of his divine nature and no diminishing or impairing of his human nature."[65] This union is the result and instrument of God's intention to bring redemption to humanity: "The Incarnation in which God gives himself to mankind takes the form of a 'hypostatic union' between divine nature and human nature in his one Person, which is the immediate ground for all Christ's mediatorial and reconciling activity in our human existence."[66]

In the perfection of his full divinity, the Son is able to take up humanity in order to redeem it. By means of the hypostatic union, the incarnate Son overcomes fallen humanity and therefore humanity's rebellion and separation from God: "This is a union which is projected, as it were, into the actual conditions of our estranged humanity where we are in conflict with God, so that the hypostatic union operates as a reconciling union in which estrangement is bridged, conflict is eradicated, and human nature taken from us is brought into perfect and sanctifying union with divine nature in Jesus Christ."[67] Over the course of the entirety of his earthly career, Jesus brings the benefits of redemption to the human nature that he has bound himself to in the hypostatic union: "The hypostatic union of divine and human nature in the oneness of his Person, far from succumbing to the onslaughts of the evil one, triumphed over them all, until through atoning

---

[64]Torrance, *Royal Priesthood*, 43.
[65]Torrance, *The Mediation of Christ* (Colorado Springs, CO: Helmers & Howard, 1992), 65.
[66]Torrance, *Mediation of Christ*, 64-65.
[67]Torrance, *Mediation of Christ*, 65.

expiation for sin Jesus Christ broke through the ultimate barrier of death and condemnation that separates man from God, and completed his mediation of reconciliation in his resurrection from the grave."[68]

The benefits of this reconciliation do not terminate with Jesus' human nature, but are extended to humanity by way of union with Christ. Thus Torrance writes, "It is only through union with Christ that we partake of the blessings of Christ, that is through union with him in his holy and obedient life."[69] This historic Reformed doctrine is central to how Torrance conceives of the nature of Christian existence. Redemption in Christ is neither a legal fiction nor a promise that is only to be realized in the future. Rather, it is a reality that is experienced in the present by the church:

> Since the Church is rooted in the hypostatic and atoning union embodied in the person of the Mediator the description of the Church as the Body of Christ is not a figurative way of speaking of some external moral union between believing people and Jesus Christ, but an expression of the ontological reality of the Church concorporate with Christ himself, who not only mediates reconciliation between man and God but constitutes and embodies it in his own divine-human Reality as Mediator.[70]

This "ontological reality," which the church receives by way of union with Christ, is crucial to Torrance's eschatology.

Torrance's conception of the particular moment the church inhabits within God's time is marked by an intention to take seriously the implications of Christ's humanity: "The crucial issue in eschatology concerns the humanity of the risen Christ."[71] For Torrance, to recognize the implications of the humanity of Christ is to understand that by way of Christ's person and work the church possesses the fruit of redemption in the present: "This is the strongest possible emphasis upon the fact that in the resurrection of Christ and in the Church's participation in Him the purpose of God in creation is brought to fulfillment. This fulfillment is no abrogation of its creatureliness but on the contrary a restoration of its creaturely reality which had

---

[68]Torrance, *Mediation of Christ*, 65-66.
[69]Torrance, "Justification: Its Radical Nature and Place in Doctrine and Life," in *Theology in Reconstruction* (Eugene, OR: Wipf & Stock, 1996), 158.
[70]Torrance, *Mediation of Christ*, 67.
[71]Torrance, *Royal Priesthood*, 43.

been impaired by sin."[72] Those who belong to Christ's body, the church, by way of union with him possess now, as a reality, participation in the perfect humanity that Jesus has secured through the hypostatic union. This, Torrance says, is what Paul meant by the "spiritual man" in 1 Corinthians: "The 'spiritual man' is no less man because he is spiritual, but on the contrary, far more man because through the Spirit he participates in the real Humanity of Jesus Christ, who is more fully Man than any other man, and who is above all the humanizing Man, the Man through whom all who believe in Him are humanized, and restored through atonement to true and perfect humanity."[73] We see here in Torrance's thought a significant emphasis upon the "already" of eschatology, the realization of redemption.

But the ontological reality of union with Christ, made available to the church by way of the humanity of Christ, is not the only theme of Torrance's eschatology or the only aspect of its christocentric character. The humanity of Christ that defines the present status of the church is at the same time the *ascended* humanity of Christ. Here again Torrance works out the implications of the distance created by the ascension: "On the one hand, then, the Church through the Spirit is joined to the Body of the risen Christ and is One Body with Him; but on the other hand, Christ has removed His Body from us so that we have to think in terms of the distance of the ascension and the nearness of His *parousia* in Glory."[74] Torrance calls this dialectic of nearness and distance the "eschatological reserve":

> There is an eschatological reserve in the relation of our union with Christ, an eschatological lag waiting for the last Word or the final Act of God. There is an element of pure immediacy in the Church's relation to the risen Body of Christ so that His *parousia* is a presence here and now through the Spirit. But there is also an element in the Church's relation to the risen Body of Christ which from our experience and our understanding is still in arrears and awaits the divine fulfillment.[75]

Thus Torrance, by way of the ascension, also emphasizes the "not yet" of eschatology.

---

[72] Torrance, *Royal Priesthood*, 44.
[73] Torrance, *Royal Priesthood*, 44-45.
[74] Torrance, *Royal Priesthood*, 45.
[75] Torrance, *Royal Priesthood*, 45.

The time of the church and the kingly office. Given the way that redemption and ascension frame the "already" and "not yet" of his eschatology, how does Torrance reconcile both into a coherent description of the "time of the Church"?[76] According to Torrance, both realities are present in the current age; the church lives in light of both the immediacy and reserve[77] of Christ's presence. This is parsed in his theology by bringing together the sacraments and eschatology precisely at the juncture of the old and new creation, the not yet and the already: "This eschatological relation of immediacy and reserve, so strong in the Epistles of the New Testament, is not easy to state precisely because it involves a twofold relation in which the sacramental and the eschatological are inseparable."[78] What Torrance discerns in his discussion of the sacraments is the same dynamic which he has already given in his account of the ascension.

In the sacraments there is both the "already" of Christ given in baptism or the Lord's Supper and also the "not yet" that they point to and promise. Thus Torrance states, "The Sacraments span the two moments [present reality and future promise] and are ordinances of Christ belonging to the eschatological reserve between the moment of the First Advent and the moment of the Final Advent."[79] We will examine Torrance's sacramentology in greater detail in our discussion of Christ's priestly office. For the purpose of our present discussion of the kingly office, however, it is important we note that Christ is present in his church (and the church enjoys its participation in him) by way of the sacraments: "This is the age . . . when by the Holy Spirit, who inhabits the Church and energizes its kerygmatic ministry, all who believe in Jesus Christ may taste the powers of the age to come through sacramental incorporation into the new creation."[80] And that sacramental presence reflects Torrance's basic commitments to eschatology. In his essay "Eschatology and the Eucharist," Torrance writes, "The sacramental signs are charted with the real presence, but it is a presence which is also yet to come, a presence whose full reality is yet to be unveiled and consummated."[81]

---

[76] Torrance, *Royal Priesthood*, 43.
[77] Torrance, *Royal Priesthood*, 46.
[78] Torrance, *Royal Priesthood*, 46.
[79] Torrance, *Royal Priesthood*, 48.
[80] Torrance, "Eschatology and the Eucharist," in *Conflict and Agreement in the Church,* vol. 2 (Eugene, OR: Wipf & Stock, 1996), 160.
[81] Torrance, "Eschatology and the Eucharist," 161.

Christ's sacramental and eschatological presence in the church provides for Torrance the foundation for the church's participation in the kingly office. When put together, Torrance's eschatology as it is determined by the ascension and his sacramentology are the articulation of how he understands the church to exist within the world as it participates in the kingly office:

> It is precisely the conjunction of these two aspects of eschatology [the ascension and the sacraments] in the doctrine of the Church that is so significant, for it means that the Church is so united to the risen Humanity of Christ that within the Church the new creation is a concrete reality reaching out through the ages of history to the *parousia* and so within the Church we are given a new orientation to the succession of time on the stage of this sinful world.[82]

In the sacraments, the church provisionally possesses the ontological reality given to it in its union with the ascended Lord: "The Church as the Body of Christ is the sphere on earth and within history where through the Spirit the redemption of the body and the redemption of time anticipate the *parousia*."[83]

Torrance understands the sacraments as the instrument whereby the church receives this foretaste of redemption. The sacraments "are the ordinances in which as far as possible, while yet remaining within empirical history, we may anticipate the resurrection of the body."[84] They are not only signs of what is to come but present participation in the reality that will arrive fully at the second advent of Christ: "In and through the Sacraments, therefore, we are given our clearest understanding of the participation of the Church in the redemption of the body and the redemption of time."[85] Torrance illustrates this by referring to a passage of the Shepherd of Hermas, an early Christian text. There, the author describes a vision where the church is personified as an elderly lady who grows younger through time. This, says Torrance, is how the church moves through time:

> The Church is a corporeal reality in this world and yet through the Spirit the same Church already participates in the new creation. Even though it

---

[82]Torrance, *Royal Priesthood*, 46.
[83]Torrance, *Royal Priesthood*, 46-47.
[84]Torrance, *Royal Priesthood*, 48.
[85]Torrance, *Royal Priesthood*, 48.

participates in the space and time of this world and this age, the life of the Church gets younger and younger because in Christ it is redeemed from the bondage and decay that characterise this world and this age. That is why to speak of the Church as the Body of Christ is to speak of it as the sphere within history where through the Spirit the redemption of the body and the redemption of time anticipate the *parousia*.[86]

As the church is renewed in its union with Christ through the sacraments, it enjoys in anticipation "the redemption of the body and the redemption of time."[87] This "sphere of redemption" that the church now knows and experiences is more than just a comforting reality to be shared by the faithful, but is instead a mode of the church's ministry to the world as it participates in the royal office: "This relation of redemption to space and time is of prime importance for the doctrine of the Church and its ministry."[88] By invoking the elements of Christ's history, which ground his understanding of the royal office—the resurrection and ascension[89]—Torrance understands this "new reality to space and time as we know them in our fallen world"[90] to be what shapes the church's ministry in that fallen world. While the church cannot escape the fallen world, it is no longer beheld to it through its union with Christ.

Torrance speaks of this royal freedom the church knows within fallen creation by way of the concept of "law." When Paul speaks of "law," Torrance states, he is speaking of "the form which this passing age assumes under the divine judgment and the means by which it seeks to entrench itself in finality."[91] When humanity experiences the law outside of participation in Christ and his royal office, it experiences bondage. To live "under the law" is to experience the closed system of the world's fallenness and our own complicity in it. Torrance calls this the "nomistic form of human existence."[92] It is "the time-form of our fallen existence within which we are fixed in our mortality, and through which we are caught in the irreversibility of guilty

---

[86]Torrance, *Royal Priesthood*, 48-49.
[87]Torrance, *Royal Priesthood*, 48.
[88]Torrance, *Royal Priesthood*, 49.
[89]Torrance, *Royal Priesthood*, 49.
[90]Torrance, *Royal Priesthood*, 49.
[91]Torrance, *Royal Priesthood*, 52.
[92]Torrance, *Atonement*, 253.

deeds and lives which have the force of 'necessity' because once lived or performed they cannot be undone. It is what St Paul called 'the curse of the law' from which we need to be redeemed."[93] And it is this "nomistic" existence that Christ's royal office overcomes.

Drawing from Paul's letter to the Galatians, Torrance sees the concepts of law (*nomos*) and order (*stoichea*) as clustered together. The Galatian Christians faced a temptation to be "dragged back again into the law."[94] In so doing, they are also drawn into the order of the fallen age—the *stoichea tou cosmou*. Central to the order of the fallen age is to live by fallen time (the "temporal succession"[95] of the fallen world), which is precisely what the church in union with the ascended Christ has been freed from: "To walk according to temporal succession . . . is not to walk according to Christ, for that is to subject oneself again to the tyrant forces from which we have been redeemed by the blood of Christ."[96] By way of its participation in Jesus' kingly office the church enjoys the *padah* redemption from bondage to the law that was displayed so clearly in Jesus' kingly ministry during his earthly career.

Torrance's depiction of the ascended Christ's kingly ministry emphasizes the freedom of the church. As they participate in Christ's royal freedom, those who belong to the church and participate in its union with Christ enjoy, on a provisional basis, victory over the "nomistic form of human existence." In a lengthy passage which is worth reading in its entirety insofar as it summarizes the effect of Christ's royal office upon the church, Torrance writes:

> Within the succession of history and its structures and forms the Church is the sphere where through the Spirit the new world breaks into the old, the arena within the limitations of the old where God acts freely upon men through Word and Spirit and men are summoned to response and obedience. If the Church were only a society within time, were but a social construct of historical succession, there would be no room for free meeting and decision, for everything would be determined by the processes of this world, the

---

[93] Torrance, *Atonement*, 253.
[94] Torrance, *Royal Priesthood*, 52.
[95] Torrance, *Royal Priesthood*, 53.
[96] Torrance, *Royal Priesthood*, 53.

stoichea tou cosmou. But the Church is the sphere where through the Cross of Christ the sovereign grace of God strikes into the heart of this world and draws all men into the sphere of His redeeming operation. In it men and women are delivered from the tyrant forces of bondage and are made free for God, so that real meeting in reconciliation and faith is effectually realised. The Church as the Body of Christ is the sphere within the time-form of this world where God and man meet in love and man is translated into the Kingdom of God's dear Son.[97]

At the close of his reflections upon this topic, Torrance signals how the concept of *hypodeigma* controls the mode of the church's participation. Using one of his favorite metaphors for *hypodeigma*, "counterpoint," Torrance states that it is by way of the church's refusal to submit to the "nomistic form of human existence"—the order of the fallen age and its "irreversibility" and "necessity"—that the church participates in the office: "As such the Church does not live within the succession of history as a self-perpetuation institution, but as the *vis-a-vis* of the Kingdom of Christ, the covenant-partner of the ascended Lord, and carries out its ministry in holy counterpoint to the heavenly session at the right hand of God the Father Almighty."[98] The dynamic of *hypodeigma* is on display: the relation between divine and ecclesial action is indirect and asymmetrical, pointing away from itself to the ascended Lord by way of the form of "service." It is in the church's refusal to submit to the order of the fallen age that the church participates in Christ's royal office.

A more complete picture of how the church participates in the kingly office of Christ by way of *hypodeigma* is demonstrated in an essay entitled, "Service in Jesus Christ."[99] Here we see the form of the church's participation in Jesus' royal ministry linked directly to the diaconal ministry. It is important to note that while Torrance understands it may be necessary to distinguish a diaconal office within the church, the form of that ministry is the mark of the entire body of Christ without distinction.

We are concerned with *diakonia* in its concrete sense as *deaconing*, both as the charge that Christ lays upon the Christian community and as the office to

---

[97] Torrance, *Royal Priesthood*, 60.
[98] Torrance, *Royal Priesthood*, 60-61.
[99] Torrance, "Service in Jesus Christ," in *Gospel, Church, and Ministry: Thomas F. Torrance Collected Studies 1*, ed. Jock Stein (Eugene, OR: Pickwick, 2012), 140-161.

which some are called within the community. *Diakonia* describes not only the relationship of service to which the whole membership of the Church and specific individuals within it bear to Jesus Christ, but the form which that relationship takes in the mutual service of members to one another and in their service to their fellow men in the world.[100]

In their relationship to Christ as Lord, the church lives out its existence and participates in that reign by way of embracing its identity as a community of *diakonoi*.

Torrance's understanding of the diaconal ministry and its relationship with Christ's kingly office is a unique contribution to the application of the *munus triplex* to the church's participation in Christ's ministry. But as we assess this contribution and consider it within the wider context of his thought, it is necessary to examine how Torrance handles one of the implications of the kingly office: the relation between the church and the state. When considering Jesus' kingly ministry, it is common for the political nature of the imagery of Christ's royal office to converge with discussions about the nature of the church and its relationship with other forms of government. The significance of Christ's ascension, the freedom from bondage to the "nomistic structure of human existence" that the office extends to the church, and the necessary parsing of the eschatological "already" and "not yet" provide a window in some of the implications of Torrance's thought at this juncture. Thus it is not surprising that we do indeed find in "Service in Jesus Christ" one of Torrance's lengthier discussions of the relationship between church and state.

Torrance frames the discussion with a question: "How can [the Church] render this service as *service* and render it *effectively* within the power-structures of humanity?"[101] Through the course of his argument it becomes clear that the particular form of service Torrance is addressing is care for the social and physical welfare of men and women. Before answering the question he has posed, Torrance notes two opposite errors. On the one hand, the church is tempted to accomplish the work of service through the improper use of power. To do so, Torrance argues, is to betray Christian service properly understood by moving to an understanding of service defined on

---

[100] Torrance, "Service in Jesus Christ," 143.
[101] Torrance, "Service in Jesus Christ," 154.

grounds other than Christ: "The Church is constantly tempted not only to institutionalize its service of the divine mercy but to build up power structures of its own, both through ecclesiastical success and prestige among the people and through social and political instruments, by means of which it can exert pressure to attain its ends and impart power to its service in order to ensure its effectiveness."[102] Torrance states this is a betrayal of the kind of service proper to the church. In his service Jesus "steadfastly resisted every temptation to use compelling demonstrations of glory and power to fulfil his ministry."[103]

The opposite error Torrance perceives is the error of abdicating responsibility for the welfare of humanity to the state. In the face of the challenge of defining the nature of its service in relation to the state, the church might simply give up this responsibility altogether: "The Church is tempted to retreat into an area where it could not come into conflict with the power-structures of organized social welfare and where it thinks to avoid the subtle snare of using its success in the relief of human suffering as a means of enhancing its own image or pressing its own claim upon the people."[104] This response is equally erroneous, for it means to "decline the burden of human need at its sharpest point and deflect the real force of Christian witness, and so run away from the agony of being merciful as God is merciful."[105] In spite of the temptations that accompany service, the church is nonetheless commanded to serve and to do so in the way of Jesus Christ.

Torrance's identification of this second "temptation" associated with service is unsurprising, but the first—the temptation "to use worldly power in order to secure the success of its service"[106]—deserves further investigation. Torrance states that on the one hand the church cannot ignore the activity of the state:

> As an organized community within the national, social, and economic structure of human life the Church cannot isolate its ministry from the organized services of the State for the welfare of its people. The Church knows

---

[102]Torrance, "Service in Jesus Christ," 154.
[103]Torrance, "Service in Jesus Christ," 155.
[104]Torrance, "Service in Jesus Christ," 155. It is interesting to note how Torrance describes the second temptation only in its relation to the first.
[105]Torrance, "Service in Jesus Christ," 155.
[106]Torrance, "Service in Jesus Christ," 154.

only too well that the need of men is bound up with the injustices inherent in the national, social, and economic structures within which people live, and is often directly traceable to them, and therefore in order to meet human need adequately and rationally attention must be given to the factors that create it and aggravate it.[107]

But Torrance stops short of saying coordination is possible. While the church does not serve in "isolation," at the same time it should not attempt to work alongside the state. From Torrance's perspective, the church must ask the question: "How can this [service] be done without economic and political power?"[108] Power, intended here by Torrance to denote political and "worldly" power, is in an antithetical relationship with true service. Indeed, as Torrance states elsewhere in "Service in Jesus Christ," there is a sharp opposition between the kinds of power and authority that worldly government and the reigning Christ dispense. Torrance asks the rhetorical question, "Can the Church go forth from Christ clad with his image in the form of a servant without laying aside the pride and glory and power of the nations, and without taking into its own mouth in triumphant agony his cry before the judgment seat of Pilate: 'My Kingdom is not of this world?'"[109] Torrance's answer is negative. The church must lay down "the pride and glory and power of the nations," because its "Kingdom is not of this world." Christian service and worldly government exist in opposition to one another.

This dichotomy that Torrance introduces between service and worldly government is intriguing: not so much in the opposition between certain forms of secular government and the kingdom of Christ, but rather in Torrance's categorical rejection of any type of action which approximates to "the forms of the world."[110] The church cannot "engage in the pressure groups of organized society . . . without compromising its real nature as the body of Jesus Christ."[111] As we have seen, the category of authority is prominent in Torrance's understanding of Christ's kingly office. In his account of the kingly office in *Atonement*, Torrance notes that there is a proper secondary authority in the order God established in creation: "God has delegated his

---

[107]Torrance, "Service in Jesus Christ," 154.
[108]Torrance, "Service in Jesus Christ," 154.
[109]Torrance, "Service in Jesus Christ," 155.
[110]Torrance, "Service in Jesus Christ," 155.
[111]Torrance, "Service in Jesus Christ," 155.

exousia to others who exercise it rightly only in obedience to God, and who can be known as 'authorities' such as rulers in the state or in the temple."[112] Of course, this authority may very well be and indeed has been misused: "They become evil 'authorities' when they usurp the *exousia* of God and claim it as their own, using it for their own ends, thus confounding their own might with the divine right."[113] And it is precisely that situation that Christ's kingly work addresses; Jesus frees humanity from the evil distortion of authority: "Evil has all its usurped *exousia* stripped away from it and humanity is free from its tyranny."[114]

We might expect, then, the possibility of the positive exercise of authority for rulers, the state, or even the church in Torrance's theology. In light of Jesus Christ's royal work and victory over the perversion of *exousia*, there would appear to be some space for the rightful exercise of state authority even if that authority was limited, still prone to be misused, and always in submission to the now-ascended Christ's royal authority. But, as we have seen, Torrance balks at this possibility.[115] Instead, authority is depicted as residing exclusively in heaven with the ascended Christ, and the corresponding human action is a form of service that Torrance carefully circumscribes with his description of the humble and suffering ministry of the incarnate Son. For Torrance it seems that the church's authority and worldly authority only exist in distinction or even in a certain type of opposition; there is neither a description of the temporary delegation of authority to the state nor a positive understanding of the relationship between the church's authority and that of the state.[116]

---

[112] Torrance, *Atonement*, 30.
[113] Torrance, *Atonement*, 30-31.
[114] Torrance, *Atonement*, 32.
[115] David Fergusson notes "the relative absence of the ethical and political significance of the ascension":
    For Torrance, the divine-human relation tends to be largely a private one, although his strong sense of the corporate nature of worship might have taken him in a different direction. Only occasionally does he give hints about the wider significance of the ascension—for example, we are told that we cannot be pessimistic about the world since it is loved by Christ. Yet the important relations and movements in Torrance are, as it were, vertical rather than horizontal. His occasional excursions into Christian ethics tend to be confined to areas of private rather than social morality. (David Fergusson, "The Ascension of Christ: Its Significance in the Theology of T. F. Torrance," *Participatio* 3 [2012]: 106).
[116] It is significant that Torrance's most extended reflection on the state and its justice, found in juridical law and physical law, is not so much a theological discussion as it is something else.

We can identify two reasons for this occlusion in Torrance's work—one eschatological, and the other christological. These categories correspond respectively to Torrance's account of the church-state relation and ecclesial authority. The extent to which Torrance's eschatology informs his understanding of the church and state relationship is visible in an address he gave that was later published under the title, "The Church in the World." There, in the course of articulating a positive vision for the church's place in the world, he presents a sharp contrast between the church and the state. The state, Torrance argues, is a part of the "old order."[117] The church, in contrast, is of the "new creation," and because of this "the Church will press toward a new order."[118] Throughout the essay Torrance advances his argument via eschatology. Because of its existence in the old order, the state is perpetually tilting toward overstepping its authority: "Every state just because it must maintain right by might, because it must maintain order in the last analysis by the power of the sword, is always on the point of developing into an authoritarian power, that is, into a fascist state."[119] The church, though it often loses grasp of its true identity, not only inhibits the state's totalitarian pretensions but is also in active opposition. "If Christianity looks toward a new creation, she cannot but be fundamentally destructive and revolutionary over against the 'fashion of this world.' Just because the Church belongs to this new creation; [sic] she cannot help but be radical in this 'present evil world.'"[120]

Torrance's eschatological description of the relationship between the church and the state inhibits any positive account of their relationship. Instead, because state and church reside in the old and new "orders," or eschatological ages, respectively, there is little place for authority to be shared or coordinated between the two entities. Torrance's rhetoric in the essay is emphatic—descriptors for the church and its nature such as "destructive," "revolutionary," and "otherworldly" are found throughout—and serves to underline the contrast between the church and the state. The fact that the

---

Torrance argues from the contingency of creation and attempts to persuade the reader on the basis of a realist epistemology. See Torrance, *Juridical Law and Physical Law: Toward a Realist Foundation for Human Law* (Eugene, OR: Wipf & Stock, 1997).

[117] Torrance, "The Church in the World," in *Gospel, Church, and Ministry: Thomas F. Torrance Collected Studies 1*, ed. Jock Stein (Eugene, OR: Pickwick, 2012), 76.
[118] Torrance, "Church in the World," 81.
[119] Torrance, "Church in the World," 77.
[120] Torrance, "Church in the World," 77.

address was given in Great Britain in 1942, at the height of the uncertainty of World War II (when there would be a natural inclination to give a more positive account, at least, of the place of one's own state within the divine economy, even while recognizing the destructive authoritarian impulses of the Axis nations), only makes Torrance's argument the more striking.

There is a second reason that Torrance locates authority within the church in such a way that it is over and against the state: his construction of the threefold office in the time after the ascension. As we have already noted, the ascension figures prominently in how the work of Christ transitions from the time of Jesus' earthly ministry to the time the church now lives in by way of union with Jesus. The event marks the transition from an ordering of Christ's office "determined by the mighty salvation events in the course of Jesus' life among us"[121]—prophet, priest, and king—to one that is determined by the ascension: "As we consider the threefold office within the period inaugurated by the ascension, it is evidently with another order that we have to work: King, Priest and Prophet."[122] This is the order that belongs to the time of the church, the time from the ascension to the parousia.

Torrance states that in between the ascension and the parousia, the kingly ministry determines the shape of Christ's ministry even as the prophetic and priestly offices continue: "His kingly ministry is supreme from ascension to *parousia*, but within that his ministry as Priest and Prophet is no less evident than before, for it is brought to fullness in the consummation of his Kingship; the priesthood of Christ is a Royal Priesthood, and the proclamation of Christ is a Royal Proclamation."[123] But supremacy does not here mean that the kingly office is the primary expression of Christ's work among the different aspects of the *munus triplex*. Instead, at the same time that the ascension determines the shape of the mediation of Christ's work, it also veils Christ and his enthronement. In his heavenly session Christ reigns, but until the *parousia* his reign is characterized by hiddenness and by gracious patience. Because of this, the priesthood of Christ occludes his kingly ministry until Christ returns and unveils his glory: "The ascension of Jesus Christ to the throne of God was the enthronement of the Word made flesh,

---

[121] Torrance, *Space, Time and Resurrection*, 106.
[122] Torrance, *Space, Time and Resurrection*, 106.
[123] Torrance, *Space, Time and Resurrection*, 106-107.

the enthronement of the Lamb.... But until the *parousia* He holds back the epiphany of Glory; He exercises His Kingdom only through His Priesthood."[124] The title of Torrance's book on the ministry of the church is telling: *royal* functions as an adjective, and *priesthood* is the substantive.

The effect of this occlusion of the kingly ministry is twofold. On the one hand, authority may be provisionally located in the community that enjoys union with the ascended Christ: the church. While Christ graciously waits until his return, his body lives in the world as his provisional presence. The church is the foretaste of his presence, the place where the world that has been inaugurated and will one day fully come can now be located: "The Church is the sphere where through the Spirit the new world breaks into the old, the arena within the limitations of the old where God acts freely upon men through Word and Spirit and where men are summoned to response and obedience."[125] But on the other hand, that same authority is not to be located anywhere else. Royal authority is delegated to the church alone through its participation in the kingly office. And even that authority is now obscured as it is seated with Christ at the right hand of the Father. The kingly reign is now hidden, exercised only by way of the priestly office and in the sphere of the church.

The combination of Torrance's christological and eschatological commitments leads to the sharp contrast we find in his thought between the respective authorities of the church and the state. The question must be put to Torrance whether such a contrast runs counter to the grain of the scriptural witness of the role of the state. Passages such as Romans 13 and 1 Peter 2:13-17, while not uncontroversial in their interpretation and clearly susceptible to abuse by those who would wish to legitimize fealty to the state, give a place to the state's authority that we would struggle to give an account of in Torrance's theology. Torrance's instinctual resistance to ceding too much authority to the state is no doubt a necessary corrective that he learned from his *Doktorvater*, Karl Barth. And yet Torrance overcorrects in a way that goes beyond his theological mentor. Thus, Torrance fails to provide a limited or circumscribed account of the authority that is given to the state before Christ's second advent. In the end, Torrance's use of the ascension claims too

---

[124]Torrance, *Royal Priesthood*, 61.
[125]Torrance, *Royal Priesthood*, 60.

much too soon, vacating earthly government of authority before Christ's return legitimizes such a reality.

There are two possible complementary responses to this perceived problem within Torrance's theology. On the one hand, it is possible to make use of the Reformed tradition's unique christological resources so as to locate the ascended Christ's authority in such a way that it can be spoken of as existing outside the church. We find this of course in Calvin who demonstrated that the *extra Calvinisticum* represents the universality of Christ's reign. Calvin refused the notion that in the incarnation the hypostatic union somehow limited the divinity of the eternal Son: "Calvin argues that though Christ's divinity is united to his humanity and is fully present therein, it nonetheless is not contained by that humanity in its finitude, but is ubiquitously present outside (*extra*) it."[126] In so doing, Calvin was able to speak of Christ's reign as existing not only beyond his earthly body, but also outside of the boundaries of his ecclesial body. In an article that makes this case, Heiko Oberman states that for Calvin the *extra* also meant *extra etiam ecclesiam*. Christ reigns not only within his church and even now exercises his reign over the world: "In the *extra etiam ecclesiam* we find it is Calvin who has the more 'progressive' or modern vision of God's rule thrusting beyond the heart of the justified sinner and beyond the boundaries of the Church, to encompass the State, Society and the whole created order."[127] Whereas an account of the church as the body of Christ might lead one to draw too narrow a circle around Christ's authority in the world, the *extra Calvinisticum* preserves the larger sense of Christ's royal authority in and over the world.

This amendment to Torrance's thought is in line with commitments he makes elsewhere in his writings. While Torrance doesn't offer an unqualified endorsement of the *extra Calvinisticum*, we have already seen that he embraced the doctrine as a corrective to a "receptacle notion of space" that placed damaging constraints upon a properly Christian view of space and time.[128] Torrance was concerned that the *extra Calvinisticum* might be used to imagine the identity of the Son of God apart from his eternal union with

---

[126]Stephen Edmondson, *Calvin's Christology* (Cambridge: Cambridge University Press, 2004), 211.
[127]Heiko A. Oberman, "The Extra Dimension in the Theology of Calvin," *Journal of Ecclesiastical History* 21.1 (1970): 64.
[128]See Torrance, *Space, Time and Incarnation* (Edinburgh: T&T Clark, 1997), 30-32.

humanity. At the same time, however, he saw the merits and the necessity of the doctrine.[129] "The Word cannot be subordinated to the flesh it assumes nor can it be limited by the creaturely reality with which it is united, and so be altered in its transcendent and divine nature."[130] We can apply a resource already present within Torrance's theology so as to demonstrate the significance of Christ's royal office both inside and outside of the church. In so doing he would reap the fruit of the *extra Calvinisticum* while at the same time avoiding some of its more speculative elements (such as an improper use of the *logos asarkos*).[131]

To this christological correction we might also add an eschatological correction. Torrance's placement of the state within the "old age" and the church within the new draws too sharp a distinction; another reading of Scripture suggests a more complicated account. One of the more complete political theologies of the twentieth century is Oliver O'Donovan's *The Desire of the Nations*.[132] There is much common ground between O'Donovan's and Torrance's projects. Both make significant use of the prophetic, priestly, and kingly offices in the biblical theologies they respectively give in their accounts of the Old Testament and then in how these same roles are fulfilled in Jesus Christ in the New.[133] For both O'Donovan and Torrance, the major events of the life of Christ provide the guide for understanding the church's place in the world.[134] But where O'Donovan differs from Torrance is in what can be extrapolated from the ascension. In particular, O'Donovan notes the mistake of losing "the balance between what has been accomplished and what remains to be accomplished." He continues, "Christ's triumph is complete, and in that event [the Ascension] mankind has been brought into the presence of God's

---

[129] "Now there can be no doubt that in this, the Reformed theologians had the agreement of the whole earthly church behind them." Torrance, *Incarnation*, 220.

[130] Torrance, *Incarnation*, 220.

[131] For an extended discussion of Torrance's use of the *extra Calvinisticum* and an argument for the merits of his use of the concept over Barth's, see Paul Molnar, *Faith, Freedom and the Spirit: The Economic Trinity in Barth, Torrance and Contemporary Theology* (Downers Grove, IL: IVP Academic, 2015), 324-354.

[132] Oliver O'Donovan, *The Desire of the Nations: Rediscovering the Roots of Political Theology* (Cambridge: Cambridge University Press, 1996).

[133] O'Donovan makes implicit but nonetheless extensive use of the *munus triplex* throughout *The Desire of the Nations*, consistently recognizing these three offices as the structure through which God worked in Israel's life and also recognizing how each is fulfilled in Jesus' work. See in particular O'Donovan, *Desire of the Nations*, 30-81, 120-157.

[134] See O'Donovan, *Desire of the Nations*, 133-146.

glory. Nothing remains to be added to what has been done; we wait only for a fuller sight of it. Yet while this is true so far as it goes, it ignores one aspect of the Ascension that should not be missed: it is a bridge between the time of Christ's life and the time of the world's future."[135] It is this "bridge" element that is missing from Torrance's thought. Even though the significance of worldly governments has been both relativized at Christ's first advent, and will inevitably expire at Christ's second advent, there remains a limited function for them in the present overlapping of the ages. So O'Donovan is right to state, "In light of Christ's ascension it is no longer possible to think of political authorities as sovereign; but neither is it possible to regard them as mere exhibitions of pride and lust for power."[136] O'Donovan goes on to give a description of the continued place of the state in the divine economy; what Torrance's account appears to have no room for is such a description.

This eschatological correction to Torrance's understanding of the royal office is significant in that it gives clarity regarding what the church should expect from the state in the present age. As we have seen, Torrance both signals the complete transfer of authority to Jesus in the ascension and also delays the expression of that authority until Jesus returns and fully unveils his kingly power. The effect of this position is to leave the church in an ambiguous relationship with the state, on the one hand claiming full authority and on the other unsure of how to exercise it before Christ's second advent. The proposed christological and eschatological corrections to Torrance's thought allow the church, on the one hand, to recognize Christ's royal reign outside of the church and, on the other hand, to understand exactly what kind of authority worldly governments should possess so that it may articulate either correlation with—or perhaps more significantly, criticism of—the state's limited and qualified exercise of authority.[137]

The importance of these christological and eschatological corrections to Torrance's thought is demonstrated in W. A. Visser 't Hooft's 1947 Stone Lectures, *The Kingship of Christ: An Interpretation of Recent European*

---

[135]O'Donovan, *Desire of the Nations*, 143.
[136]Oliver O'Donovan, *The Ways of Judgment* (Grand Rapids, MI: Eerdmans, 2005), 5.
[137]"The church will frame its political witness with authenticity, avoiding the characteristic evils of abstract idealism and colourless assimilation, when it stands self-consciously before that horizon and confesses that it looks for the resurrection of the dead and the life of the world to come." O'Donovan, *Desire of the Nations*, 288.

Theology. In a poignant chapter titled "The Kingship of Christ in the Years of Struggle," Visser 't Hooft traces the lack of a coherent understanding of Christ's kingship through the time between World War I and World War II. In his diagnosis of the church's silence in the face of the rise of the Nazi party, Visser 't Hooft notes that the problem was not merely a lack of a doctrine of Christ's kingship. When the confessing church courageously articulated Christ's lordship over and against the claims of National Socialist ideology, its stance was, according to Visser 't Hooft, primarily defensive. The concern then was primarily with preventing the encroachment of Nazi ideology into the church's proclamation of the gospel: "The Church belongs to Christ and to him alone and cannot possibly leave its order to be shaped according to the changing ideologies of the world. The state has a specific divine vocation but the doctrine that it is the sole and total order of human life is a pernicious heresy."[138] But a truncated doctrine of Christ's kingship prevented the full exposition of the church's proclamation:

> To carry out the Barmen declaration in its full implications would have meant ... to start a battle along the line in which the Church would not only defend its own purity but also counteract the totalitarian claim of National Socialism with the even more comprehensive and absolute gospel of the Kingship of Christ.... The Confessing Church has on the whole found a defensive rather than an aggressive battle and concentrated its attention so largely on the issues of Church life that the wider issue of the battle for the nation and for the world has been neglected.[139]

Visser 't Hooft's diagnosis is addressed with a chapter (following one that details "The Kingship of Christ in the Church") that considers the implications of Christ's kingship for the world—its political realities and the church's faithful mission within it.

Visser 't Hooft's critique is significant not in that we might cast aspersions upon those who witnessed bravely to the gospel in their own time, but rather as a reminder of the significance of these doctrines for the church's life in the world. Torrance's description of Christ's kingly office emphasizes the reality of Christ's royal reign; his exercise of it is a source of the church's strength in

---

[138] W. A. Visser 't Hooft, *The Kingship of Christ: An Interpretation of Recent European Theology* (New York: Harper & Brothers, 1948), 45.

[139] Visser 't Hooft, *Kingship of Christ*, 47.

its mission, and by faith the church reminds itself that worldly powers and structures do not control its ministry. But the church is also compelled to understand what its mission looks like in relation to those authorities which bridge the time between Christ's first and second advents.[140]

Conclusion

In this chapter we have begun to see how Torrance's doctrine of God, christology, and ecclesiology unfold in a positive vision of the ongoing work of the ascended Christ through the ministry of the church. Torrance is keen to avoid simply identifying the ministry of the church with the work of Christ as some kind of extension of the incarnation. But at the same time he also seeks to establish a proper relationship between Christ and the church. The church's ministry is only efficacious because it is a participation in the work of Christ. For Torrance, the concept that frames the relationship between the ascended Christ and the church is *hypodeigma*. As it follows the example of its Lord, the church participates in his work while acknowledging its dependence and pointing to his very real and active presence.

We have also begun to understand what concrete shape this ministry takes through an examination of Torrance's account of the church's participation in one of the threefold offices: the royal office. Torrance's description here allows us to see how the various commitments that he makes across his corpus—from christology to eschatology to political theology—are consistently applied in a positive vision of the church's royal identity in its king. And yet we have also seen that this consistency reveals problems in Torrance's constructive doctrine of ministry and mission. Though these problems are significant, they can be addressed from resources within Torrance's own thought.

Having explored these two aspects of Torrance's understanding of the church's ministry, we now turn to the other two offices of the *munus triplex*: the prophetic and priestly offices.

---

[140]For a similar account, see Philip G. Ziegler, "Witness to Christ's Dominion: The Political Service of the Church," *Theology* 116.5 (2013): 323-331. "By their political service, Christians announce the assurance and claim of the God of the gospel, and thereby bear witness 'for government to their common Lord'; in this way they call the state to genuine exercise of its divine appointment to secure measures of human peace and justice and thereby also to safeguard the free mission of the Church" (325).

5

The Ministry of the Ascended Lord

THE CHURCH'S PARTICIPATION IN CHRIST'S PROPHETIC AND PRIESTLY OFFICES

CHRIST'S PROPHETIC MINISTRY AND THE CHURCH

Given Torrance's description of the church's ministry as the "royal priesthood," it may appear difficult to provide a description of the church's participation in Christ's prophetic ministry.[1] The kingly (royal—significantly in adjectival form) and priestly (priesthood—possessing the substantival form) ministries are clearly present, but the prophetic office appears to be occluded. How then are we to speak of this office in Torrance's theology?

To answer this question, we must return to the biblical theology that grounds Torrance's reflection on the *munus triplex*. In Torrance's reading, the prophetic office does not possess a distinct place in the history of salvation in the same way that the kingly and priestly offices do. In a dogmatic decision that he credits to the early editions of Calvin's *Institutes*, Torrance argues for a *munus duplex* composed only of the royal and priestly offices. The prophetic office, Torrance states, arose only later within Israel's history and did so *from* the priestly office as a protest against Israel's abuse of the priesthood: "Against the independence and perversion

---

[1] Torrance is referencing 1 Peter 2:9, but it is nonetheless striking that he chooses this particular description when his doctrine of ministry draws extensively on the *munus triplex*.

of priesthood and priestly liturgy God sent the prophets, most of them out of the priesthood itself."[2] While Torrance accepts the category of the prophetic office and the framework of the threefold office, he at the same time understands it to be a derivative of the priestly office. This is why Torrance is comfortable with articulating the church's ministry as a "royal priesthood" while at the same time providing a description of the church's prophetic ministry.

For Torrance, the prophetic office emerges from the concept of *goel* as an image to describe redemption within Scripture. Torrance's use of *goel* is a unique decision within the Christian tradition's reflection on the prophetic office. As we have already seen, it has been more common to identify the prophetic office with Jesus' teaching as it addresses humanity's ignorance and epistemological blindness. In contrast, Torrance does not limit the prophetic office to Jesus' teaching ministry but instead subsumes all of his earthly ministry leading up to the cross under the office within the category of Jesus' "incarnational assumption."[3] "It is this *goel* aspect of redemption that we have been considering in the incarnate life and work of the Word and Son of God leading up to the crucifixion, that is, incarnational redemption through the Word."[4] Or, as Torrance states elsewhere, "Here in the *gaal* type of redemption the emphasis is laid upon the nature of the *redeemer*, upon the person of the *goel*."[5] While Torrance's description of the prophetic office attains its goal of focusing upon the person of the redeemer, in so doing it rejects the broader tradition's use of the office to address humanity's blindness or ignorance.

Torrance's use of the *goel* redemption concept as a foundation of the prophetic office means that the office is to be understood in its connection to the vicarious humanity of Christ. This doctrine—so central to Torrance's thought and a key aspect of his efforts both to preserve a balance between Jesus' person and work and also to prevent the instrumentalization of Jesus' humanity—is, as we shall see in our next section, also a

---

[2]Thomas F. Torrance, *Royal Priesthood: A Theology of Ordained Ministry* (Edinburgh: T&T Clark, 1955), 5.
[3]Torrance, *Atonement: The Person and Work of Christ* (Downers Grove, IL: IVP Academic, 2009), 60.
[4]Torrance, *Atonement*, 61.
[5]Torrance, *Atonement*, 45.

central aspect of the priestly office. Because of the way both are shaped by the vicarious humanity of Christ, it is not uncommon to find Torrance speaking of the prophetic office in a way that is nearly identical to how he elsewhere speaks of the priestly office. Thus in the introduction to *The School of Faith*, which he considers to be a survey of his theological project,[6] Torrance states, "The Prophetic Office refers above all to Christ's work as the Word made flesh, as He who brings the Word of the Father to bear upon man in his darkness and sin, but also as He who from within our darkness and alienation bears the Word before God."[7] It is perhaps unsurprising that there is significant overlap between the priestly and prophetic offices given his understanding of the prophetic office's derivative relationship to the priestly office. But does the church participate in the prophetic office in a way that has not already been subsumed under the priestly office? Does Torrance completely occlude the church's participation in the prophetic office by way of what he provides in his description of the priestly office?

We are tempted to ask these questions because Torrance makes Christ's *person* a central aspect within an otherwise traditional understanding of the prophetic office's place in the church's preaching ministry. Here the meaning of the prophetic office cannot be understood by a simple survey of prophetic speech in Scripture; rather, it is understood through the person of Christ who gathers up and fulfills the office: "Just as the concepts of king and priest are essentially changed when they are applied to Christ, inasmuch as he makes himself their Subject and Content, so the concept of the prophet is also changed." In what way is the concept changed? Torrance continues, "He is Prophet in a unique sense, for he is in himself the Word he proclaims."[8]

Torrance's statement that Christ "is in himself the Word he proclaims" prevents the abstraction of Jesus' teaching from his person and the abstraction

---

[6]The introduction was used by Torrance as a survey of his theology and methodology for students at New College in preparation for his lectures.
[7]Torrance, *School of Faith: The Catechisms of the Reformed Church* (Eugene, OR: Wipf & Stock, 1996), lxxxix.
[8]Torrance, *Space, Time and Resurrection* (Edinburgh: T&T Clark, 2019), 118-119.

of revelation from reconciliation within the economy of redemption.[9] The person of Christ cannot be separated from the mediation of revelation that takes place in the church's proclamation. Leading up to the ascension, Christ fulfills both sides of the God-human relation by way of the hypostatic union, mediating humanity to God in his perfect human response and the things of God to humanity in the fullness of his deity. The ascended Christ, still preserving the now-glorified humanity in the unity of his person at the right hand of the Father, continues to minister out of the perfection of the hypostatic union: "Christ, ascended, then, as the Word made flesh, as he is both Word from God to man and word from man to God."[10] And the unity of the fully human and fully divine person of Christ is essential to his prophetic ministry: "He is God's own Word translated into human form and reality and returning back to the Father as answering Word in perfect fulfilment of his Will. It is in that identity of Word of God and Word of man that Christ's prophetic ministry is fulfilled."[11] Upon the completion of his earthly ministry, it is Christ as fully God and fully human who exercises the prophetic office, and only in this way.

Torrance's identification of the prophetic ministry with the revelation of the reconciliation accomplished by Jesus Christ bears some similarity to that of Karl Barth. Like Barth, Torrance describes the prophetic ministry as the proclamation of what Jesus accomplished as the mediator between God and humanity. As Kimlyn Bender writes in his study of Barth's ecclesiology,

---

[9]John Webster notes a similar concern in Barth's account of the prophetic office:

> In post-Reformation Protestant dogmatics, both Reformed and Lutheran, Jesus' *munus propheticum* was largely identified with his revealing of the will of God in his earthly teaching, sealed by his miracles. This handling of the topic goes hand in hand with the tendency to disintegrate the three offices, so that they are no longer what they were for Calvin—three aspects of the unitary saving person and work of Christ—but a linear scheme, executed in the order prophet-priest-king. Expounded in these terms, the prophetic office threatens to become isolated from its incarnational and soteriological context, and can serve simply as a way of talking of Jesus as herald of divine truth, thereby preparing the way for rationalistic Christologies. Barth, by contrast, pushes the *munus propheticum* much more deeply into the structure of Christology and soteriology. (John Webster, "Eloquent and Radiant: The Prophetic Office of Christ and the Mission of the Church," in *Barth's Moral Theology: Human Action in Barth's Thought* [Grand Rapids, MI: Eerdmans, 1998], 130-131.)

[10]Torrance, *Space, Time and Resurrection*, 119.
[11]Torrance, *Space, Time and Resurrection*, 119.

> The atonement, as God's supreme act of reconciliation in Jesus Christ, is comprised of two elements, or movements, the obedience of the Son of God, and the exaltation of the Son of man, unified in the history of one person, Jesus Christ. Materially, these two movements comprise the doctrine of reconciliation, though from a formal standpoint a third element must be added, the revelation of the reality and unity of the history of the atonement of Jesus Christ in its two movements. . . . This third element is characterized in terms of Christ's prophetic office and is as such the revelation of the material content of the doctrine.[12]

While the priestly and kingly offices do not function in precisely the same way as they do in Barth's description of the *munus triplex*, it is apparent that there are formal resonances between how Barth and Torrance understand the prophetic office.[13]

As we stated at the beginning of this chapter, Torrance understands the church to participate in Christ's prophetic office through its own proclamation of the gospel. He notes the way that Scripture speaks of the activity of the early church in Mark 16:20: "And [the apostles] went out and preached everywhere, while the Lord worked with them and confirmed the message by accompanying signs." This description points to a "relation between the Church's proclamation of Christ and the activity of Christ himself in that proclamation where, through their common objective and dynamic content, the proclamation of the Gospel in the name of Christ and Christ's own proclamation are one and the same."[14] But rather than restricting his description to the church's preaching, Torrance presses beyond the act of preaching to what he perceives to be a more fundamental topic.

Torrance's unique contribution to the prophetic office is to begin his description of the office with the apostolic foundation of Holy Scripture. Rather than focusing upon the ecclesial act of preaching, he instead traces this act to its fundamental grounding upon Holy Scripture. This is demonstrated in his discussion of the ascended Christ's prophetic office in *Space, Time and Resurrection*, where Torrance moves from his exegesis of Mark 16:19-20 and

---

[12]Kimlyn J. Bender, *Karl Barth's Christological Ecclesiology* (Eugene, OR: Wipf & Stock, 2013), 131.
[13]For a summary of Barth's use of the *munus triplex* in the *Church Dogmatics*, see Phil Butin, "Two Early Reformed Catechisms, the Threefold Office, and the Shape of Karl Barth's Christology," *Scottish Journal of Theology* 44.2 (1991): 195-214.
[14]Torrance, *Space, Time and Resurrection*, 119.

the previous quote directly to a reference of the importance of the apostolic foundation.[15] The unity between Christ and the church's proclamation has "in an important sense . . . happened once for all in the fulfillment of the apostolic office, for it was the special function of the Apostles to translate the self-witness of Christ into witness to Christ, the self-proclamation of Christ into proclamation of Christ by the Church."[16] Here our discussion of the apostolic foundation does not revolve around the deposit's function in renewing the church and driving it out in mission as we saw in the previous chapter, but rather the centrality of this idea in Torrance's understanding of Christ's prophetic office.

Torrance's reflection on the formation and nature of Scripture is a part of, in the words of John Webster, "one of the most promising bodies of material on the Christian theology of the Bible and its interpretation from a Protestant divine of the last five or six decades."[17] Rather than moving directly from an account of Christ's prophetic ministry to the church's participation in it by way of the preaching of Holy Scripture, Torrance instead turns to a discussion of the formation of the New Testament.[18] In so doing, he explores how the church's proclamation is united to Christ's. Here, as elsewhere, the ascension is crucial, as is the event of Pentecost. Christ's withdrawal from human sight and hearing in the ascension enables the gift of the Spirit at Pentecost, which in turn allows the disciples to understand and then to communicate what had taken place in the incarnation: "It was only after Pentecost when the Spirit was sent upon them in fullness after Christ had opened the kingdom of heaven for them by his ascension, that the apostles were able at last fully to take in, assimilate and understand all that Christ had taught them by word and deed."[19]

---

[15]Torrance, *Space, Time and Resurrection*, 119.
[16]Torrance, *Space, Time and Resurrection*, 119.
[17]John Webster, "*Verbum mirificum*: T. F. Torrance on Scripture and Hermeneutics," in *The Domain of the Word: Scripture and Theological Reason* (London: Bloomsbury, 2012), 87.
[18]Torrance's discussion of the formation of the Old Testament has some formal differences from what is discussed here, but is materially basically the same. The Old Testament is formed out of Israel's covenant struggle with God and his use of that relationship to make Israel a fit bearer of revelation. See Torrance, "The Mediation of Revelation," in *The Mediation of Christ* (Colorado Springs, CO: Helmers & Howard), 1992.
[19]Torrance, *Atonement*, 324.

One of the unique features of Torrance's account of the apostolic foundation is his consideration of how Christ's prophetic office is coordinated with the persons of the apostles in the creation of the New Testament. The persons of the apostles are not incidental to revelation, but are instead taken up in the process of revelation so that the scriptural text can have its proper place in the mediation of revelation.[20] "It was to the understanding and teaching of this *word* that the apostles gave themselves daily immediately after Pentecost, so fulfilling their function as the earthen vessels specially chosen and trained by Christ and then specially endowed by his Spirit to understand and assimilate his teaching and his actions that they might bear it forth as *word* and *kerygma* creative of the church."[21] The effect of this is to emphasize the immediacy of Christ's communication to the church not first by way of the church's preaching but instead in the word of Scripture itself: "The response of the apostles was assumed by Christ into oneness with His own to form the means by which the Word of Christ reached out into history. Thus, through the apostolic witness and proclamation, it was Christ Himself who was at work testifying to the mighty acts whereby He had redeemed the world and offering Himself to men as their Saviour and Lord."[22] By way of the formation of the apostolic foundation, Christ addresses the church through Scripture.[23]

Torrance's description of Christ's prophetic office in the church—both in the formation of the apostolic foundation of the New Testament and also in the church's own act of proclamation—unfolds by way of the concept of kerygma. The formation of the apostles that took place in Jesus' earthly ministry and the subsequent gift of the Holy Spirit by the ascended Jesus combine to create a relation of identity between Jesus' own proclamation and the proclamation of the apostles: "It is because *the content of the apostolic kerygma is the living Christ himself,* that their *kerygma* is identical with Jesus Christ's own *kerygma,* in which he proclaimed himself and through

---

[20] Here Torrance's account of the apostolic witness is similar to what John Webster has proposed with respect to the "sanctification" of the creaturely agents of Scripture. See John Webster, *Holy Scripture: A Dogmatic Sketch* (Cambridge: Cambridge University Press, 2003), 26-30.
[21] Torrance, *Atonement*, 325.
[22] Torrance, "The Word of God and the Response of Man," in *God and Rationality* (Oxford: Oxford University Press, 1971), 152.
[23] Thus Webster states of Torrance's doctrine of Scripture, "This extension of the communicative presence of Christ is basic to the ontology of Scripture." Webster, "*Verbum mirificum,*" 93.

which he confronted men and women with his own person, so that the apostolic *kerygma* is an extension of Christ's own *kerygma*."[24] Torrance understands the formation of the apostolic witness to take place in such a way that it is Christ himself who speaks in their kerygma. The apostolic kerygma that makes up the New Testament is not only *about* Jesus Christ, but instead is the vehicle that Jesus uses for his own self-communication: "The supremely distinctive thing about the apostolic *kerygma*, therefore, is that it not only enshrines Christ's own *kerygma* of himself, not only contains witness to Christ based on the great events of his life and work, but has for its content nothing less than *Jesus Christ* the living Lord."[25]

Torrance devotes comparatively little time to the nature of the church's proclamation than he does to the formation of the apostolic foundation and certainly to the sacraments. One of the few places where he does discuss preaching is in his 1950 essay "A Study in New Testament Communication." Alongside the themes we have already seen in his account of the formation of the New Testament we find Torrance moving past an account of Christ's prophetic presence in Scripture to the presence of Christ in the church's own proclamation. The same emphasis is present here as elsewhere: it is Christ who is at work in the church's preaching. In this essay Torrance speaks of the original "event" of Christ reoccurring in the church's preaching by way of the Holy Spirit: "The original event becomes event all over again through the power of the Spirit so that in *kerygma* a man encounters the living Christ, Christ crucified but risen."[26] The language of "event" is later displaced within Torrance's writings as he presses traditional christological categories into deeper service in his theology (his essay "Amsterdam—The Nature and Mission of the Church," written four years later in 1954, is demonstrative of this shift away from "event" language), but nonetheless the same theological instincts are present. While later Torrance will qualify Christ's presence by way of the doctrine of the ascension rather than the language of "event," kerygma nonetheless functions to stress the divine presence at work in the church's proclamation: "*Kerygma* is objective, sacramental

---

[24]Torrance, *Atonement*, 323 (emphasis original).
[25]Torrance, *Atonement*, 323.
[26]Torrance, "A Study in New Testament Communication," in *Conflict and Agreement in the Church*, vol. 2 (Eugene, OR: Wipf & Stock, 1996), 72.

preaching with an eschatological result such that the original event (Christ crucified) becomes event all over again in the hearer."[27]

In contrast to Torrance's description of the church's participation in Christ's priestly ministry, the extent to which the concept of *hypodeigma* helps distinguish between Christ and the church's action is difficult to discern. In *Space, Time and Resurrection*, Torrance states that the Christ's kerygma is "echoed" in the church's proclamation—a word that Torrance frequently uses in connection with *hypodeigma*.[28] But beyond this hint of a reference, Torrance appears to be less interested in providing a description of the relation between the divine and ecclesial action as he is elsewhere. And where he does display this interest, it is done by way of the deposit of faith rather than by *hypodeigma*.

We may make a few observations regarding Torrance's understanding of the continuing prophetic ministry of Christ by way of a summary. First, of each of the threefold offices, Torrance devotes the least amount of space to Christ's continuing exercise of the prophetic office and the church's participation in it.[29] This slim—though still substantive—description that may be traced back to Torrance's account of the *munus triplex* is perhaps due to his belief in the derivative nature of the office within the priestly office and the *munus duplex*. As we noted in chapter two, Torrance understands

---

[27]Torrance, "Study in New Testament Communication," 72.

[28]Interestingly, Torrance continues on in the same sentence to say that the church's proclamation is "made one" with Christ's: "Primarily, it is Christ's own *kerygma*, in which through the Spirit he allows to be echoed and heard through the preaching of the Church, so that their *kerygma* about Jesus Christ is made one with his own *kerygma*." Torrance, *Space, Time and Resurrection*, 119.

[29]Of this trend within modern ecclesiologies, John Webster writes,

> Modern ecumenical ecclesiology has shown surprisingly little interest in [the ministry of the Word], and tends to have concentrated its energies elsewhere, on the sacraments (especially the Eucharist) and on the theology of ministerial order. An effect of this has been to promote a theology of the church in which the ministry of the Word does not always play a determinative role in understanding of the church's action. Sacramental agency has usually been assumed to be paradigmatic of the church's action, and fundamental questions about the relation of God's work to the work of the church have commonly been approached by trying to sort out a number of issues in Eucharistic theology. (John Webster, "The Visible Attests the Invisible," in *The Community of the Word*, ed. Mark Husbands and Daniel Treier [Downers Grove, IL: IVP Academic, 2005], 107-108).

While Torrance is not fully guilty of such an accusation due to the significant amount of attention he gives to the doctrine of Scripture, it is likely that his early extensive involvement in both the ecumenical movement and his ecclesial responsibilities (such as the Church of Scotland report, *The Biblical Doctrine of Baptism*) skewed his work away from reflection on the ministry of the Word and to sacramental theology.

the prophetic office to have arisen due to the decline of the priesthood in Israel's history, and thus he underemphasizes the office within the more fundamental framework of a twofold office. Second, Torrance's placement and description of the apostolic deposit within the church's participation in Christ's prophetic office is a unique and promising contribution to the doctrine and one that provides the foundation for Torrance's understanding of the church's preaching. Whereas other theological systems might place Holy Scripture in an awkward place somewhere outside of the mediation of reconciliation, Torrance gives it a coherent place within Christ's redemptive work. Third, preaching finds its place within the prophetic office as the church proclaims the apostolic and biblical kerygma and Christ then makes it his own. This is "a prophetic ministry in which Christ is himself its living, actual and full content, or in which Christ effectively ministers himself to us."[30] Even if it is possible to criticize the relative paucity of reflection upon preaching by Torrance, the act is nonetheless properly founded upon Jesus' redemptive work by way of the prophetic office.

But in addition to the strengths of Torrance's doctrine of the prophetic office, we may also note a relative lack of reflection upon the actual act of preaching. In his essay, "*Verbum mirificum*: T. F. Torrance on Scripture and Hermeneutics," John Webster notes the need for Torrance to provide "a more spacious account of the creaturely coefficient of revelation."[31] While Webster is referring more generally to Torrance's doctrine of Scripture, and in particular the lack of attention to textual formation and reception, the criticism can also be applied to preaching. Torrance is likely concerned that prolonged attention to the practice of preaching runs against the grain of his emphasis upon Christ's agency in speaking through the text.[32] But an account of the prophetic office that gives greater attention to what precisely is the nature of the *hypodeigma* by which the church participates in Christ's own prophetic proclamation would do much to strengthen what is already a slim description.

As a point of distinction, we can contrast Torrance's reflection upon the act of preaching with that of Karl Barth. In his aforementioned essay,

---

[30]Torrance, *Space, Time and Resurrection*, 120.
[31]Webster, "*Verbum mirificum*," 110.
[32]"So firm is [Torrance's] conception of the ostensive nature of Scripture that he does not linger over the textual sign, fearing, no doubt, that this may arrest the movement of hermeneutical intelligence in pressing through to the *res*." Webster, "*Verbum mirificum*," 110.

Webster notes the comparative lack of extended exegesis in Torrance's corpus in contrast to Barth's own extended exegetical departures in the *Church Dogmatics* and "the suffusion of his rhetoric by biblical idioms."[33] But the distinction between Torrance and Barth, while more a difference of species than genus, goes beyond this. There is nothing among Torrance's work that approximates Barth's work in *Homiletics*.[34] There, Barth expands upon the definition of the sermon,[35] the necessity of expository preaching,[36] and the way that the preacher's speech should relate to, reflect, and honor the biblical passage.[37] These kinds of reflections are missing from Torrance's corpus, even when he speaks straightforwardly about the task of preaching, as he does in the address to the Scottish Church Society later published as "Preaching Christ Today."[38] Webster is correct in stating that the problem here is "one of execution, not principle."[39] But it is also the case that his driving concern to establish the direct connection between Jesus Christ, the apostolic deposit of faith, and the church's encounter with the ascended Christ in its preaching[40] causes Torrance to pass over what are equally significant matters. Thus, in Torrance's account of the church's participation in the prophetic office, we find comparatively little attention given to the nature of the *hypodeigma* that guides this participation.

Christ's priestly ministry and the church. As we have already noted, Torrance emphasizes the priestly aspect of the church's ministry by describing it as a "royal priesthood." Of course, for Torrance the church has a priestly ministry only insofar as it participates in Christ's own priestly ministry. And

---

[33] Webster, "*Verbum mirificum*," 111.
[34] Karl Barth, *Homiletics*, trans. Geoffrey W. Bromiley and Donald E. Daniels (Louisville, KY: Westminster John Knox, 1991).
[35] Barth, *Homiletics*, 44-46.
[36] Barth, *Homiletics*, 49-50.
[37] Barth, *Homiletics*, 75-81.
[38] Torrance, *Preaching Christ Today: The Gospel and Scientific Thinking* (Grand Rapids, MI: Eerdmans, 1994), 1-40.
[39] Webster, "*Verbum mirificum*," 111.
[40] Joel Scandrett neatly describes the way that so many ecclesial loci cluster together in Torrance's thought: "A proper understanding of the deposit of faith ascertains that the very existence and authority of the church, the truth of Scripture, the proper orientation and character of Christian worship, the ontology and teleology of Christian catechesis, and the rationale and motive for Christian mission all coinhere in the sacred deposit of 'Christ clothed with his Gospel,' which is the apostolic faith." Joel Scandrett, "'Christ Clothed with His Gospel': Apostolicity and the Deposit of Faith in the Thought of T. F. Torrance," in *Marking the Church: Essays in Ecclesiology*, ed. Greg Peters and Matt Jenson (Eugene, OR: Wipf & Stock, 2016), 196.

just as with his kingly and prophetic ministries, that priestly ministry cannot be understood except within the biblical conception of redemption that begins in the Old Testament. As was noted in chapter two, Torrance links the priestly work of Christ with the Hebrew word *kipper*, which draws together cultic, legal, and covenantal language in its description of the redeeming work of God. Here the priestly act describes "an expiatory sacrifice for sin made in the offering of Christ's life for our life in obedience to the divine Will and Mercy."[41] Significantly, the redemptive act takes place in the context of a covenant relationship wherein the initiative is taken by God: God is not appeased, but rather takes initiative in providing the means of reconciliation so that the fractured relationship can be healed.

When *kipper* is integrated into the New Testament, a multivalent picture emerges. Torrance notes four different aspects of Christ's priestly mediation, and we will summarize them briefly here.[42] First, Christ's priestly work is *propitiatory* in that it is directed toward the reconciliation of two alienated parties. It is not only propitiatory in its origin from God's side, but also in its assumption of humanity in order to secure the reconciliation that is desired. Second, the priestly work of Christ is also marked by *penitence*: it is not merely forensic in nature, but also works to transform and bring to repentance human nature—not only substitutionally for humanity in its place, but representatively "within" humanity on its behalf. Third, Christ's priestly mediation should be understood within a *liturgical* framework—following the book of Hebrews, Christ's work is likened to his act of intercession on behalf of humanity. For Torrance, redemption has a fundamentally liturgical frame of reference: "The mediatorial and priestly nature of Christ's Person and work, in the unity of his divine and human agency . . . had the effect of making the whole event of our redemption one which is properly understood within the context of worship."[43] And finally priestly mediation is understood within the context of *sonship*, a basic descriptor of the relationship between God and his people.

The ascension establishes Christ's priestly ministry in heaven so that it does not come to an end at the close of Jesus' earthly ministry. Rather than

---

[41]Torrance, *School of Faith*, lxxxvii.
[42]See chapter two for a more extended description.
[43]Torrance, *The Trinitarian Faith: An Evangelical Theology of the Ancient Catholic Church* (Edinburgh: T&T Clark, 1995), 154.

ceasing, priestly ministry continues at the right hand of the Father, though still shaped by Jesus' earthly ministry. As we have seen, the priestly ministry of the ascended Jesus is a ministry marked by his "endless self-oblation," his "eternal advocacy," and his "eternal benediction." These three marks of Jesus' continuing ministry point in turn to the continuing efficacy of Jesus' reconciling priestly ministry, the continuing nature of his intercessory work on behalf and through the church, and his ongoing commissioning and strengthening of the church for ministry. For Torrance, each of these three aspects of the priestly ministry find their primary expression in the sacrament of the Lord's Supper by way of the particular form of the vicarious humanity of Jesus Christ: "The immediate key to the understanding of the Eucharist is to be sought in *the vicarious humanity of Jesus Christ, the priesthood of the Incarnate Son*."[44] Throughout his work, Torrance consistently draws each of these three doctrines together: the Lord's Supper, the vicarious humanity of Christ, and the priestly office. In order to understand the third of these doctrines, we will need to understand the first two.

The vicarious humanity of Jesus Christ. The doctrine of Jesus' vicarious humanity[45] holds such a central and foundational place in Torrance's thought that it may surprise some readers that our study has not dealt with it until now. However, given the way that the doctrine is so significant in informing human participation in Christ's work, it is fitting to leave the work of understanding it and its implications until this juncture in our project. The vicarious humanity of Jesus Christ is linked to a number of concerns that drive Torrance's thought: his historical reconstruction of patristic doctrine, his concerns about both liberal Protestantism as well as Reformed scholasticism, and his existential concerns about the experience of the Christian life. In summarizing Torrance's thought, we will explore each of these concerns in order to understand the place of Jesus' vicarious humanity as it relates to his ongoing priestly ministry before considering the doctrine's

---

[44]Torrance, "The Paschal Mystery of Christ and the Eucharist: General Theses," *Liturgical Review* 6 (1976): 6 (emphasis original).

[45]Various accounts of this doctrine can be found in Christian Kettler, *The Vicarious Humanity of Christ and the Reality of Salvation* (Eugene, OR: Wipf & Stock, 2011); Alexandra S. Radcliff, *The Claim of Humanity in Christ: Salvation and Sanctification in the Theology of T. F. and J. B. Torrance* (Eugene, OR: Wipf & Stock, 2016), 48-83; Elmer M. Colyer, *How to Read T. F. Torrance: Understanding His Trinitarian and Scientific Theology* (Eugene, OR: Wipf & Stock, 2001), 100-112; Paul Molnar, *Thomas F. Torrance: Theologian of the Trinity* (Burlington, VT: Ashgate, 2009), 119-120.

relation to the Lord's Supper and the church's participation in that priestly and eucharistic ministry.

The concerns that drive Torrance's understanding of the vicarious humanity of Christ are the same as those that shape the theological realism of his doctrine of God. In the same way that the *homoousios* functions as a way of healing the dualisms that Torrance traces within Western culture, Jesus' vicarious humanity is consciously articulated against soteriologies that are less than fully realist.[46] He describes these competing soteriologies as functioning "externally" and failing to take seriously the implications of Jesus' true humanity. This is a judgment that parallels his understanding of the *homoousion* and is similarly informed by Torrance's extensive engagement with the Nicene Fathers and also the theology of Karl Barth.[47]

In his 1976 essay "The Paschal Mystery of Christ and the Eucharist: General Theses" (not to be confused with the more well-known and similarly titled 1974 essay later collected in *Theology In Reconciliation*), Torrance makes claim to the patristic heritage of the vicarious humanity by situating the doctrine within the competing christologies of the early church:

> If the vicarious humanity or the human priesthood of Christ is to be taken in its full seriousness, nothing must be allowed to detract from the *perfection, fullness and integrity of Christ's human nature*. Thus Eutychian and monophysite tendencies in Christology and the liturgy leave no room for the human priesthood of Christ, while Apollinarian tendencies which replace the human mind and soul of Jesus with the divine mind of the eternal Son or Word, make Jesus only a bodily instrument in the hands of God, and detract from the integrity of his human agency in the whole man-Godward movement of the Incarnation.[48]

---

[46]Thus Torrance states, "A realist approach to the fact that in Jesus Christ God the Son has united himself with us in our actual existence, combine with the view that atonement takes place within the incarnate life and being of the Mediator, led Nicene theology to give full place to the teaching of St Paul about the way in which God in Christ has substituted himself for us in making our sin and death his own that we may partake of his divine life and righteousness." Torrance, *Trinitarian Faith*, 161.

[47]See in particular Torrance's discussion of the Nicene Fathers and Barth on the topic of reconciliation in "Karl Barth and the Latin Heresy," in *Karl Barth: Biblical and Evangelical Theologian* (Edinburgh: T&T Clark, 1990), 227-240.

[48]Torrance, "The Paschal Mystery of Christ and the Eucharist: General Theses," *Liturgical Review* 6 (1976): 7.

Each of these christological options in its own way failed to honor Jesus' full humanity, and the church rightly discerned that each possessed a fatal error with respect not only to Christ's person but also to his work. This commitment, gleaned from the Nicene Fathers, to take seriously the "*perfection, fulness and integrity of Christ's human nature*" leads Torrance to place such emphasis upon Gregory Nazianzen's statement, "The unassumed is the unhealed."[49] In order to conceive of a full redemption, we must at the same time conceive of Jesus' full assumption of human nature.[50]

It is this logic, traced back to the christological controversies by way of which the church articulated its understanding of the person and work of Jesus Christ, that brings Torrance to his doctrine of the vicarious humanity of Christ. Thus, Torrance states in a section of *The Mediation of Christ* entitled "The Vicarious Life and Death of the Mediator":

> Perhaps the most fundamental truth which we have to learn in the Christian Church, or rather relearn since we have suppressed it, is that the Incarnation was the coming of God to save us in the heart of our *fallen* and *depraved humanity*, where humanity is at its wickedest in its enmity and violence against the reconciling love of God. That is to say, the Incarnation is to be understood as the coming of God to take upon himself our fallen nature, our actual human existence laden with sin and guilt, our humanity diseased in mind and soul in its estrangement or alienation from the Creator.[51]

But Torrance's doctrine of the vicarious humanity of Jesus Christ is not simply Jesus' full identification with humanity by taking on human flesh. Rather, it is both his assumption of sin and guilt and also his perfect response in humanity's stead: "We are to think of the whole life and activity of Jesus from the cradle to the grave as constituting the vicarious human

---

[49] Torrance, *Trinitarian Faith*, 164.
[50] For a full-length assessment of the specific claim of the assumption of fallen humanity in Torrance's theology, see Daniel J. Cameron, *Flesh and Blood: A Dogmatic Sketch Concerning the Fallen Nature View of Christ's Human Nature* (Eugene, OR: Wipf & Stock, 2016); E. Jerome Van Kuiken, *Christ's Humanity In Current and Ancient Controversy: Fallen or Not?* (London: T&T Clark, 2017); Kevin Chiarot, *The Unassumed is the Unhealed: The Humanity of Christ in the Christology of T. F. Torrance* (Eugene, OR: Wipf & Stock, 2013); and Myk Habets, *Theology in Transposition: A Constructive Appraisal of T. F. Torrance* (Minneapolis, MN: Fortress, 2013), 163-195. For a more general discussion of the topic, see Kelly M. Kapic, "The Son's Assumption of a Human Nature: A Call for Clarity," *International Journal of Systematic Theology* 3.2 (2001): 154-166.
[51] Torrance, *Mediation of Christ*, 39 (emphasis original).

response to himself which God has freely and unconditionally provided for us."[52]

For Torrance, the logic of the christological controversies leads to a fully "realistic" understanding of Jesus' mediation of humanity's response to God. In the same way that Torrance understands Athanasius to have deployed the *homoousios* so as to secure an epistemological realism about the divine life, the concept of the vicarious humanity secures a similar kind of realism by way of Jesus Christ's obedience as a fully human representative and substitute for humanity. This is a point clarified by way of Torrance's contrast of his position with "liberals" and "fundamentalists." "Liberals" understand Jesus as a representative, modeling for humanity the way of response to the Father. The historical Jesus is celebrated but his concrete humanity is ignored, particularly as it functions within a substitutionary atonement: "Liberal theology tends to reject the concept of substitution with contempt, and concentrates upon the historical Jesus, but . . . it regularly tends to lose the humanity of Jesus for what is important for it is not Jesus himself but what he symbolises."[53] "Fundamentalists," on the other hand, focus on substitution but do so to the exclusion of a full understanding of Jesus' human life: "Fundamentalist theology . . . readily accepts the idea of substitution, and concentrates upon the saving work of God in Jesus Christ, and again tends to lose the humanity of Jesus for the Incarnation is regarded as merely instrumental and not internally related to the atonement."[54] The doctrine of the vicarious humanity is understood when the church seriously considers Jesus both as a representative of humanity (vicariously living the life that humanity should have but did not) and also a substitute (fully human in our place): "If representation and substitution are combined and allowed to interpenetrate each other within the incarnational union of the Son of God with us . . . then we may have a profounder and truer grasp of the vicarious humanity in the mediatorship of Christ, as one in which he acts in our place, in our stead, on our behalf but out of the ontological depths of our actual human being."[55]

---

[52]Torrance, *Mediation of Christ*, 80.
[53]Torrance, *Mediation of Christ*, 81.
[54]Torrance, *Mediation of Christ*, 81.
[55]Torrance, *Mediation of Christ*, 80-81.

Torrance believes a proper understanding of the vicarious humanity of Christ is to have a marked effect upon the church's articulation of the gospel and its practice of worship. Torrance is persistently concerned about an understanding of the gospel that throws humanity back upon its own resources to actualize in some way the reality of Jesus' life, death, and resurrection. In a warmly pastoral section of *The Mediation of Christ*, Torrance applies the vicarious humanity of Christ to the act of faith in Jesus Christ, to the idea of conversion, to the practice of evangelism and, significantly for our purposes, to worship and to the sacraments. Thus Torrance understands Jesus both as representative and substitute in worship, writing, "Jesus Christ embodied in himself in a vicarious form the response of human beings to God, so that all their worship and prayer to God henceforth became grounded and centred in him."[56] In the same way Torrance understands baptism and the Eucharist are for us "sacraments of the vicarious human response to God effected by Jesus Christ in his representative and substitutionary capacity in our place and on our behalf."[57]

The significance of the vicarious humanity of Jesus Christ for worship and the sacraments is an excellent segue to considering the second foundational aspect of Christ's continuing priesthood—the sacraments and in particular the Lord's Supper. But before doing so, it should be pointed out just why the vicarious humanity of Jesus Christ is so significant in Torrance's thought, not only in understanding the continuing exercise of the priestly office but also a nodal point for much of Torrance's entire theology.[58] The incarnation—and specifically the hypostatic union—is both the controlling concept for understanding divine-human relations and, by way of the vicarious humanity of Jesus, the objective, realistic site of humanity's mediated relationship back to the Father. If one wishes to consider the ecclesial activity and participation in Christ's ongoing ministry, it can only be done via the framework established here. That this is the case has implications not only for the shape of the church's ministry, but also for Torrance's construction of the threefold office. To these points we will return

---

[56] Torrance, *Mediation of Christ*, 87.
[57] Torrance, *Mediation of Christ*, 90.
[58] Thus Chiarot argues that "there is virtually no aspect of [Torrance's] theology 'downstream' from his doctrine of the Trinity which is untouched by [the assumption of fallen humanity and the vicarious humanity of Christ]." Chiarot, *Unassumed is the Unhealed*, 224.

in our assessment of Torrance's vision for ecclesial ministry at the end of this chapter.

Baptism, the Lord's Supper, and the church's priestly ministry. Throughout Torrance's writing there is a clear link between the ongoing priestly ministry of Jesus Christ and the Lord's Supper as the fundamental expression of the church's participation in that office. The chapter of *Royal Priesthood* titled "The Priesthood of the Church" is representative of this link: it is a sustained meditation on the place of the Lord's Supper in the ministry given to the church by Christ. There Torrance writes, "Thus in the Eucharist the Church assumes true form and order in obedience to the Word, but as such that order is not static, but dynamic, not a state but action."[59] The church's priestly ministry is a ministry understood as participation in Christ's priestly office and this is so primarily by way of the Lord's Supper.

But as soon as this is said, we must at the same time remember that Torrance's emphasis upon the Lord's Supper is not made to the exclusion or neglect of the sacrament of baptism. Thus while baptism may not receive the same material emphasis in Torrance's description of the church's priestly ministry, it is nonetheless closely linked by way of its shared status as a sacrament of the church and also because of the profound link between baptism and the vicarious humanity of Jesus Christ in Torrance's thought: "Jesus was baptised with the baptism of repentance not for his own sake but for ours, and in him it was our humanity that was anointed by the Spirit and concerted in sonship to the Father."[60] Because the Lord's Supper shares such close proximity to baptism by way of Torrance's sacramental theology and his understanding of the vicarious humanity of Jesus Christ, it is helpful to place the two sacraments in relation to one another in order to better understand Torrance's thought at this juncture.

Baptism. Torrance's sacramental theology of baptism and the Lord's Supper has its foundation in his understanding of the "dimension of depth" that both ecclesial acts contain. Baptism, Torrance states, "must be interpreted in coherence with the whole Gospel of the Incarnation, *in a*

---

[59]Torrance, *Royal Priesthood*, 72.
[60]Torrance, "One Baptism Common to Christ and His Church," *Theology in Reconciliation* (Eugene, OR: Wipf & Stock, 1996), 86.

dimension of depth going back to the saving work of God in Jesus Christ, and as grounded so objectively in the work that it has no content, reality or power apart from it."[61] In the same way Torrance states regarding the Lord's Supper, "The mystery of the Eucharist is objectively grounded in the Paschal mystery of Christ which gives it meaning. Therefore the Eucharist is to be understood not by looking *at* it, but by looking *from* it and *through* it to the paschal Mystery of Christ."[62] Both baptism and the Lord's Supper are properly understood only in their shared relation to the person and work of Jesus. He is the dimension of depth within which both find their proper place. Thus Torrance states at the beginning of his essay "The One Baptism Common to Christ and His Church"—in what amounts to a programmatic statement for Torrance's sacramental theology—"The primary *mysterium* or *sacramentum* is Jesus Christ himself, the incarnate reality of the Son of God who has incorporated himself into our humanity and assimilated the people of God into himself as his own Body, so that the sacraments have to be understood as concerned with our *koinonia* or participation in the mystery of Christ and his Church through the *koinonia* or communion of the Holy Spirit."[63]

Torrance's understanding of Jesus Christ himself as the "primary *sacramentum*" is crucial in establishing the relationship between baptism and the Lord's Supper in his thought and in their place in the church's ministry. Baptism is essential to understanding the church's priesthood because it is the sign of our incorporation into Christ and his priesthood. Therefore Torrance states in his chapter on "The Priesthood of the Church" in *Royal Priesthood*, "Baptism . . . is the sacrament of the general or corporate priesthood of the Church, for it is through Baptism that we are incorporated into the Body of Christ and are inserted into the ministry of His Body. All who are baptised into Christ are baptised into the Royal Priesthood."[64] Torrance's understanding of the place of baptism draws from the same christological resources that permeate all of his theology—namely, the vicarious humanity of Jesus Christ: "Here we have . . . a doctrine of the priesthood of the whole Church through its participation in the substitutionary

---

[61] Torrance, "One Baptism Common," 82-83 (emphasis original).
[62] Torrance, "Paschal Mystery of Christ," 6 (emphasis original).
[63] Torrance, "One Baptism Common," 82.
[64] Torrance, *Royal Priesthood*, 74.

Self-consecration of Christ our High Priest.... In the last analysis it is Christ Himself who is the one Priest, and men are ordained only in the sense that He gives them to share in His Priesthood."[65]

There are two implications of Torrance's understanding of baptism and the church's ministry that are worth noting within his understanding of the church's ministry. First, by making baptism the sign of incorporation into Christ, it is also the sign of incorporation into his *ministry* and indeed the sign of the church's earthly existence. Baptism, Torrance states, is representative of the shape of Jesus' ministry as a suffering servant and thus provides the pattern (*hypodeigma*)[66] for the church's life in the world: "The Church through Baptism into the death of Christ is made to grow together with Him ... so that in a very real sense Christ comes to be formed within the Church giving it conformity with Him."[67] Second, the place Torrance gives to baptism as the sign of incorporation into Christ's ministry and specifically his priestly ministry establishes the corporate nature of the church's ministry. Torrance provocatively states that there is no such thing as "the priesthood of all believers"; it is a title that belongs only to Jesus Christ. "The expression 'priesthood of all believers' is an unfortunate one as it carries with it a ruinous individualism. 'Priest' in the singular is never found in the NT applied to the believer, any more than 'king' in the singular. In the singular these words could only apply to Christ Himself."[68] But this is a statement made on the way to establishing the corporate nature of priesthood shared by the entire church and its participation in Christ's singular priestly ministry: "The participation of the Church in the ministry of Christ is *primarily corporate*. Thus the ministry of the Church refers primarily to the royal priesthood which pertains to the whole membership of Christ's Body."[69] The result is to emphasize the corporate character of ministry within the body of Christ and the shared participation in Christ's ministry laid upon all who have been baptized into Jesus Christ.

---

[65] Torrance, *Royal Priesthood*, 80-81.
[66] Torrance, *Royal Priesthood*, 35. "It is now clear that, as the ministry is grounded upon the whole relation of the Church to Christ, the doctrine of ministry must be formulated in terms of the Christological pattern (*hypodeigma*)."
[67] Torrance, *Royal Priesthood*, 34.
[68] Torrance, *Royal Priesthood*, 35n1.
[69] Torrance, *Royal Priesthood*, 35n1 (emphasis original).

Before we consider Torrance's understanding of the Lord's Supper within Christ's priestly ministry, it is worth noting a curiosity in how Torrance writes of baptism in relation to Christ's threefold ministry. While the passages quoted above demonstrate that one can locate baptism within the priestly office in *Royal Priesthood*, elsewhere Torrance is consistently silent regarding the connection between this sacrament and the priestly office. There are clearly connections due to the way the vicarious humanity of Christ, the priestly office, and the sacraments cluster together in Torrance's thought. And yet in the overwhelming majority of Torrance's writings on baptism—"The One Baptism Common to Christ and His Church," "The Origins of Baptism," "Aspects of Baptism in the New Testament," "The Meaning of Baptism," and *The Biblical Doctrine of Baptism*—Torrance refrains from making an explicit connection between the priestly office and baptism. This is perhaps nowhere more obvious than in Torrance's masterful essay, "The Mind of Christ in Worship: The Problem of Apollinarianism in the Liturgy." There, within the course of a sweeping argument about the implications of a proper understanding of the vicarious humanity of Christ and the priestly office for the church's liturgy and worship, Torrance is silent about baptism. The Lord's Supper, on the other hand, is given a prominent place in the discussion. This silence is perhaps only demonstrative of the occasional nature of Torrance's writings. His treatment of baptism may also be affected by the disproportionate relationship between how often the two sacraments are celebrated in the life of the church. But it is nonetheless significant, and it helps to explain why Torrance's treatment of the relation between the priestly office and the Lord's Supper will receive the seemingly disproportionate (but actually reflective of Torrance's corpus) attention that we shall now give to it.

The Lord's Supper. As we have seen, baptism sets the terms for the church's participation in Christ and his ministry. Through that sacrament, the church is incorporated into the pattern of his ministry as a suffering servant and given participation in his priestly office. But it is through the Lord's Supper that the church is renewed and sustained as it enacts that ministry. For Torrance, the singular nature of baptism is understood in its correspondence with the church's continuing eucharistic ministry: "By Baptism we are incorporated into One Body but that unity is preserved (1 Cor. 10.16f; 12.12f) and made visible in the Lord's Supper (1 Cor. 11.18ff). Here the whole life and form of the Church's life are seen to derive from a source beyond the Church, in the Blood and Body of Christ, and can only be maintained by continual return to that source."[70] It is in the Lord's Supper that we see the church renewed in the ministry it receives through baptism: "We have two sacraments; one which seals His once-for-all work of salvation, and one which continually seals our renewal in that finished work and gives us to participate in its effective operation."[71]

What is the particular shape of the renewal that is found in the Lord's Supper? We recall first that Torrance understands the priestly office, which undergirds the Lord's Supper, now to be exercised in three distinct ways: "endless self-oblation," "eternal intercession and advocacy," and "eternal benediction."[72] Given the way in which the priestly office and the Lord's Supper are linked in Torrance's thought, we should expect to find the church participating in the office via the table in ways that coordinate with each of these acts. And that, as detailed below, is indeed what may be found when the strands of Torrance's reflection on the Lord's Supper are untangled. Moreover, if Torrance is consistent with what we have already said about the priestly office, we should expect the vicarious humanity of Christ to feature prominently in his writing on the Eucharist. And this is also the case:

> In so far as the Eucharist is the act of the Church in [Jesus'] name and is also a human rite, it must be understood as an act of prayer, thanksgiving, and worship, i.e., as essentially *eucharistic* in nature, but as act in which through the Spirit we are given to share in the vicarious life, faith, prayer, worship, thanksgiving and self-offering of Jesus Christ to the Father, for in the final resort it is Jesus Christ himself who is our true worship.[73]

To these three forms of the Church's participation in Christ's priestly office do we now turn.

Self-oblation. Jesus' "eternal self-oblation" is understood by Torrance to be the way in which humanity is offered up to the Father in the life of the

---

[70]Torrance, *Royal Priesthood*, 64.
[71]Torrance, "Toward a Doctrine of the Lord's Supper," in *Conflict and Agreement in the Church*, vol. 2 (Eugene, OR: Wipf & Stock, 1996), 146.
[72]Torrance, *Space, Time and Resurrection*, 115-118.
[73]Torrance, "Paschal Mystery of Christ," 109.

incarnate Son.⁷⁴ "In the humanity of the ascended Christ there remains for ever before the Face of God the Father the one, perfect, sufficient Offering for mankind. . . . He represents us before the Father as those who are incorporated in him and consecrated and perfected together with him in one for ever."⁷⁵ Torrance is here expanding upon the propitiatory aspect of the priestly office, one of the four aspects of Christ's priestly action that he draws from his biblical-theological exposition of *kipper*: "Propitiation is wrought out in Jesus Christ himself. . . . He is . . . the man who in our place draws near to God and so submits himself to the divine judgement, offering himself in sacrifice to God."⁷⁶ This same propitiatory action is represented in the Lord's Supper as it points to Jesus' death on the cross: "When on the night in which he was betrayed, Jesus celebrated the passover with his disciples, he linked it with his passion in the inauguration of the new covenant for the remission of sins, and when he said 'this is my body,' 'this is my blood,' he constituted himself the mystery of the Supper."⁷⁷

The Lord's Supper points to Jesus' self-offering, but it is not in and of itself that offering. Just as with baptism, the "dimension of depth" that the sacrament contains is crucial to grasping Torrance's understanding of how the Eucharist partakes of this aspect of the priestly office. As we have already seen, Torrance is suspicious of any description of ecclesial action that would approach something like *ex opere operato* or any other kind of symmetry between divine and human action:

> The Eucharist is what it is not because of what it is in itself as an act of the Church but because of what it is in its grounding beyond in what God in Christ has done, does do, and will do for us in his Spirit. Very serious problems

---

⁷⁴It is worth noting the resonances between Torrance's understanding of the ascended Christ's priestly work and that of recent biblical scholarship on the Epistle to the Hebrews. David M. Moffitt's groundbreaking *Atonement and the Logic of Resurrection in the Epistle to the Hebrews*, Supplements to the Novum Testamentum 141 (Leiden: Brill, 2013) argues that the center of Christ's priestly work is to be found in the presentation of his life before the Father at the ascension. There Moffitt presents a compelling account of how "it is not ultimately Jesus' death that is his sacrifice, but his life. Jesus' living presence in heaven, predicated on the resurrection and ascension of his human body, was the sacrifice that he offered to God in the heavenly holy of holies. . . . The offering of Jesus' body, blood, and self is the presentation of his life before God" (284). This account parallels Torrance's description of Christ's ongoing exercise of his priestly office that we find here.
⁷⁵Torrance, *Space, Time and Resurrection*, 115.
⁷⁶Torrance, *Atonement*, 68-69.
⁷⁷Torrance, "Paschal Mystery of Christ," 106.

arise when the focus of attention is shifted from that objective ground to the ritual act in the foreground, that is, from the person of the Mediator, God manifest in the flesh, to the sacramental rite as a means of saving grace.[78]

Rather Torrance's understanding of the church's action in the Lord's Supper seeks to follow the asymmetrical depiction of divine and human action that is found in his account of *hypodeigma*: "The Lord's Supper or the Eucharist is both the act of Christ and the act of the Church in his name, but in the nature of the case the act of the Church is one which serves the act of Christ and directs us away from itself to Christ."[79] The "dimension of depth" complements Torrance's use of *hypodeigma*, emphasizing the divine action that grounds ecclesial action: "In this perspective [the dimension of depth] the Eucharist by its very nature points us beyond itself to its constitutive reality in Jesus Christ himself."[80]

The Lord's Supper is intelligible as a participation in Christ's "eternal self-oblation" through the vicarious humanity of Christ. Christ's priestly office is exercised in the ascension "as the act of Christ's self-offering to the Father in which his self-sacrifice on the Cross is backed up by his own resurrection and endless Life, and made a self-offering to God through the Eternal Spirit." But Jesus offers not only himself, but humanity within himself. Any sense in which the Eucharist is considered an act of offering does not terminate with the act itself but instead is enclosed within Jesus' act on the church's behalf: "The Eucharist is not to be regarded as an independent act on our part in response to what God has already done for us in Christ (i.e., not as the *Church's* supper, but as the *Lord's* supper), but as act towards the Father already fulfilled in the humanity of Christ in our place and on our behalf."[81]

Therefore, over and against conceptions of the Lord's Supper, which would describe the act as in some sense propitiatory, Torrance understands the church's action at the table to be a participation in the priestly act of propitiation that Christ continues to exercise in his "eternal self-offering" in heaven. Through the Eucharist, the church enjoys the fruits of that propitiation: access to the Father and the communion of the Holy Trinity.

---

[78]Torrance, "Paschal Mystery of Christ," 107.
[79]Torrance, "Paschal Mystery of Christ," 107.
[80]Torrance, "Paschal Mystery of Christ," 108.
[81]Torrance, "Paschal Mystery of Christ," 109 (emphasis original).

> The Eucharist, while being the worship of men on earth, is essentially a participation in the worship of the heavenly sanctuary which Jesus Christ their ascended High Priest renders to the Father in the oblation of His endless life, for it is worship in the same Spirit by whom we are made one with the Son as he is one with the Father, in whom we have access to the Father, and through whom we are taken up into the eternal communion of the Father, the Son and the Holy Spirit.[82]

As a participation in Christ's self-oblation, the Lord's Supper is a means by which the church enjoys the access and communion that Christ has secured for it in his life, death, and resurrection.

Eternal intercession and advocacy. Torrance's description of the ascended Christ's priestly work of intercession and advocacy is intelligible by way of the liturgical framework within which he understands Christ's saving work. In *The Trinitarian Faith*, Torrance acknowledges the Nicene Fathers as the source of this idea, stating, "The mediatorial and priestly nature of Christ's Person and work, in the unity of his divine and human agency . . . had the effect of making the whole event of our redemption one which is properly understood within the context of worship."[83] That emphasis upon worship is most evident in Torrance's aforementioned idea of Christ's "advocacy and intercession": "Here is an Advocacy in which Christ is the eternal Leader of our prayer and intercession, in which he makes himself the true content and sole reality of the worship and prayer of man."[84]

For Torrance, this intercession and advocacy finds its ecclesial location in the Lord's Supper. Even in the foundational work of the opening chapters of *Atonement*, Torrance draws attention to this connection: "It is this aspect of the atonement that is particularly evident in the worship and sacramental life of the church—and not least in the eucharist which must be regarded as a dramatic prayer in union with the mediation and intercession of our ascended high priest at the right hand of the Father."[85] But in what way does the Lord's Supper serve the church's participation in this advocacy and intercession?

---

[82] Torrance, "Paschal Mystery of Christ," 110.
[83] Torrance, *Trinitarian Faith*, 154.
[84] Torrance, *Space, Time and Resurrection*, 116.
[85] Torrance, *Atonement*, 71.

Here again the vicarious humanity of Christ establishes the proper relation between divine and ecclesial action, here by way of Torrance's liturgical description of the atonement. According to Torrance, Christ's redemptive work is a liturgical work. His life is a kind of prayer that obtains mercy in the heavenly throne room: "Let us now think of this as the self-offering of Christ, in which he prays for us not only with his words but with his life and life-blood for us sinners—the prayer of priestly self-sacrifice."[86] This "prayer" is prayed not only on behalf of humanity but also in our place: he is both representative and substitute for humanity. If Christ was merely humanity's representative, he would pray only in our place: "If he were only our representative before God, he would represent us in *our* prayer and worship and would be, so to speak, their instrument."[87] But these would not actually be humanity's prayers—they would only be Christ's. Torrance's use of the vicarious humanity of Christ, however, means that Christ prays not only as substitute but also as representative: "He acts in our place and offers worship and prayer which we could not offer, yet offers them in such a vicarious way that while in our stead and on our behalf they are made to issue out of our human nature to the Father as our own worship and prayer to God."[88] The church's prayer is Christ's prayer (in the comprehensive sense that Torrance uses this concept), but it is at the same time its own prayer: "That identification is so profound that through the Spirit Christ's prayers and intercessions are made to echo in our own, and there is no disentangling of them."[89]

In his ecumenical writings Torrance expands upon the concept of "echo"[90] as a way of describing the relationship between Christ and the church's intercession. For Torrance, "echo" is a way of filling out precisely what the traditional eucharistic concept *anamnesis* means as a descriptor of the church's action: "The action of the Church is the *anamnesis* of an act that is once and for all, and enduring before the Face of the Heavenly Father; but

---

[86] Torrance, *Atonement*, 71.
[87] Torrance, *Space, Time and Resurrection*, 116.
[88] Torrance, *Space, Time and Resurrection*, 116-117.
[89] Torrance, *Space, Time and Resurrection*, 117.
[90] He attributes the concept to Donald MacKinnon and its use in a report written for the Sixth Anglo Catholic Congress. Torrance, "Eschatology and the Eucharist," in *Conflict and Agreement in the Church*, vol. 2 (Eugene, OR: Wipf & Stock, 1996), 176n1.

it is no more than *anamnesis*, for it is not the act itself. It is the living echo of that act which Christ alone performs as Mediator and Savior."[91] It is clear that Torrance is working out again the concept of *hypodeigma*, seeking to describe the asymmetrical relationship between divine and human action. At the Lord's Supper, the church witnesses to and remembers (*anamnesis*) the supremacy and singularity of Christ's intercession. And yet at the same time, the church also itself intercedes, its own action bound up with Christ's as it points to his action.

For Torrance, proper celebration of the Lord's Table through the eucharistic liturgy points to this eternal advocacy and intercession, and the church's echo of Christ's prayer. His landmark essay, "The Mind of Christ in Worship: The Problem of Apollinarianism in the Liturgy," is representative of his attempts to work toward reforming the church's worship. There, he draws from the work of J. A. Jungmann to argue that certain changes in the church's liturgical practice have obscured the full extent of Christ's mediatorial work, an error that has had profound functional effects upon christology and ecclesial practice. What is needed is a liturgy and eucharistic practice that is grounded on the truth of the full extent of Christ's vicarious work to facilitate the church's full understanding of the benefits of the priestly office. This is worship that is *through* and *with* Christ, not simply *to* Christ.[92] Worship that is in this spirit is worship that reflects the participation in Christ's intercession that is given to the church through Christ's priestly ministry.

While Torrance believes that the entirety of eucharistic liturgy and worship serves as a witness to Christ's intercession and advocacy, his favorite example of this is the Lord's Prayer. As an essential part of the church's worship and eucharistic liturgy, the prayer is indicative of the central dynamic of Christ and the church's priestly intercession. Thus, in his description of Christ's continuing priestly work of intercession in *Space, Time and Resurrection*, Torrance writes,

> It is in this light that we have to understand Eucharistic worship and prayer, and are to think of the heart of it all in the Lord's Prayer which we take into

---

[91]Torrance, "Eschatology and the Eucharist," 176.
[92]Torrance, "Mind of Christ in Worship: The Problem of Apollinarianism in the Liturgy," *Theology in Reconciliation* (Eugene, OR: Wipf & Stock, 1996), 185-198.

our mouths at his command. It is Prayer backed up with the pledges of His broken body and shed blood which he puts into our hands, with which to appear before the Father, for it is his one sufficient and once for all offering of himself for us that is our only sacrifice before God. This is neither a Pelagian offering of the immolated Christ by man nor a Pelagian offering of ourselves in addition to the sacrifice of Christ, but the pleading of a sacrifice which by its very nature is offered on our behalf and in our place and in our stead, so that it is not we but Christ himself who here stands in for us as our Mediator and Advocate, while we take refuge in his sole sacrifice, finding shelter in his prayer and intercession and not our own. "Nothing in my hands, I bring, simply to Thy Cross I cling."[93]

The place of the Lord's Prayer within the eucharistic liturgy provides the appropriate context for understanding ecclesial intercession. It is grounded upon Christ, dependent upon his own intercession so as to secure its efficacy. And it is also Christ's own prayer (the *Lord's* Prayer), which he has taken upon his own lips in our place. It is, according to the framework of Christ's vicarious priestly ministry, a prayer that is made in our place, on our behalf.

By way of its participation in Christ's intercession, the church enters into intercession for the world and participation in his servant-shaped ministry. Because Christ's intercession is on behalf of humanity, the church's participation is an intercession of the same kind: "Through the *anamnesis* the Church enters into the passion of the Redeemer, and in His name travails in prayer for all mankind."[94] Torrance views the church's participation in Christ's intercessory prayer as the driving force behind its mission in the world. In his essay "Service in Christ," Torrance connects Christ's high priestly ministry of intercession to the church's mission by way of the church's intercession: "The Church does not minister through the power of its own action but only through the power of its Lord, and therefore cannot fulfill its *diakonia* on earth without continuous engagement in intercession through its great high Priest at the right hand of God almighty."[95] It is not only true that the church is unable to accomplish the task of ministry without its action being taken up in the divine action, but even its prayers

---

[93]Torrance, *Space, Time and Resurrection*, 117.
[94]Torrance, "Eschatology and Eucharist," 177.
[95]Torrance, "Service in Jesus Christ," in *Gospel, Church, and Ministry: Thomas F. Torrance Collected Studies 1*, ed. Jock Stein (Eugene, OR: Pickwick, 2012), 158-159.

for and on behalf of the world must participate in Jesus' intercession. And this intercession is itself a real work of engaging with the powers of the fallen world. Torrance continues, stating, "The intercessory prayer of the Church is direct engagement in the mighty apocalyptic battle between the Kingdom of Christ and the kingdoms of this world and in the triumphant reign of the enthroned Lamb over all the forces of evil and darkness in history. The Church's great need is to *believe again* in the intercession of Christ and to find through prayer the sole source of power in its mission."[96] For Torrance, the church's mission finds its expression as it joins Christ in his high priestly intercession on behalf of humanity.

Eternal benediction. The final aspect of the ascended Christ's continuing priestly ministry is his benediction,[97] which is the gift of the Holy Spirit. Although Torrance does not provide the biblical theology for this concept in the same way that he does for other aspects of the threefold office, he acknowledges the work of Scottish theologian William Milligan and his *The Ascension of the Lord* for laying the groundwork for his own ideas. The connection between priestly action and blessing is drawn from the Old Testament accounts of Melchizedek and Aaron: "The language which the Old Testament uses to speak of these aspects of Christ's heavenly priesthood is taken from the Old Testament accounts of Melchizedek's blessing of Abraham, and from the Aaronic blessing of God's people after the completion of the sacrificial liturgy on the Day of Atonement."[98] Jesus' own blessing of the disciples, with the promise of the Holy Spirit and its subsequent fulfillment at Pentecost, are the fulfillment of those Old Testament "shadows": "Pentecost is the content and actualization of that high priestly blessing. He ascended in order to fill all things with his presence and to bestow gifts of the Spirit upon men."[99]

Torrance's description of the Lord's Supper as the location of the benediction of the Spirit has significant implications for the place of the table in

---

[96]Torrance, "Service in Jesus Christ," 159.
[97]For a more extended account of the biblical roots of the priestly benediction, which also draws attention to its significance to John Calvin, see Kelly M. Kapic, "Receiving Christ's Priestly Benediction: A Biblical, Historical, and Theological Exploration of Luke 24:50-53," *Westminster Theological Journal* 67.2 (2005): 247-260.
[98]Torrance, *Space, Time and Resurrection*, 117.
[99]Torrance, *Space, Time and Resurrection*, 118.

the church's mission and ministry. For Torrance, the Lord's Supper is the central place where the real presence of Jesus Christ is made available to the church and where Jesus both ministers in the power of the Spirit and also empowers the church for mission. In his essay "Eschatology and the Eucharist," Torrance calls the Lord's Supper "the sacramental enactment of the real presence of Christ."[100] "When we say . . . that the Eucharist is the sacramental enactment of the real presence of Christ, we must make clear that it is the real presence of the God-Man. No doubt it is through the eternal Spirit, through an act issuing from the Godhead, but it is the divine enactment of the Incarnate Presence in the Church."[101] In the Lord's Supper, the ascended Jesus is present through the Holy Spirit to the church in full divinity and humanity in a unique and exclusive way. And Torrance describes two specific ways the church participates in this eternal benediction in its ministry: the sacramental relation to the crucified and risen Jesus Christ and the distribution of spiritual gifts.

The sacramental relation. Torrance understands the sacraments to have a crucial place in the church's existence "between the times." They are at the same time a part of the old order of the cosmos and also the new order that Jesus Christ has established and will one day bring to completion. They serve as gifts to the church, pointing backwards to Jesus' first advent and pointing ahead to his second: "On one side the Sacraments belong very much to earth and its on-going space and time. . . . But on the other side they are signs of the new order which has once and for all broken into our world in Jesus Christ and in which we have constant participation through the Spirit even though since the ascension that new order is veiled from our sight."[102] For Torrance the sacraments are understood by way of eschatology as they serve to work out the implications of the continuing ministry of Christ in the church: "Eschatology properly speaking is the application of Christology to the Kingdom of Christ and to the work of the Church in history. . . . The crucial issue in eschatology concerns the Humanity of the risen Christ, and our participation in His Humanity through Word and Sacrament in the Church."[103]

---

[100]Torrance, "Eschatology and Eucharist," 186.
[101]Torrance, "Eschatology and Eucharist," 186.
[102]Torrance, *Space, Time and Resurrection*, 148.
[103]Torrance, *Royal Priesthood*, 43.

We recall that for Torrance one of the implications of Christ's ascension is that it establishes his earthly career as the only place where we may understand the witness of Jesus Christ: "By withdrawing himself from visible and physical contact with us as our contemporary throughout history, Jesus Christ sends us back by his ascension to the Gospels and to their witness to the historical Jesus Christ."[104] But the church has more than just a historical relationship with Jesus by way of the witness of the Gospels. It is through the sacraments that the church encounters the continued ministry of Jesus.

Because he gives the witness of the historical Jesus descriptive control over the church's mission and ministry, Torrance must then provide an account of ecclesial action that is in accord with what we find in the Gospels. We have already seen that this is at least partially accomplished through his use of *hypodeigma*. The concept of the "Suffering Servant" provides continuity between the form of Christ's ministry as well as that of the church. But Torrance recognizes that this concept does not exhaust the description that is found in the Gospels: "With the immediate presence of the Son of God in the Incarnation the authoritative signs of that new order were his acts of healing and of forgiveness taken together, signs that pointed ahead to the crucifixion and the resurrection, as the mighty acts of cosmic significance that constituted the ground for all acts of healing and forgiveness in the Name of Christ."[105] Torrance has in mind specifically miraculous acts of healing that were an essential part of the ministry of Jesus. How then does Torrance give continuity between the Christ and the church at this point?

Torrance's answer is to locate Christ's healing ministry with his presence in the sacraments and, in particular, at the Lord's Supper. The continuity is somewhat muted by Torrance's claim that these miraculous acts are no longer prominent in the same way because much of their purpose terminated in the establishment of the apostolic deposit of faith. They "are no longer prominent, for their unique revelatory function is fulfilled in what came to be handed on as the New Testament."[106] Indeed Torrance argues that the dominant mode of Christ's ministry is one in which "Christ holds back the physical transformation of the creation to the day when he will return

---

[104]Torrance, *Space, Time and Resurrection*, 147.
[105]Torrance, *Space, Time and Resurrection*, 149.
[106]Torrance, *Space, Time and Resurrection*, 149.

to make *all things new*, and that in the meantime he sends the Church to live and work in the form of a servant."[107] And yet these acts are nonetheless a part of Christ's ministry through the church, only now by way of the sacraments: "Now in on-going history his healing and forgiving work is normally mediated through the Holy Sacraments which are given to the historical Church to accompany the proclamation of the Gospel and to seal its enactment in the lives of the faithful."[108] Christ is free to exercise his ministry outside of the sacraments through miraculous intervention, but the "normal" place for the mediation of his forgiveness and healing is the no less miraculous ministry of sacraments: "With his resurrection and ascension these sacraments were constituted by the power and presence of the Spirit as the 'miraculous signs' of the Church's forgiveness and healing, of its crucifixion and resurrection with Christ, to be used perpetually throughout the course of its historical existence."[109] In particular, the Lord's Supper is where we see this ministry continue to be enacted. In contrast to baptism, which is the "Sacrament of Justification" and therefore "is not to be repeated,"[110] the church continuously participates in Christ's ministry at the table: "The Eucharist is the Sacrament of our continuous participation in Christ and may be spoken of as the Sacrament of Sanctification."[111] When we wish to see the continuation of the ministry of the ascended Jesus through the church, we look to the Lord's Supper. It is there that Christ continues his work of benediction, blessing the church with the gifts that he has won in the atonement.

The distribution of gifts. The other place where we observe Christ's work of eternal benediction is in Torrance's concept of the distribution of spiritual gifts at the Lord's Supper. In his discussion of the eternal benediction of Christ, Torrance gives this aspect of Christ's continuing priestly ministry a prominent place: "This [Christ's eternal benediction] is, again, an aspect of Christ's royal priestly ministry which is especially relevant to the Church's Communion in the body and blood of Christ through the Spirit. It is through the Church's *koinonia* with Christ that various gifts are distributed to members of the Church which in their manifold character and working

---

[107]Torrance, *Space, Time and Resurrection*, 149.
[108]Torrance, *Space, Time and Resurrection*, 149.
[109]Torrance, *Space, Time and Resurrection*, 149.
[110]Torrance, *Space, Time and Resurrection*, 149.
[111]Torrance, *Space, Time and Resurrection*, 149.

together in the one Body are made to echo the one Priesthood of Christ."[112] It is through the Lord's Supper that spiritual gifts are both given to the church and also that these gifts find their proper order.

In order to grasp Torrance's reasoning here, we must understand the exegetical reasoning that undergirds it. In his chapter on "The Priesthood of the Church" in *Royal Priesthood*, Torrance gives a reading of 1 Corinthians 10-14, which notes the significance of how Paul's argument moves from the Lord's Supper to spiritual gifts to the superintending goal of love within the body of Christ.[113] The ordering of Paul's argument—from the discussion of the Lord's Supper in chapter eleven to the counsel regarding spiritual gifts in chapter twelve—is suggestive of a deeper, theological connection between the two topics in Paul's thought: "In the eleventh and twelfth chapters he speaks of the ordering of the Church as it comes together to celebrate the Lord's Supper. . . . It is made clear in the twelfth chapter that the Lord's Supper and the *charismata* belong inseparably together, and that the charismatic gifts are to be used in accordance with the promulgation of God's will in the New Covenant or Testament."[114]

At the Lord's Table two distinct events are accomplished simultaneously. First, spiritual gifts are given at the table: "In the ordering of the Eucharist, and for the Church at the Eucharist, special *charismata* or gifts are given."[115] But they are not merely given; they are also properly ordered. This second act is just as significant. Here Torrance draws upon Paul's transition to the discussion of love in 1 Corinthians 13: "In the thirteenth chapter St. Paul goes on to describe the nature of the new divine order as Love for *Agape*. That divine Love is manifest in the ordering of the Supper in the midst of the love-feast or *Agape* and in the mutual service the charismatic gifts involve."[116] As we have already seen in chapter three, *agape* love is intrinsic to the church's nature as the body of Christ. When the gathered church celebrates the Lord's Supper, that love is enacted in the ordered distribution of spiritual gifts: "That love is the very *esse* of the Church given to it through union with

---

[112]Torrance, *Space, Time and Resurrection*, 118.
[113]Torrance acknowledges Ernst Kasemann and H. Doebert for their influence on his reading. See Torrance, *Royal Priesthood*, 63n1.
[114]Torrance, *Royal Priesthood*, 65.
[115]Torrance, *Royal Priesthood*, 65.
[116]Torrance, *Royal Priesthood*, 65.

Christ, and manifests in the Church in the form of self-denial, suffering and service (1 Cor. 13.3ff). This love which is given to the Church in history is *charismata* and operates through *diakonia*, reaches out to the divine *telos* of the eternal Kingdom."[117] Through the benediction of the Spirit in the Eucharist, the church is both gifted and ordered to this end.

Beyond the general description of Christ's eternal benediction and the Spirit's work of ordering to the end of love and service, Torrance's account of how the Lord's Supper accomplishes these things is short on specifics. But he is at the same time concerned with distinguishing between Christ's priestly ministry and the church's corresponding activity. While Christ does distribute spiritual gifts by way of his continuing priestly ministry through the Lord's Supper, he does not at the same time give over his priestly ministry to the church. Here again, Torrance is concerned to distinguish between divine and human action by way of the concept of *hypodeigma*. The church's use of the various spiritual gifts is "service": "The Church is thus also a 'royal priesthood' on earth through the Spirit, but a real priesthood in a secondary sense, participating in the one Priesthood of the ascended King through its *service* of him."[118] It is not possible to add up the various *charismata* distributed by Christ so as to comprehend Christ's priestly ministry. To do so would be to give the church an improper control over the priestly ministry. Instead, for Torrance, the spiritual gifts given at the table facilitate the kind of indirect participation that governs Torrance's understanding of divine and human action: "The priesthood of the Church is not constituted through the aggregation of the priestly function of its individual members but is only a reflection of the one indivisible Priesthood of Christ. Through the Spirit Christ's own priestly ministry is at work in and through the Church which is his Body."[119]

For Torrance, Christ's continuing exercise of his priestly office is at the very center of the church's ministry and mission. The centrality of the priestly office in Torrance's organization of the *munus triplex* is reflected in the church's participation in Christ's continuing ministry. Christ exercises his priestly office through the sacraments, the place where the church is both

---

[117] Torrance, *Royal Priesthood*, 66.
[118] Torrance, *Space, Time and Resurrection*, 118 (emphasis original).
[119] Torrance, *Space, Time and Resurrection*, 118.

incorporated into Christ and his ministry and also renewed in that relation. While not to the exclusion of baptism, the church participates in Christ's ministry chiefly as it gathers for the Lord's Supper. There, Christ exercises the three aspects of his ascended ministry: his oblation, his advocacy, and his benediction. In the Eucharist, the church is renewed in the access and communion that Christ has won for his people through his exclusive propitiation, it participates in the intercession that Christ undertakes for the church and on behalf of the world, and it receives the gifts that Christ possesses and freely gives while at the right hand of the Father.

The scope of Torrance's theology of the priestly office is a significant accomplishment and a synthesis of many of the central aspects of his thought. Given the importance of the vicarious humanity of Christ for Torrance's understanding of the relationship between divine and human action—and how closely Torrance draws together this doctrine and the Lord's Supper—it is unsurprising that we should find a number of ecclesial actions clustered around the Lord's Supper. And, indeed, we do: the church's spiritual gifting for ministry, its intercession for the world, the continued healing ministry of Christ, and the church's renewal of its union with Christ are all found in this sacrament. Ecclesiologies that desire to incorporate mission as a meaningful category and end of the church often empty the Lord's Supper of the real presence of Christ so that they may functionalize the sacrament as a demonstration of some more seemingly fundamental value.[120] These kinds of sociological explanations of ecclesial acts are significant departures from the kind of objective realism Torrance rightly is concerned to protect. In Torrance we find married together a commitment to sacramental realism and an exploration of the missional implications of the Lord's Supper.

And yet the importance of the priestly office for Torrance's understanding of the church's participatory ministry bears the signs of a lack of proportion to the other offices of Christ's work. The priestly office is so fundamental to Torrance's description of the church's participation in Christ's ongoing ministry that it threatens to crowd out the significance of the other two. In Torrance's most systematic presentation of the impact of the three offices in

---

[120]See, for example, the chapter, "Disciples Break Bread Together" from John Howard Yoder's *Body Politics: Five Practices of the Christian Community Before the Watching World* (Scottsdale, PA: Herald Press, 1992).

Space, Time and Resurrection, the kingly and prophetic offices receive one and five paragraphs of treatment, respectively. The priestly office, in contrast, receives six full pages. And, as we have already noted, Torrance's shorthand description of the church's ministry, "royal priesthood," is also telling.

It is not necessarily the case that each office should be considered equally important in the mediation of redemption. Beginning with Calvin, the Reformed tradition has often understood the priestly office to have a central importance among the other offices.[121] But there is in Torrance's work an occlusion of each of the other two offices by the priestly office. It is not just the case that Christ's priestly office "opens the way" for the kingly and prophetic offices.[122] Rather, as we have already seen in our initial discussion of the threefold office, the prophetic office is subsidiary to the priestly office within an original schema of a *munus duplex*, and additionally the implications of the kingly office are muted as it is now exercised "through his priestly mediation before God."[123] There is an underdevelopment of the prophetic and kingly offices in Torrance's theology here, and insofar as this lack of development leads the church into a misunderstanding of its own proclamation of and service to the gospel, it deserves scrutiny and critical evaluation. Torrance's constructive proposal for the church's mission and ministry should not therefore be dispensed with entirely, but rather might serve as a crucial conversation partner along the way toward a more well-proportioned account of Christ's ministry and the church's participation in it.

Conclusion

In his essay, "Ministry in Union with Christ: A Constructive Critique of Incarnational Ministry," Todd Billings laments the lack of theological depth in many contemporary articulations of the church's ministry. Well-meaning

---

[121] See, for example, Edmundson's evaluation of Calvin:
> Calvin has a great deal to say about Christ's office as king and prophet, but he is nevertheless clear that Christ's work as priest is the foundation to a proper understanding of his role as Mediator.... If we are to understand Christ's purpose, we must begin with his offer of himself through his death to reconcile the Church to God; that is, we must begin with his work as priest. It is only by means of this reconciliation that way is open for the broader covenant relation between God and the Church. Through his priestly work, Christ opens the way for his work as prophet and king. (Stephen Edmondson, *Calvin's Christology* [Cambridge: Cambridge University Press, 2004], 89.)

[122] Edmundson, *Calvin's Christology*, 89.

[123] Torrance, *Space, Time and Resurrection*, 112.

advocates of "incarnational ministry" commit the unintentional error of conflating the work of Christians serving Christ with the work of Christ. These advocates move past the imperative of imitating Christ in ministry and slip into language which identifies their own activities of imitation as itself redemptive. "Incarnation" is no longer a singular act of Jesus Christ, it is instead a description of what is to be normative for every minister of Christ. To this, Billings says, "Instead of seeing the incarnation as a process we undergo, we should seek to be very clear about a central doctrinal point: the power of incarnation is precisely in its uniqueness—that Jesus Christ is God's incarnate one, and no other."[124]

As an alternative, Billings proposes a "a theology of ministry in union with Christ the servant."[125] Drawing on Calvin, Ursinus, and Barth, he proposes a work of theological retrieval from the church's tradition that better utilizes the ample resources that can be found within the Reformed tradition and the doctrine of ministry and mission therein. The *munus triplex* is central to the argument he sketches: "It is an extraordinary gift given to all who share Christ's anointing—all Christians—to participate in Christ as the true prophet, priest, and king. For through faith Christians are 'engrafted' into Christ as members to the head, that we may be continuously sustained, governed, and quickened by him; and because he makes us prophets, priests, and kings unto God and his Father, by making us partakers of his anointing.'"[126]

In the extensive writings of T. F. Torrance on the church's participation in Christ's ongoing ministry through the *munus triplex*, we have a valuable contribution to the tradition that Billings references. The creative organization of the threefold office, the robust sacramental vision that funds the church's mission, the union with and yet asymmetrical distinction between Christ and the church, the unique contribution of the prophetic office to the church's doctrine of Scripture: each of these is a significant contribution to the church's reflection upon its mission and ministry in the world.

---

[124] J. Todd Billings, *Union with Christ: Reframing Theology and Ministry for the Church* (Grand Rapids, MI: Baker, 2011), 135-136.
[125] Billings, *Union with Christ*, 143-165.
[126] Billings, *Union with Christ*, 162. Billings is quoting Ursinus's commentary on the Heidelberg Catechism.

Conclusion

THE CENTRAL ARGUMENT of this book has been that T. F. Torrance's theology is not only consistently informed by his own sense of theological vocation "to help the church evangelize the entire culture,"[1] but also that he provides a comprehensive and constructive theology of the missional church. Whereas Torrance scholars such as Stanley S. MacLean have argued that, "Torrance's doctrine of the mission of the church is a small part of his theology, and the theologian's ruminations on mission are confined to the earlier stages of his career,"[2] we have demonstrated that mission—both as a driving motivation and as a persistent concern—is a central aspect of Torrance's theology. Beginning with his doctrine of God and continuing on through christology, ecclesiology, and finally an account of the church's participation in the continuing ministry of the ascended Christ, Torrance's thought is a compelling articulation of the church's mission, and one that serves as a valuable contribution to an ongoing conversation about the church's existence and ministry. In contrast to proposals that focus primarily on sociological realities or that are truncated by only focusing upon ecclesiology, Torrance provides an example of a truly *theological* engagement with the church's mission.

Why is this attempt at a theological engagement with the church's ministry and mission significant and thus deserving of the attention that we

---

[1] Michael Bauman, "Interview with Thomas Torrance," in *Roundtable: Conversations with European Theologians* (Grand Rapids, MI: Baker, 1990), 114.
[2] Stanley S. MacLean, "A Radical New Humanism: Thomas Torrance's Mission of the Church," *Participatio* 6 (2017): 193.

have devoted to it in this book? Why are all the elements of Torrance's theology—from the objective realism of his doctrine of God to his creative reworking of Reformed christology to the various elements of his ecclesiology and finally his constructive proposal for how the church can participate in each of the threefold offices of Christ—worth not only our study but also critical appreciation and constructive amendment? To put it simply, Torrance's missional theology is founded on the conviction that *the living God acts*. And if it is God who acts in the church's witness, then the church would be foolish not to call upon all of the resources of the various loci of systematic theology so that it may speak truthfully in its witness. As John Webster writes in his essay "Principles of Systematic Theology," "Systematic apprehension of the Christian gospel is necessary. . . . Theological system is rendered necessary by the comprehensiveness and singularity of the object of Christian confession and praise. God is one; all other things are held together and have their several natures in relation to God."[3]

Torrance's theological engagement with the church's ministry and mission is not without its weaknesses and thus in need of correction. But if there is dissatisfaction with elements of his project, this is only because the larger vision is so important and vital. In his understanding of his own vocation as an ecclesial theologian working toward the evangelization of Western culture, Torrance grasped that simply proposing alterations to church practice in light of cultural or sociological shifts is an implicit denial that the subject of theology is the most important object of the church's attention. Similarly, to move directly from the doctrine of God to ecclesiology or mission is to ignore the important relationships between doctrines and the way that careful consideration of this prevents the church from falling into error by way of ignorance. Torrance understood this and worked with zeal and love to refine the church's witness.

THE PRIESTLY MISSION OF THE CHURCH: STRENGTHS AND WEAKNESSES

The centrality of the sacraments in Torrance's account of the church's mission and ministry provides an excellent nodal point from which we may provide

---

[3]John Webster, "Principles of Systematic Theology," in *The Domain of the Word: Scripture and Theological Reason* (London: Bloomsbury, 2012), 144.

a concluding evaluation of his proposal. By describing the church as a "Royal Priesthood," a description that privileges the body of Christ's participation in Christ's priestly office (and therefore the significance of the sacraments), we can better understand what Torrance's missional ecclesiology accomplishes as well as what unintentional weaknesses should be noted as this proposal serves as a contribution to the church's own proclamation of and service to the gospel of Jesus Christ.

As our first chapter demonstrates, a driving and even organizing concern of Torrance's theology is a theological objective realism that overcomes the persistently dualistic habits of mind of the West. The *homoousion* is important to Torrance because it provides, with passionate singularity, a way to conceptualize God both in his action and in his availability to human knowing. God speaks and acts, and in so doing God is unfettered by any separation between the divine and the human. In Jesus Christ and in his Spirit, God is freely available to the world to act and to be known.

The centrality of the priestly office and of the Lord's Supper is simply the unfolding of Torrance's theological objective realism through his doctrine of God and his ecclesiology, to his understanding of ecclesial action in mission and ministry. The Lord's Supper is central to Torrance's theology because it is here more than anywhere else that Torrance discerns the church's ability to speak of Christ's very real presence: "When we in the Eucharist remember his passion and plead for his atoning sacrifice, this is not a mere recollection of what he has done for us once and for all on the Cross but the setting forth of a memorial or *anamnesis*, according to his command, which through the Spirit is filled with the presence of Christ in the indivisible unity of all his vicarious work and his glorified Person."[4] In the Lord's Supper, Christ is really and objectively present, not only descending to humanity but also gathering up humanity in his ascent back to the Father, "the mutual involution of his *God-manward* and *man-Godward* activity."[5] The significance of the vicarious humanity of Christ for the Lord's Supper is indicative of the objectivity of salvation for the church. For Torrance, it is at the Lord's Table that the church encounters Jesus Christ.

---

[4]Torrance, "Paschal Mystery of Christ and the Eucharist: General Theses," *Liturgical Review* 6 (1976): 136. It is significant that throughout this essay, Torrance addresses the problem of dualism as it relates to a proper understanding of Christ's presence at the table.
[5]Torrance, "Paschal Mystery of Christ," 136.

At the same time, the centrality of the priestly office and its connection to the Lord's Supper preserves the important distinction between Christ and the church and prevents the complete collapse of the church into christology. The church exists not only *enhypostatically* in Jesus, receiving its life and being from its communion with him, but also *anhypostatically*, looking for its life outside of itself in its Lord. The Lord's Supper preserves for Torrance this ontological and eschatological dialectic: "The Sacrament of the Eucharist . . . is the form which our sacramental union with Christ takes within the brokenness and the divisions of history, and yet mediates the wholeness of that union as such an abiding reality that the brokenness and the divisions of history, in which the church inevitably partakes, are revealed to be but the shell of the old life which passes away."[6] With this dialectic in place and preserved through the Lord's Supper, the church cannot be described as an "extension of the incarnation" or any similar term that would somehow obscure the distinction between Christ and the church. Through Christ's priesthood, the church is continually receiving its identity as a "royal priesthood."

It is also this concern to safeguard a theological objective realism that leads Torrance to the particular set of emphases that organizes his understanding of the *munus triplex*. Torrance's emphasis upon the priestly office is the result of the theological objective realism that drives his concerns about epistemology, soteriology, and the church's mission. The vicarious humanity of Jesus Christ, the nature of Jesus' relation to the church, and the objective reality of his presence each coordinate with the emphases of the priestly office and do not straightforwardly find the same correlation with the kingly and prophetic offices. The "already and not yet" dialectic that governs the church's participation in the kingly office has an uneasy relation to Torrance's concerns. Rather than offering an account of the provisional authority that earthly rulers are given in the overlap of the ages like that found in O'Donovan, Torrance emphasizes both the objective reality of Christ's kingship and yet also insists on the veiling of this reign until Christ returns.[7] His decision to subordinate the exercise of the kingly office to the

---

[6]Torrance, "Eschatology and the Eucharist," in *Conflict and Agreement in the Church*, vol. 2 (Eugene, OR: Wipf & Stock, 1996), 173.
[7]Torrance, *Space, Time and Resurrection* (Edinburgh: T&T Clark, 2019), 112.

priestly office is a result of this deeper theme of objective realism that runs throughout his theology.[8] The priestly office is again more amenable to the concerns that drive his project.

The prophetic office is similarly underdetermined by the priority of the priestly office. As we have already noted, Torrance deviates from many traditional Reformed accounts of the prophetic office which, like Calvin, conceive of the office in their God-humanward dimension in the interpretation and proclamation of the salvation accomplished for humanity. What we find in Torrance is instead a description of the prophetic office that is founded upon the *goel* conception of redemption, the "incarnational assumption"[9] of humanity. Torrance's uneasiness with traditional Reformed doctrine at this point is a result of his sensitivity to any description of redemption that does not include with it the objective reality of its accomplishment. Thus Torrance moves beyond the God-humanward movement so that the prophetic office also includes the human-Godward movement. His interpretation of the prophetic office's subordination to the priestly office within the salvation history of Israel and his relative lack of attention to the "creaturely coefficient of revelation" likewise bear the imprint of Torrance's nervousness on this account: the appearance of revelation without reconciliation and the arresting "of hermeneutical intelligence in pressing through to the *res*,"[10] namely, the objective reality of Jesus Christ present to and vicariously for humanity.

The emphasis upon the priestly office and the sacramental enactment of the church's mission also invites us to reflect upon whether or not the church's mission is unintentionally delaicized by such a description. An early interlocutor with Torrance's *Royal Priesthood*, Hendrik Kraemer, thought that this was the case in his engagement with Torrance in *A Theology of the Laity*. While Kraemer heaps praise upon Torrance for his use of the *munus triplex* to describe the shape of the church's mission, he also reserves criticism for what he sees as an unintentional privileging of ordained ministry.

---

[8]"Even in ascension the power of Christ is exercised through his sacrifice, through his atoning expiation of guilt, through his priestly mediation before God." Torrance, *Space, Time and Resurrection*, 112.

[9]Torrance, *Atonement: The Person and Work of Christ* (Downers Grove, IL: IVP Academic, 2009), 60.

[10]John Webster, "*Verbum mirificum*: T. F. Torrance on Scripture and Hermeneutics," in *The Domain of the Word: Scripture and Theological Reason* (London: Bloomsbury, 2012), 110.

Commenting on the tendency of theologians to demonstrate a "reticence" to speak of the ministry of the laity, Kraemer remarks,

> A striking example of this magnetic attraction towards the ordained ministry is T. F. Torrance's book: *Royal Priesthood*. The more striking, because the basic assumption in this book, full of profound remarks, is that all that has to be said about the Church regards the Church *as the whole Body*, but the real purpose of the book turns out to be to define a "corporate" conception of the ordained Ministry. The other sector of "the Body," viz. the laity, vanishes out of sight.[11]

Kraemer's critique identifies a significant lack of development of a crucial aspect of the church's ministry and mission. In a classic section of *The Gospel in a Pluralist Society*, one of the central texts of the missional theology movement, Lesslie Newbigin speaks of the necessity of the church equipping men and women to exercise their calling in the world. The church's priestly calling, Newbigin says, is to be exercised by its members in their individual callings: "This priesthood has to be exercised in the life of the world. It is in the ordinary secular business of the world that the sacrifices of love and obedience are to be offered to God. . . . The Church gathers every Sunday . . . to renew its participation in Christ's priesthood. But the exercise of this priesthood is not within the walls of the Church but in the daily business of the world."[12] This priestly calling is to be given structure by the church's teaching office, Newbigin says, as men and women are instructed in how their secular work is included in God's mission to the world.[13]

Such an emphasis is not entirely absent from Torrance. In his writings on the relationship between theology and science, Torrance makes brief mention of humanity's mediatorial and priestly role in the cosmos. Humanity's "priestly function" is to mediate the meaning and order that is embedded within the universe: "The universe as a whole is formed in such a way that man constitutes that intelligent ingredient in it through whose heuristic inquiry and creative activity the universe knows and unfolds itself in developing rational order and expression. This is man's priestly function

---

[11]Hendrik Kraemer, *A Theology of the Laity* (Philadelphia: Westminster Press, 1958), 161n1. I am indebted to Andy Cornett for pointing out this volume to me.
[12]Lesslie Newbigin, *The Gospel in a Pluralist Society* (Grand Rapids: Eerdmans, 1989), 230.
[13]Newbigin, *Gospel in a Pluralist Society*, 230.

in the universe, as man of faith and man of science."[14] But beyond this sketch of how scientists might understand their own vocation through a priestly lens, Torrance does not emphasize or expand upon this aspect of the church's mission. We have also seen Torrance's discussion of the Lord's Table as the site of the Holy Spirit's distribution of spiritual gifts, but this as well is given without much comment or description. What is lacking is an account of the human person as an ethical agent in the world, living in response to and in the light of Christ's vicarious work.

Once again we find Karl Barth to be a helpful point of reference for understanding Torrance's position. What we find in Barth that we do not find in Torrance is something like the concept of vocation that Barth discusses in IV/3 of the *Church Dogmatics*. Organized under the framework of the prophetic office, Barth discusses the nature of the calling placed upon each Christian in their relation to Jesus Christ. Vocation is "the event in which man is set and instituted in actual fellowship with Jesus Christ, namely, in the service of His prophecy, in the *ministerial Verbi divine*, of the Word of reconciliation, and therefore in the service of God and his fellowmen."[15] Here vocation is inclusive of the shape and nature of Christian existence in the world. This description is governed by the concept of witness, which for Barth captures a range of actions but preserves the same kind of asymmetry between divine and human action that is also important to Torrance.[16] It is significant (but a point that should not be pressed too far) that Barth discusses vocation before he considers the sending of the Christian community in a subsequent paragraph of the *Church Dogmatics*. For Barth, the shape of Christian witness in the world is a pressing question that must be answered for men and women so that they might live faithfully in "the light of life" that is Jesus Christ.

While there is not space within this study to explore the reason behind this divergence between Torrance and Barth, such an observation does align with similar comments made about Torrance's theology and the place of the human person as an ethical agent within it. These discussions have usually

---

[14]Torrance, *Divine and Contingent Order* (Edinburgh: T&T Clark, 1981), 129-130. See also Torrance, *The Christian Frame of Mind: Reason, Order, and Openness in Theology and Natural Science* (Eugene, OR: Wipf & Stock, 2010), 59-63.
[15]Karl Barth, *CD* IV/3.2, 482.
[16]Barth, *CD* IV/3.2, 597-600.

clustered around a different aspect of ecclesiology, Barth and Torrance's disagreement regarding the nature of baptism.[17] Here the same question surfaces: Does Torrance provide within his theology a thick description of the shape of Christian existence alongside his account of the vicarious humanity of Christ? John Webster comments on what he perceives to be a difference between Torrance and Barth at precisely this point:

> Barth and Torrance part company because the latter allows little substance to the notions of covenant partnership and reciprocal agency which are deeply embedded in the structure of Barth's account. Torrance, indeed, explicitly repudiates what he calls the trapping of grace within "reciprocity between God and man." Behind this lies a deeper incompatibility at the level of Christology; where Torrance sees the acts of Jesus as solely vicarious, Barth sees them as representative acts which are nevertheless more than simply completed events containing proleptically our involvement: they are "really an imperative."[18]

At question is not the viability of the concept of the vicarious humanity of Christ but rather the space that it occupies within the architectonic of Torrance's thought. The linked concepts of the vicarious humanity and priestly office of Christ both appear out of proportion to other aspects of the work of Christ and the nature of the Christian life.

While it is outside the scope of this study to pursue Webster's analysis of the competing christologies within Torrance and Barth, our own work suggests that there is some merit to Webster's argument. In R. Michael Allen's study of the concept of the role of the faith of Jesus Christ in theology, he makes an argument that is for the most part sympathetic to the concept of the vicarious humanity of Jesus Christ. But his study identifies the same reticence to provide a thick description of humanity's corresponding faith and obedience that Webster identifies above.[19] This desire to emphasize

---

[17] John Webster, *Barth's Ethics of Reconciliation* (Cambridge: Cambridge University Press, 1995), 170-173; W. Travis McMaken, "Actualism, Dualism, and Onto-Relations: Interrogating Torrance's Criticism of Barth's Doctrine of Baptism," *Participatio* 6 (2016): 1-31.
[18] John Webster, "The Christian in Revolt: Some Reflections on The Christian Life," in *Reckoning with Barth: Essays in Commemoration of the Centenary of Karl Barth's Birth*, ed. Nigel Biggar (London: Mowbray, 1988), 126. For a vigorous reply, see Todd Speidell, *Fully Human in Christ: The Incarnation as the End of Christian Ethics* (Eugene, OR: Wipf & Stock, 2016), especially 1-37.
[19] R. Michael Allen, *The Christ's Faith: A Dogmatic Account* (London: T&T Clark, 2009), 195-200.

divine action as a primary over and against theologies that simply throw the church back upon its own resources is not only admirable, but is also a necessary response to the various missional theologies that provide so thin an account of the work of the ascended Christ that one could imagine that they would carry on quite the same without his presence! But the reticence to provide a thicker description of the moral ontology that God's action creates for human creatures—the *imatatio* that rests within Christ's vicarious work—overcorrects and leaves imbalanced descriptions of the kingly and prophetic offices and how the church participates with them.

THE CONTRIBUTION OF TORRANCE'S MISSIONAL ECCLESIOLOGY

This observation about Torrance's theology is not fatal to the argument that we have made about the significance of his missional ecclesiology. While future interlocutors with his understanding of the church's ministry and mission will need to grapple with the issues above, Torrance's contribution to the current conversation remains significant. As we conclude, it is worth enumerating the contribution that Torrance makes to the current discussion regarding the nature of the church's mission.

First, and perhaps most significantly, Torrance provides a decidedly systematic and catholic contribution to a discussion that has been impoverished by a lack of attention to both the church's tradition as well as the resources of systematic theology. Rather than relying merely upon sociological analysis of Western culture or providing a truncated theological account that both begins and ends in ecclesiology, in Torrance we find an account of the church's mission that keeps as its first language the grammar of the triune God of the gospel. For Torrance, to speak of the church's mission is to speak of God, a goal to which all missional theologies should aspire but few have attained. The theological objective realism that is at the center of Torrance's thought ensures that the church points to the ascended Lord as the source of its life and not to its own efforts or resources.

Second, Torrance's methodology demonstrates the importance of the church's christological resources for the articulation of the church's mission. Christ's redemptive work does not cease with the resurrection but instead continues by way of the ascension and the gift of the Holy Spirit. The nature of the work of Christ, described in the *munus triplex*, is therefore important so as to prevent the church's self-understanding of its ministry from drifting into abstraction or falling into *a priori* judgments made apart from the primary grammar of the Holy Trinity. Calvin and Torrance are both motivated by the same concern in their use of the *munus triplex*—"that faith may find a firm basis for salvation in Christ, and thus rest in him,"[20]—for Calvin in the understanding of what Christ's work has secured for the church, and for Torrance in the application of this work for the church's self-understanding of its participation in Christ's continued ministry. While Torrance's construction of the threefold office is not without weaknesses, in its methodology it is exemplary.

Third, Torrance presents unique contributions for understanding the intrinsic relationship between the church and its mission. In particular, the connection Torrance draws between the deposit of faith and the church's renewal in its mission deserves consideration as theologians of the church's mission attempt to formulate how the church is to understand itself. Missional theologies claim the priority of mission for the church's life, but often do so with little reflection upon how this claim is to be understood within theology's principles and proportions. Torrance's proposal is an example of how this might be done in such a way that does not infringe upon claims of God's aseity and that rests upon the church's foundation on the deposit of faith.

Fourth and finally, Torrance's description of the church's participation in the ascended Jesus' continued ministry is an important contribution to the growing number of missional ecclesiologies presented to the church. Torrance's use of the concept of *hypodeigma*, while in need of some development and refinement, is a helpful concept for understanding the correspondence of divine and human action. Torrance's description of the priestly office places the sacraments of baptism and the Lord's Supper at the center of the church's mission and does so in a way that reinforces the theological objective realism that are at the center of his thought, avoiding falling back upon sociological explanations of "practice" that lose the primary grammar of the Holy Trinity.[21] While not without need of correction, Torrance's

---

[20]John Calvin, *Institutes of the Christian Religion*, ed. John T. McNeill, trans. Ford Lewis Battles (Louisville, KY: Westminster John Knox, 1960), 494.

[21]For a discussion of this, see Nicholas M. Healy, "Practices and the New Ecclesiology: Misplaced Concreteness?," *International Journal of Systematic Theology* 5.3 (2003): 287-308.

presentation of the church's participation in the *munus triplex* is an example of the kind of considered presentation of the shape of the church's ministry that can guide the church to greater faithfulness in its mission and ministry.

It is to this end that this work argues. As a missional theologian, Torrance has been an undervalued conversation partner to this point. The work done here provides both a contribution to the continued understanding of his own thought and body of work as well as a contribution to the wider discussion about the nature of the church's mission. My prayer is that it will serve as an aid and service to those who lead and labor for the church's work in the world.

Bibliography

Allen, R. Michael. *The Christ's Faith: A Dogmatic Account*. London: T&T Clark, 2009.
———. *Justification and the Gospel: Understanding the Contexts and Controversies*. Grand Rapids, MI: Baker Academic, 2013.
Anatolios, Khaled. "Yes and No: Reflections on Lewis Ayres, *Nicaea and its Legacy*." *Harvard Theological Review* 100.2 (2007): 153-158.
Augustine. *The Trinity*. 2nd ed. Introduction, translation and notes by Edmund Hill OP. Hyde Park, NY: New City Press, 1991.
Ayres, Lewis. *Augustine and the Trinity*. Cambridge: Cambridge University Press, 2010.
———. *Nicaea and its Legacy: An Approach to Fourth-Century Trinitarian Theology*. Oxford: Oxford University Press, 2004.
Barrett, Lois Y. *Treasure in Clay Jars: Patterns in Missional Faithfulness*. Grand Rapids, MI: Eerdmans, 2004.
Barth, Karl. *The Doctrine of the Word of God*. Vol. 1, bk. 1 of *Church Dogmatics*, translated by G. T. Thomson. Edinburgh: T&T Clark, 1936.
———. *The Doctrine of God*. Vol. 2, bk. 1 of *Church Dogmatics*, translated by T. H. L. Parker et al. Edinburgh: T&T Clark, 1957.
———. *The Doctrine of Reconciliation*. Vol. 4, bk. 3 of *Church Dogmatics*, edited by G. W. Bromiley and T. F. Torrance. London: T&T Clark, 2009.
———. *God in Action: Theological Addresses*. Translated by Elmer George Homrighausen and Karl J. Ernst. New York: Round Table Press, 1936.
———. *Homiletics*. Translated by Geoffrey W. Bromiley and Donald E. Daniels. Louisville, KY: Westminster John Knox, 1991.
Bauman, Michael. "Interview with Thomas Torrance." In *Roundtable: Conversations with European Theologians*. Grand Rapids, MI: Baker, 1990.
Bavinck, Hermann. *Sin and Salvation in Christ*. Vol. 3 *of Reformed Dogmatics,* edited by John Bolt. Translated by John Vriend. Grand Rapids, MI: Baker Academic, 2006.
Bender, Kimlyn J. *Karl Barth's Christological Ecclesiology*. Eugene, OR: Wipf & Stock, 2013.
Billings, J. Todd. *Union with Christ: Reframing Theology and Ministry for the Church*. Grand Rapids, MI: Baker Academic, 2011.
Bosch, David J. *Transforming Mission: Paradigm Shifts in Theology of Mission*. 20th anniv. ed. Maryknoll, NY: Orbis Books, 2011.
Brownson, James V., Inagrace T. Dietterich, Barry A. Harvey, and Charles C. West. *Stormfront: The Good News of God*. Grand Rapids, MI: Eerdmans, 2003.
Brunner, Emil. *The Christian Doctrine of Creation and Redemption*. Vol. 2 of *Dogmatics*. Eugene, OR: Wipf & Stock, 2014.
Burgess, Andrew. *The Ascension in Karl Barth*. Hampshire, UK: Ashgate, 2004.

Butin, Phil. "Two Early Reformed Catechisms, the Threefold Office, and the Shape of Karl Barth's Christology." *Scottish Journal of Theology* 44.2 (1991): 195-214.
Calvin, John. *Institutes of the Christian Religion*. Edited by John T. McNeill. Translated by Ford Lewis Battles. 2 vols. Louisville, KY: Westminster John Knox, 1960.
Cameron, Daniel J. *Flesh and Blood: A Dogmatic Sketch Concerning the Fallen Nature View of Christ's Human Nature*. Eugene, OR: Wipf & Stock, 2016.
Chiarot, Kevin. "T. F. Torrance and Apostolic Succession." *Participatio* 6 (2017): 112-150.
———. *The Unassumed is the Unhealed: The Humanity of Christ in the Christology of T. F. Torrance*. Eugene, OR: Wipf & Stock, 2013.
Chung, Titus. *Thomas Torrance's Mediations and Revelation*. Farnham, UK: Ashgate, 2011.
Colyer, Elmer M. *How to Read T. F. Torrance: Understanding His Trinitarian & Scientific Theology*. Downers Grove, IL: InterVarsity Press, 2001.
———. *The Nature of Doctrine in T. F. Torrance's Theology*. Eugene, OR: Wipf & Stock, 2001.
———, ed. *The Promise of Trinitarian Theology: Theologians in Dialogue with T. F. Torrance*. Lanham, MD: Rowman and Littlefield, 2001.
Davidson, Ivor. "Theologizing the Human Jesus: An Ancient (and Modern) Approach to Christology Reassessed." *International Journal of Systematic Theology* 3.2 (2001): 129-153.
Deddo, Gary W. *Karl Barth's Theology of Relations: Trinitarian, Christological, and Human; Towards an Ethic of the Family*. New York: Peter Lang, 1999.
———. "T. F. Torrance: The Onto-Relational Frame of His Theology." *Princeton Theological Review* 15.2 (2008): 35-48.
———. "The Realist and Onto-Relational Frame of T. F. Torrance's Incarnational and Trinitarian Theology." *Theology in Scotland* 16 (2009): 105-136.
Dolezal, James. *All That Is in God: Evangelical Theology and the Challenge of Classical Theism*. Grand Rapids, MI: Reformation Heritage Books, 2017.
Edmondson, Stephen. *Calvin's Christology*. Cambridge: Cambridge University Press, 2004.
Emery, Gilles. *The Trinitarian Theology of St Thomas Aquinas*. Translated by Francesca Murphy. Oxford: Oxford University Press, 2007.
Farrow, Douglas. "T. F. Torrance and the Latin Heresy." *First Things*, 238 (2013): 25-31.
Fergusson, David. "The Ascension of Christ: Its Significance in the Theology of T. F. Torrance." *Participatio* 3 (2012): 92-107.
Flett, John G. *Apostolicity: The Ecumenical Question in World Christian Perspective*. Downers Grove, IL: IVP Academic, 2016.
———. *The Witness of God: The Trinity, Missio Dei, Karl Barth, and the Nature of Christian Community*. Grand Rapids: MI: Eerdmans, 2010.
Frost, Michael, and Alan Hirsch. *The Shaping of Things to Come: Innovation and Mission for the 21st-Century Church*. Peabody, MA: Hendrickson, 2003.
Guder, Darrell L. *Be My Witnesses: The Church's Mission, Message, and Messengers*. Grand Rapids, MI: Eerdmans, 1985.
———. *Called to Witness: Doing Missional Theology*. Grand Rapids, MI: Eerdmans, 2015.
———. *The Continuing Conversion of the Church*. Grand Rapids, MI: Eerdmans, 2000.
———, ed. *Missional Church: A Vision for the Sending of the Church in North America*. Grand Rapids, MI: Eerdmans, 1998.
Gunton, Colin E. *Act and Being: Towards a Theology of the Divine Attributes*. Grand Rapids, MI: Eerdmans, 2002.
———. *The One, the Three and the Many: God, Creation and the Culture of Modernity*. Cambridge: Cambridge University Press, 1993.

Habets, Myk. *Theology in Transposition: A Constructive Appraisal of T. F. Torrance*. Minneapolis: Fortress, 2013.

———. *Theosis in the Theology of Thomas Torrance*. Farnham, UK: Ashgate, 2009.

Hasker, William. *Metaphysics and the Tri-Personal God*. Oxford: Oxford University Press, 2013.

Hastings, Ross. *Missional God, Missional Church: Hope for Re-Evangelizing the West*. Downers Grove, IL: IVP Academic, 2012.

Healy, Nicholas M. "Practices and the New Ecclesiology: Misplaced Concreteness?," *International Journal of Systematic Theology* 5.3 (2003): 287-308.

Heron, Alasdair I. C. "*Homoousios* with the Father." In *The Incarnation: Ecumenical Studies in the Nicene-Constantinopolitan Creed A.D. 381*. Edited by Thomas F. Torrance, 58-87. Edinburgh: Handsel Press, 1998.

Hesselink, I. John. "A Pilgrimage in the School of Christ: An Interview with T. F. Torrance." *Reformed Review* 38.1 (1984): 49-64.

Holmes, Stephen R. *The Quest for the Trinity: The Doctrine of God in Scripture, History and Modernity*. Downers Grove, IL: IVP Academic, 2012.

Hunsberger, George R. *Bearing the Witness of the Spirit: Lesslie Newbigin's Theology of Cultural Plurality*. Grand Rapids, MI: Eerdmans, 1998.

———. *The Story that Chooses Us: A Tapestry of Missional Vision*. Grand Rapids, MI: Eerdmans, 2015.

Hunsinger, George. *How to Read Karl Barth: The Shape of His Theology*. Oxford: Oxford University Press, 1991.

Hunter, James Davison. *To Change the World: The Irony, Tragedy, and Possibility of Christianity in the Late Modern World*. Oxford: Oxford University Press, 2010.

Jansen, J. F. *Calvin's Doctrine of the Work of Christ*. London: James Clarke, 1956.

Jüngel, Eberhard. *God's Being is in Becoming: The Trinitarian Being of God in the Theology of Karl Barth; A Paraphrase*. Translated by John Webster. Edinburgh: T&T Clark, 2001.

Kapic, Kelly M. "Receiving Christ's Priestly Benediction: A Biblical, Historical, and Theological Exploration of Luke 24:50-53." *Westminster Theological Journal* 67 (2005): 247-260.

———. "The Son's Assumption of a Human Nature: A Call for Clarity." *International Journal of Systematic Theology* 3.2 (2002): 154-166.

Kettler, Christian. *The Vicarious Humanity of Christ and the Reality of Salvation*. Eugene, OR: Wipf & Stock, 2011.

Kraemer, Hendrik. *A Theology of the Laity*. Philadelphia: Westminster, 1958.

Lane, Anthony N. S. *John Calvin: Student of the Church Fathers*. Edinburgh: T&T Clark, 1999.

Lee, Kye Won. *Living in Union with Christ: The Practical Theology of Thomas F. Torrance*. New York: Peter Lang, 2003.

Luoma, Tapio. *Incarnation and Physics: Natural Science in the Theology of Thomas F. Torrance*. Oxford: Oxford University Press, 2002.

MacKinnon, Donald M. "Substance in Christology—A Cross-Bench View." In *Christ, Faith and History: Cambridge Studies in Christology*. Edited by S. W. Sykes and J. P. Clayton, 279-300. Cambridge: Cambridge University Press, 1972.

MacLean, Stanley S. "A Radical New Humanism: T. F. Torrance's Mission of the Church." *Participatio* 6 (2017): 178-194.

———. *Resurrection, Apocalypse, and the Kingdom of Christ: The Eschatology of Thomas F. Torrance*. Eugene, OR: Wipf & Stock, 2012.

McCall, Thomas H. *Which Trinity? Whose Monotheism? Philosophical and Systematic Theologians on the Metaphysics of Trinitarian Theology*. Grand Rapids, MI: Eerdmans, 2010.

McCormack, Bruce. "Grace and Being." In *The Cambridge Companion to Karl Barth*. Edited by John Webster, 92-110. Cambridge: Cambridge University Press, 2000.

———. *Orthodox and Modern: Studies in the Theology of Karl Barth*. Grand Rapids, MI: Baker Academic, 2008.

McGrath, Alister. *T. F. Torrance: An Intellectual Biography*. Edinburgh: T&T Clark, 1999.

McMaken, W. Travis. "Actualism, Dualism, and Onto-Relations: Interrogating Torrance's Criticism of Barth's Doctrine of Baptism." *Participatio* 6 (2016): 1-31.

———. *The Sign of the Gospel: Toward and Evangelical Doctrine of Infant Baptism after Karl Barth*. Minneapolis: Fortress, 2013.

Moffitt, David M. *Atonement and the Logic of Resurrection in the Epistle to the Hebrews*. Supplements to the Novum Testamentum 141. Leiden: Brill, 2013.

Molnar, Paul D. *Faith, Freedom and the Spirit: The Economic Trinity in Barth, Torrance and Contemporary Theology*. Downers Grove, IL: IVP Academic, 2015.

———. *Thomas F. Torrance: Theologian of the Trinity*. Burlington, VT: Ashgate, 2009.

———. "Was Barth a Pro-Nicene Theologian? Reflections on *Nicaea and its Legacy*." *Scottish Journal of Theology* 64 (2011): 347-359.

Molnar, Paul D. and Myk Habets, eds. *T&T Clark Handbook of Thomas F. Torrance*. New York: T&T Clark, 2020.

Muller, Richard A. "The Barth Legacy: New Athanasius or Origen Redivivus? A Response to T. F. Torrance." *The Thomist* 54.4 (1990): 673-704.

———. *Christ and the Decree: Christology and Predestination in Reformed Theology from Calvin to Perkins*. Grand Rapids, MI: Baker Academic, 1986.

———. "Not Scotist: Understandings of Being, Univocity, and Analogy in Early-Modern Reformed Thought." *Reformation and Renaissance Review* 14.2 (2012): 127-150.

———. *The Unaccommodated Calvin: Studies in the Foundation of a Theological Tradition*. Oxford: Oxford University Press, 2000.

Myers, Benjamin. "The Stratification of Knowledge in the Thought of T. F. Torrance." *Scottish Journal of Theology* 61.1 (2008): 1-15.

Newbigin, Lesslie. *Foolishness to the Greeks: The Gospel and Western Culture*. Grand Rapids, MI: Eerdmans, 1986.

———. *The Gospel in a Pluralist Society*. Grand Rapids, MI: Eerdmans, 1989.

———. *The Open Secret: Sketches for a Missionary Theology*. London: SPCK, 1978.

———. *Proper Confidence: Faith, Doubt, and Certainty in Christian Discipleship*. Grand Rapids, MI: Eerdmans, 1995.

———. *The Relevance of Trinitarian Doctrine for Today's Mission*. Eugene, OR: Wipf & Stock, 2006.

Noble, Thomas A., and Jason S. Sexton, eds. *The Holy Trinity Revisited: Essays in Response to Stephen R. Holmes*. Milton Keynes: Paternoster, 2015.

O'Collins, Gerald, S. J., and Michael Keenan Jones. *Jesus Our Priest: A Christian Approach to the Priesthood of Christ*. Oxford: Oxford University Press, 2010.

O'Donovan, Oliver. *The Desire of the Nations: Rediscovering the Roots of Political Theology*. Oxford: Oxford University Press, 1996.

———. *The Ways of Judgment*. Grand Rapids: Eerdmans, 2005.

Oberman, Heiko A. "The Extra Dimension in the Theology of Calvin." *Journal of Ecclesiastical History* 21.1 (1970): 43-64.

Purves, Andrew. *Reconstructing Pastoral Theology: A Christological Foundation*. Louisville, KY: Westminster John Knox, 2004.

Radcliff, Alexandra S. *The Claim of Humanity in Christ: Salvation and Sanctification in the Theology of T. F. and J. B. Torrance*. Eugene, OR: Wipf & Stock, 2016.

Radcliff, Jason Robert. *Thomas F. Torrance and the Church Fathers: A Reformed, Evangelical, and Ecumenical Reconstruction of the Patristic Tradition*. Eugene, OR: Wipf & Stock, 2014.
Sanders, Fred. "The Trinity." In *The Oxford Handbook of Christian Theology*. Edited by John Webster, Kathryn Tanner, and Iain Torrance, 35-53. Oxford: Oxford University Press, 2007.
Scandrett, Joel. "'Christ Clothed with His Gospel': Apostolicity and the Deposit of Faith in the Thought of T. F. Torrance." In *Marking the Church: Essays in Ecclesiology*. Edited by Greg Peters and Matt Jenson, 184-197. Eugene, OR: Wipf & Stock, 2016.
Schrenk, Gottlob. "ἱερός." Vol 3. of *Theological Dictionary of the New Testament*, edited by Gerhard Kittel. Translated by Geoffrey W. Bromiley. Grand Rapids, MI: Eerdmans, 1965.
Sexton, Jason S. "A Confessing Trinitarian Theology for Today's Mission." In *Advancing Trinitarian Theology: Explorations in Constructive Dogmatics*. Edited by Oliver D. Crisp and Fred Sanders, 171-189. Grand Rapids, MI: Zondervan, 2014.
———. "Missional Theology's Missing Ingredient: The Necessity of Systematic Theology for Today's Mission." *Mission Studies* 32 (2015): 384-397.
Shepherd, Albert L. "The Body of Christ: T. F. Torrance's Ecclesial Ontology." PhD diss., University of Aberdeen, 2015.
Sherman, Robert. *King, Priest, and Prophet: A Trinitarian Theology of Atonement*. New York: T&T Clark, 2004.
Shults, Leon. "A Dubious Christological Formula: From Leontius of Byzantium to Karl Barth." *Theological Studies* 57 (1996): 431-446.
Sonderegger, Katherine. *The Doctrine of God*. Vol. 1 of *Systematic Theology*. Minneapolis: Fortress, 2015.
Speidell, Todd. *Fully Human in Christ: The Incarnation as the End of Christian Ethics*. Eugene, OR: Wipf & Stock, 2016.
Stamps, Robert J. *The Sacrament of the Word Made Flesh: The Eucharistic Theology of Thomas F. Torrance*. Edinburgh: Rutherford House, 2007.
Sykes, Stephen W., ed. *The Way of Theology in Karl Barth: Essays and Comments*. Eugene, OR: Wipf & Stock, 1986.
Torrance, Alan J. *Persons in Communion: Trinitarian Description and Human Participation*. Edinburgh: T&T Clark, 1996.
———. "Reclaiming the Continuing Priesthood of Christ: Implications and Challenges." In *Christology Ancient and Modern: Explorations in Constructive Dogmatics*. Edited by Oliver Crisp and Fred Sanders, 184-204. Grand Rapids, MI: Zondervan, 2013.
Torrance, Thomas F. *Atonement: The Person and Work of Christ*. Edited by Robert T. Walker. Downers Grove, IL: InterVarsity Press, 2009.
———. "The Atonement: The Singularity of Christ and the Finalist of the Cross; The Atonement and the Moral Order." In *Universalism and the Doctrine of Hell*. Edited by Nigel M. de S. Cameron, 223-254. Grand Rapids, MI: Baker Academic, 1992.
———, ed. *Belief in Science and in Christian Life: The Relevance of Michael Polanyi's Thought for Christian Faith and Life*. Eugene, OR: Wipf & Stock, 1998.
———. *The Christian Doctrine of God: One Being Three Persons*. 2nd ed. With an introduction by Paul D. Molnar. Edinburgh: T&T Clark, 2016.
———. *The Christian Frame of Mind: Reason, Order, and Openness in Theology and Natural Science*. Eugene, OR: Wipf & Stock, 2010.
———. *Christian Theology and Scientific Culture*. Eugene, OR: Wipf & Stock, 1998.
———. "The Deposit of Faith." *Scottish Journal of Theology* 36.1 (1983): 1-28.
———. *Divine and Contingent Order*. Edinburgh: T&T Clark, 1998.

———. *Divine Meaning: Studies in Patristic Hermeneutics.* Edinburgh: T&T Clark, 1995.
———. *The Doctrine of Grace in the Apostolic Fathers.* Eugene, OR: Wipf & Stock, 1996.
———. *The Doctrine of Jesus Christ.* Eugene, OR: Wipf & Stock, 2002.
———. *God and Rationality.* London: Oxford University Press, 1971.
———. *Gospel, Church, and Ministry: Thomas F. Torrance Collected Studies 1.* Edited by Jock Stein. Eugene, OR: Pickwick, 2012.
———. *The Ground and Grammar of Theology: Consonance Between Theology and Science.* Edinburgh: T&T Clark, 2001.
———. *The Hermeneutics of John Calvin.* Edinburgh: Scottish Academic Press, 1988.
———. *Incarnation: The Person and Life of Christ.* Edited by Robert T. Walker. Downers Grove, IL: InterVarsity Press, 2008.
———. *Juridical Law and Physical Law: Toward a Realist Foundation for Human Law.* Eugene, OR: Wipf & Stock, 1997.
———. *Karl Barth: An Introduction to His Early Theology 1910-1931.* London: T&T Clark, 2000.
———. *Karl Barth: Biblical and Evangelical Theologian.* Edinburgh: T&T Clark, 1990.
———. *Kingdom and Church: A Study in the Theology of the Reformation.* Eugene, OR: Wipf & Stock, 1996.
———. *The Mediation of Christ.* Colorado Springs, CO: Helmers & Howard, 1992.
———. *The Ministry and Sacraments of the Gospel.* Vol. 2 of *Conflict and Agreement in the Church.* Eugene, OR: Wipf & Stock, 1996.
———. "The Mission of the Church." *Scottish Journal of Theology* 19 (1966): 129-143.
———. "My Interaction With Karl Barth." In *How Karl Barth Changed My Mind.* Edited by Donald K. McKim, 52-64. Grand Rapids, MI: Eerdmans, 1986.
———. *Order and Disorder.* Vol. 1 of *Conflict and Agreement in the Church.* Eugene, OR: Wipf & Stock, 1996.
———. "The Paschal Mystery of Christ and the Eucharist: General Theses." *Liturgical Review* 6 (1976): 6-12.
———. *Preaching Christ Today: The Gospel and Scientific Thinking.* Grand Rapids, MI: Eerdmans, 1994.
———. *Reality & Evangelical Theology: The Realism of Christian Revelation.* Downers Grove, IL: InterVarsity Press, 1999.
———. *Reality and Scientific Theology.* Eugene, OR: Wipf & Stock, 2001.
———. *Royal Priesthood: A Theology of Ordained Ministry.* Edinburgh: T&T Clark, 1993.
———. *The School of Faith: The Catechisms of the Reformed Church.* Eugene, OR: Wipf & Stock, 1996.
———. "Scientific Hermeneutics According to St Thomas Aquinas." *Journal of Theological Studies* 13.2 (1962): 259-89.
———. *Scottish Theology: From John Knox to John McLeod Campbell.* Edinburgh: T&T Clark, 1996.
———. *Space, Time and Incarnation.* Edinburgh: T&T Clark, 1997.
———. *Space, Time and Resurrection.* 2nd ed. Introduction by Paul D. Molnar. Edinburgh: T&T Clark, 2019.
———. "'The Substance of Faith': A Clarification of the Concept in the Church of Scotland." *Scottish Journal of Theology* 36.3 (1983): 327-338.
———, ed. *Theological Dialogue Between Reformed and Orthodox Churches.* Edinburgh: Scottish Academic Press, 1985.
———. "Theological Realism." In *The Philosophical Frontiers of Christian Theology: Essays Presented to D. M. MacKinnon.* Edited by Brian Hebblethwaite and Stewart Sutherland, 169-196. Cambridge: Cambridge University Press, 1982.

———. *Theological Science*. Edinburgh: T&T Clark, 1996.
———. *Theology in Reconciliation: Essays Towards Evangelical and Catholic Unity in East and West*. Eugene, OR: Wipf & Stock, 1996.
———. *Theology in Reconstruction*. Eugene, OR: Wipf & Stock, 1996.
———. *The Trinitarian Faith: The Evangelical Theology of the Ancient Catholic Church*. 2nd ed. Introduction by Myk Habets. London: T&T Clark, 2016.
———. *Trinitarian Perspectives: Toward Doctrinal Agreement*. Edinburgh: T&T Clark, 1994.
———. "The Triunity of God in the Nicene Theology of the Fourth Century." In *Theological Dialogue Between Orthodox and Reformed Churches*. Vol. 2 of *Theological Dialogue Between Orthodox and Reformed Churches*, edited by Thomas F. Torrance, 3-60. Edinburgh: Scottish Academic Press, 1993.
———. "Urgent Call to the Kirk." Accessed March 23, 2017. www.tftorrance.org/call-to-kirk.php.
Turretin, Francis. *Eleventh Through Seventeenth Topics*. Vol. 2 of *Institutes of Elenctic Theology*. Philadelphia: Presbyterian and Reformed, 1994.
Tyler, Kate. *The Ecclesiology of Thomas F. Torrance: Koinonia and the Church*. Lanham, MD: Lexington Books/Fortress, 2019.
Van Gelder, Craig. *Confident Witness—Changing World*. Grand Rapids, MI: Eerdmans, 1999.
Van Kuiken, E. Jerome. *Christ's Humanity in Current and Ancient Controversy: Fallen or Not?* London: T&T Clark, 2017.
Visser 't Hooft, W.A. *The Kingship of Christ: An Interpretation of Recent European Theology*. New York: Harper & Brothers, 1948.
Wainwright, Geoffrey. *Lesslie Newbigin: A Theological Life*. Oxford: Oxford University Press, 2000.
Webster, John. *Barth's Ethics of Reconciliation*. Cambridge: Cambridge University Press, 1995.
———. *Barth's Moral Theology: Human Action in Barth's Thought*. Grand Rapids, MI: Eerdmans, 1998.
———. "The Christian in Revolt: Some Reflections on *The Christian Life*." In *Reckoning with Barth*. Edited by Nigel Biggar, 110-144. London: Mowbray, 1988.
———. Introduction to *God's Being is in Becoming: The Trinitarian Being of God in the Theology of Karl Barth* by Eberhard Jüngel, ix-xxiii. Edinburgh: T&T Clark, 2001.
———. *God Without Measure: Working Papers in Christian Theology*. Vol. 1 of *God and the Works of God*. London: T&T Clark, 2016.
———. *Holy Scripture: A Dogmatic Sketch*. Cambridge: Cambridge University Press, 2003.
———. *Karl Barth*. 2nd ed. London: Continuum, 2004.
———. "The Self-Organizing Power of the Gospel." In *Word and Church: Essays in Christian Dogmatics*, 191-210. London: T&T Clark, 2006.
———. "*Verbum mirificum*: T. F. Torrance on Scripture and Hermeneutics." In *The Domain of the Word: Scripture and Theological Reason*, 86-112. London: Bloomsbury, 2012.
———. "The Visible Attests the Invisible." In *The Community of the Word*. Edited by Mark Husbands and Daniel Treier, 96-113. Downers Grove, IL: IVP Academic, 2005.
Wigley, Stephen D. "Karl Barth on St Anselm: The Influence of Anselm's 'Theological Scheme' on T. F. Torrance and Eberhard Jüngel." *Scottish Journal of Theology* 46.1 (1993): 79-97.
Wisse, Martin. *Trinitarian Theology Beyond Participation: Augustine's De Trinitate and Contemporary Theology*. London: T&T Clark, 2011.
Wright, Christopher J. H. *The Mission of God: Unlocking the Bible's Grand Narrative*. Downers Grove, IL: IVP Academic, 2006.

Yocum, John. *Ecclesial Mediation in Karl Barth*. Hampshire, UK: Ashgate, 2004.
Yoder, John Howard. *Body Politics: Five Practices of the Christian Community Before the Watching World*. Scottsdale, PA: Herald, 1992.
Ziegler, Philip G. "Witness to Christ's Dominion: The Political Service of the Church." *Theology* 116.5 (2013): 323-331.
Zizioulas, John D. *Being as Communion: Studies in Personhood and the Church*. Crestwood, NY: St. Vladimir's Seminary Press, 1985.

General Index

Allen, R. Michael, 50-51, 224-25
anhypostasia/enhypostasia distinction, 108-9, 112-14, 220
apostolicity. *See* faith, deposit of
Arian controversy, 21-24
ascension, doctrine of, 89-100, 144-52, 210
Athanasius, 18-24, 31
Augustine, 24-25
Ayres, Lewis, 17, 21, 25, 29, 31
baptism, 197-200
Barth, Karl, 27-29, 35-38, 45-47, 53-54, 56-57, 114, 140, 183-84, 189-90, 223-24
Bavinck, Herman, 145
Bender, Kimlyn J., 184
Billings, J. Todd., 98-99, 215-16
Bosch, David, 2, 8, 12
Burgess, Andrew, 90
Butin, Phil, 63, 184
Calvin, John, 62-64, 73, 75, 85, 87-89, 226
Cameron, Daniel J., 194
Chiarot, Kevin, 138, 194, 196
Christ
  analogy of, 109-14
  vicarious humanity of, 192-97, 205
Colyer, Elmer, 17, 192
Cornett, Andrew, 222
Deddo, Gary W., 23
Dolezal, James E., 56
dualism, 14-18
Edmondson, Stephen, 69, 72, 88, 89, 175, 215

election, doctrine of, 56-57
eschatology, 159-75
  and sacraments, 164-65, 209-11
extra Calvinisticum, 94, 175-76
faith, deposit of, 134-42
Fergusson, David, 171
Flett, John, 4, 11-13, 51-55, 141-42
Guder, Darrell, 1-3, 52
Habets, Myk, 19, 112, 194
Hastings, Ross, 3, 4, 13, 132
Healy, Nicholas M., 226
Hesselink, I. John, 5
Holmes, Stephen R., 35, 50
homoousion, 22-23, 26-35, 37-39, 40-44, 49-51, 219
hypodeigma, 153-56, 167-71, 203, 205-6, 210, 226
incarnational ministry, 215-16
Jansen, J. F., 72
Jones, Michael Keenan, 87
Kapic, Kelly M., 194, 208
Kettler, Christian, 192
Kraemer, Hendrik, 8, 221-22
Lee, Kye Won, 6
Lord's Supper, 200-214
Maclean, Stanely S., 6-7, 113, 122, 217
McCormack, Bruce L., 5, 39, 54
McGrath, Alister M., 5, 16, 35-36
missio Dei, 11-13, 51-57
missional ecclesiology, 116-23, 224-27
missional theology, 1-5, 98-99, 215-16, 224-27
Moffit, David M., 202

Molnar, Paul, 14, 56-57, 176, 192
Muller, Richard, 17, 29, 45-46, 63, 88
munus triplex, 62-64, 69-89, 145-52, 214-15, 220-22, 227
  kingly office, 83-86, 146-47, 156-79
  priestly office, 79-83, 147-50, 190-215
  prophetic office, 75-78, 150-55, 180-90
Myers, Benjamin, 40
Newbigin, Lesslie, 1, 8, 12, 124-29, 132-33, 222
Oberman, Heiko, 175
O'Collins, Gerald, 87
O'Donovan, Oliver, 9, 87, 176-77
Purves, Andrew, 99
Radcliff, Alexandra S., 192
Radcliff, Jason, 14, 35, 46
Scandrett, Joel, 190
Sexton, Jason S., 4, 13
Shepherd, Albert L., 7, 133
Sonderegger, Katherine, 38
Torrance, Alan J., 37, 72
Tyler, Kate, 7
Van Kuiken, E. Jerome, 194
Visser't Hooft, W. A., 8, 177-79
Wainwright, Geoffrey, 124, 125
Webster, John B., 38, 99, 102, 155-56, 183, 185, 186, 188, 189-90, 218, 221, 224
Wisse, Maarten, 49-50
Wright, Christopher J. H., 3
Yoder, John Howard, 214
Ziegler, Philip G., 179

Scripture Index

OLD TESTAMENT

Numbers
12, *71*

Psalms
2, *85*

Isaiah
53, *153*

NEW TESTAMENT

Mark
16:19, *151*
16:20, *184*

Luke
24:50-53, *208*

John
13, *153*
15:9, *118*

16:8-11, *128*
16:12-15, *128*

Acts
2, *122*

Romans
6:7, *134*
8, *155*
13, *174*

1 Corinthians
10–14, *212*
11:23, *134*
13, *212*
15:3, *134*

2 Corinthians
11:2-4, *134*

Galatians
1:9, *134*
2:2, *134*
2:9, *134*

Ephesians
1, *146*
1:22-23, *121*
4:10, *121*

2 Thessalonians
2:15, *134*
3:6, *134*

1 Timothy
4:6, *134*
6:20, *134*

2 Timothy
1:12-14, *134*
2:2, *134*
2:4, *134*
4:3, *134*

Titus
1:9, *134*
1:13, *134*

Hebrews
3:1, *134*
4:14, *134*
7, *83*
10:23, *134*

1 Peter
2:9, *180*
2:13-17, *174*

Jude
3, *134*

New Explorations in Theology

Theology is flourishing in dynamic and unexpected ways in the twenty-first century. Scholars are increasingly recognizing the global character of the church, freely crossing old academic boundaries and challenging previously entrenched interpretations. Despite living in a culture of uncertainty, both young and senior scholars today are engaged in hopeful and creative work in the areas of systematic, historical, practical and philosophical theology. New Explorations in Theology (NET) provides a platform for cutting-edge research in these fields.

In an age of media proliferation and academic oversaturation, there is a need to single out the best new monographs. IVP Academic is committed to publishing constructive works that advance key theological conversations. We look for projects that investigate new areas of research, stimulate fruitful dialogue, and attend to the diverse array of contexts and audiences in our increasingly pluralistic world. IVP Academic is excited to make this work available to scholars, students and general readers who are seeking fresh new insights for the future of Christian theology.

NET ADVISORY BOARD:

Daniel Castelo, *Seattle Pacific University*
Tom Greggs, *University of Aberdeen*
Kristen Johnson, *Western Theological Seminary*
Beth Jones, *Wheaton College*
Veli-Matti Karkkainen, *Fuller Theological Seminary*
Tom McCall, *Trinity Evangelical Divinity School*
Kyle Strobel, *Biola University*

VOLUMES INCLUDE:

- *Chrysostom's Devil: Demons, the Will, and Virtue in Patristic Soteriology,* Samantha L. Miller
- *Reading Scripture as the Church: Dietrich Bonhoeffer's Hermeneutic of Discipleship,* Derek W. Taylor
- *T. F. Torrance as Missional Theologian: The Ascended Christ and the Ministry of the Church,* Joseph H. Sherrard
- *The Making of Stanley Hauerwas: Bridging Barth and Postliberalism,* David B. Hunsicker